W9-BVR-183

𝔉rontenac 𝔈dition

FRANCIS PARKMAN'S WORKS

VOLUME NINE

Copyright, 1897, by Little, Brown, & Co.

Goupil & Cⁱᵉ Paris.

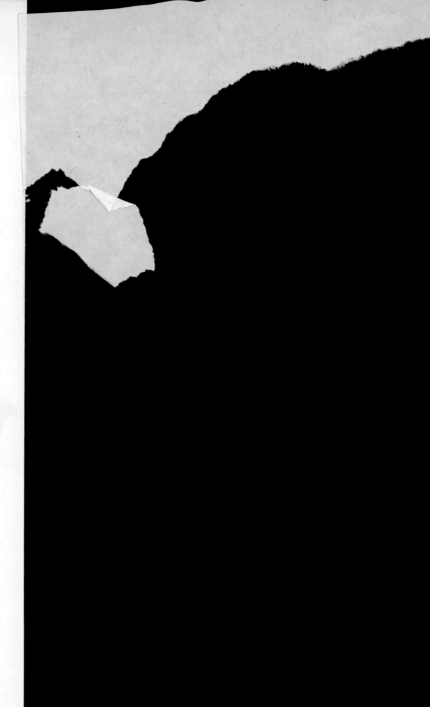

The Return from Deerfield.

The Return from Deerfield.

Frontenac Edition

A Half-Century

of

Conflict

*[France and England in North America
Part Sixth]*

BY

FRANCIS PARKMAN

IN TWO VOLUMES

VOLUME ONE

NEW YORK

CHARLES SCRIBNER'S SONS

1915

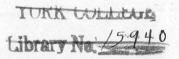
YORK COLLEGE
Library No. 15940

F
1030
.P24
1915

973.Y
P249w
v.9

67396

Copyright, 1892,
By Francis Parkman.

Copyright 1897,
By Little, Brown, and Company.

All rights reserved.

Printers
S. J. Parkhill & Co., Boston, U.S.A.

PREFACE.

THIS book, forming Part VI. of the series called France and England in North America, fills the gap between Part V., "Count Frontenac," and Part VII., "Montcalm and Wolfe;" so that the series now forms a continuous history of the efforts of France to occupy and control this continent.

In the present volumes the nature of the subject does not permit an unbroken thread of narrative, and the unity of the book lies in its being throughout, in one form or another, an illustration of the singularly contrasted characters and methods of the rival claimants to North America.

Like the rest of the series, this work is founded on original documents. The statements of secondary writers have been accepted only when found to conform to the evidence of contemporaries, whose writings have been sifted and collated with the greatest care. As extrem-

ists on each side have charged me with favoring the other, I hope I have been unfair to
neither.

The manuscript material collected for the
preparation of the series now complete forms
about seventy volumes, most of them folios.
These have been given by me from time to time
to the Massachusetts Historical Society, in whose
library they now are, open to the examination
of those interested in the subjects of which they
treat. The collection was begun forty-five years
ago, and its formation has been exceedingly
slow, having been retarded by difficulties which
seemed insurmountable, and for years were so
in fact. Hence the completion of the series has
required twice the time that would have sufficed
under less unfavorable conditions.

BOSTON, March 26, 1892.

CONTENTS.

CHAPTER I.
1700–1713.

EVE OF WAR.

PAGE

CHAPTER II.
1694–1704.

DETROIT.

CHAPTER III.
1703–1713.

QUEEN ANNE'S WAR.

CHAPTER IV.

1704–1740.

DEERFIELD.

CHAPTER V.

1704–1713.

THE TORMENTED FRONTIER.

CHAPTER VI.

1700–1710.

THE OLD RÉGIME IN ACADIA.

CHAPTER VII.

1704–1710.

ACADIA CHANGES HANDS.

CHAPTER XIV.

1700–1732.

THE OUTAGAMIE WAR.

CHAPTER XV.

1697–1741.

FRANCE IN THE FAR WEST.

Illustrations

VOLUME I.

A HALF-CENTURY OF CONFLICT.

A HALF-CENTURY OF CONFLICT.

CHAPTER I.

1700–1713.

EVE OF WAR.

The Spanish Succession. — Influence of Louis XIV. on History. — French Schemes of Conquest in America. — New York. — Unfitness of the Colonies for War. — The Five Nations. — Doubt and Vacillation. — The Western Indians. — Trade and Politics.

The war which in the British colonies was called Queen Anne's War, and in England the War of the Spanish Succession, was the second of a series of four conflicts which ended in giving to Great Britain a maritime and colonial preponderance over France and Spain. So far as concerns the colonies and the sea, these several wars may be regarded as a single protracted one, broken by intervals of truce. The three earlier of them, it is true, were European contests, begun and waged on European disputes. Their American part was incidental and apparently subordinate, yet it involved questions of prime importance in the history of the world.

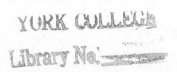
YORK COLLEGE
Library No.

The War of the Spanish Succession sprang from the ambition of Louis XIV. We are apt to regard the story of .that gorgeous monarch as a tale that is told; but his influence shapes the life of nations to this day. At the beginning of his reign two roads lay before him, and it was a momentous question for posterity, as for his own age, which one of them he would choose, — whether he would follow the wholesome policy of his great minister Colbert, or obey his own vanity and arrogance, and plunge France into exhausting wars; whether he would hold to the principle of tolerance embodied in the Edict of Nantes, or do the work of fanaticism and priestly ambition. The one course meant prosperity, progress, and the rise of a middle class; the other meant bankruptcy and the Dragonades,— and this was the King's choice. Crushing taxation, misery, and ruin followed, till France burst out at last in a frenzy, drunk with the wild dreams of Rousseau. Then came the Terror and the Napoleonic wars, and reaction on reaction, revolution on revolution, down to our own day.

Louis placed his grandson on the throne of Spain, and insulted England by acknowledging as her rightful King the son of James II., whom she had deposed. Then England declared war. Canada and the northern British colonies had had but a short breathing time since the Peace of Ryswick; both were tired of slaughtering each other, and both needed rest. Yet before the declaration of war, the Canadian officers of the Crown prepared, with their usual energy, to meet

the expected crisis.   One of them wrote: "If war be
declared, it is certain that the King can very easily
conquer and ruin New England."   The French of
Canada often use the name "New England" as apply-
ing to the British colonies in general.   They are
twice as populous as Canada, he goes on to say; but
the people are great cowards, totally undisciplined,
and ignorant of war, while the Canadians are brave,
hardy, and well trained.   We have, besides, twenty-
eight companies of regulars, and could raise six thousand warriors from our Indian allies.   Four thousand
men could easily lay waste all the northern English
colonies, to which end we must have five ships of
war, with one thousand troops on board, who must
land at Penobscot, where they must be joined by
two thousand regulars, militia, and Indians, sent
from Canada by way of the Chaudière and the
Kennebec.   Then the whole force must go to Portsmouth, take it by assault, leave a garrison there, and
march to Boston, laying waste all the towns and
villages by the way; after destroying Boston, the
army must march for New York, while the fleet follows along the coast.   "Nothing could be easier,"
says the writer, "for the road is good, and there is
plenty of horses and carriages.   The troops would
ruin everything as they advanced, and New York
would quickly be destroyed and burned."[1]

Another plan, scarcely less absurd, was proposed

[1] *Premier Projet pour L'Expédition contre la Nouvelle Angleterre,*
1701.   *Second Projet,* etc.   Compare *N. Y. Col. Docs.,* ix. 725.

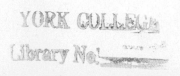
YORK COLLEGE

Library No.

about the same time by the celebrated Le Moyne d'Iberville. The essential point, he says, is to get possession of Boston; but there are difficulties and risks in the way. Nothing, he adds, referring to the other plan, seems difficult to persons without experience; but unless we are prepared to raise a great and costly armament, our only hope is in surprise. We should make it in winter, when the seafaring population, which is the chief strength of the place, is absent on long voyages. A thousand Canadians, four hundred regulars, and as many Indians should leave Quebec in November, ascend the Chaudière, then descend the Kennebec, approach Boston under cover of the forest, and carry it by a night attack. Apparently he did not know that but for its lean neck — then but a few yards wide — Boston was an island, and that all around for many leagues the forest that was to have covered his approach had already been devoured by numerous busy settlements. He offers to lead the expedition, and declares that if he is honored with the command, he will warrant that the New England capital will be forced to submit to King Louis, after which New York can be seized in its turn.[1]

In contrast to those incisive proposals, another French officer breathed nothing but peace. Brouillan,

---

[1] *Mémoire du Sieur d'Iberville sur Boston et ses Dépendances*, 1700 (1701?). Baron de Saint-Castin also drew up a plan for attacking Boston in 1702, with lists of necessary munitions and other supplies.

governor of Acadia, wrote to the governor of Massachusetts to suggest that, with the consent of their masters, they should make a treaty of neutrality. The English governor being dead, the letter came before the council, who received it coldly. Canada, and not Acadia, was the enemy they had to fear. Moreover, Boston merchants made good profit by supplying the Acadians with necessaries which they could get in no other way · and in time of war these profits, though lawless, were greater than in time of peace. But what chiefly influenced the council against the overtures of Brouillan was a passage in his letter reminding them that, by the Treaty of Ryswick, the New England people had no right to fish within sight of the Acadian coast. This they flatly denied, saying that the New England people had fished there time out of mind, and that if Brouillan should molest them, they would treat it as an act of war.[1]

While the New England colonies, and especially Massachusetts and New Hampshire, had most cause to deprecate a war, the prospect of one was also extremely unwelcome to the people of New York. The conflict lately closed had borne hard upon them

[1] *Brouillan à Bellomont,* 10 *Août,* 1701. *Conseil de Baston à Brouillan,* 22 *Août,* 1701. Brouillan acted under royal orders, having been told, in case of war being declared, to propose a treaty with New England, unless he should find that he can "se garantir des insultes des Anglais" and do considerable harm to their trade, in which case he is to make no treaty. *Mémoire du Roy au Sieur de Brouillan,* 23 *Mars,* 1700.

through the attacks of the enemy, and still more
through the derangement of their industries. They
were distracted, too, with the factions rising out of
the recent revolution under Jacob Leisler. New
York had been the bulwark of the colonies farther
south, who, feeling themselves safe, had given their
protector little help, and that little grudgingly, seem-
ing to regard the war as no concern of theirs. Three
thousand and fifty-one pounds, provincial currency,
was the joint contribution of Virginia, Maryland,
East Jersey, and Connecticut to the aid of New York
during five years of the late war.[1] Massachusetts
could give nothing, even if she would, her hands
being full with the defence of her own borders.
Colonel Quary wrote to the Board of Trade that New
York could not bear alone the cost of defending herself; that the other colonies were "stuffed with com-
monwealth notions," and were "of a sour temper in
opposition to government," so that Parliament ought
to take them in hand and compel each to do its part
in the common cause.[2] To this Lord Cornbury adds
that Rhode Island and Connecticut are even more
stubborn than the rest, hate all true subjects of the
Queen, and will not give a farthing to the war so
long as they can help it.[3] Each province lived in
selfish isolation, recking little of its neighbor's
woes.

[1] Schuyler, *Colonial New York*, i. 431, 432.
[2] *Colonel Quary to the Lords of Trade*, 16 *June*, 1703.
[3] *Cornbury to the Lords of Trade*, 9 *September*, 1703.

New York, left to fight her own battles, was in a wretched condition for defence. It is true that, unlike the other colonies, the King had sent her a few soldiers, counting at this time about one hundred and eighty, all told;[1] but they had been left so long without pay that they were in a state of scandalous destitution. They would have been left without rations had not three private gentlemen — Schuyler, Livingston, . and Cortlandt — advanced money for their supplies, which seems never to have been repaid.[2] They are reported to have been "without shirts, breeches, shoes, or stockings," and "in such a shameful condition that the women when passing them are obliged to cover their eyes." "The Indians ask," says the governor, "'Do you think us such fools as to believe that a king who cannot clothe his soldiers can protect us from the French, with their fourteen hundred men all well equipped?'"[3]

The forts were no better than their garrisons. The governor complains that those of Albany and Schenectady "are so weak and ridiculous that they look more like pounds for cattle than forts." At Albany the rotten stockades were falling from their own weight.

If New York had cause to complain of those whom she sheltered, she herself gave cause of complaint to those who sheltered her. The Five Nations of the Iroquois had always been her allies against the

---

[1] *Bellomont to the Lords of Trade, 28 February,* 1700.
[2] *Ibid.*
[3] Schuyler, *Colonial New York,* i. 488.

French, had guarded her borders and fought her
battles. What they wanted in return were gifts,
attentions, just dealings, and active aid in war; but
they got them in scant measure. Their treatment by
the province was short-sighted, if not ungrateful.
New York was a mixture of races and religions not
yet fused into a harmonious body politic, divided in
interests and torn with intestine disputes. Its Assembly was made up in large part of men unfitted
to pursue a consistent scheme of policy, or spend the
little money at their disposal on any objects but
those of present and visible interest. The royal governors, even when personally competent, were hampered by want of means and by factious opposition.
The Five Nations were robbed by land-speculators,
cheated by traders, and feebly supported in their
constant wars with the French. Spasmodically, as
it were, on occasions of crisis, they were summoned
to Albany, soothed with such presents as could be
got from unwilling legislators, or now and then
from the Crown, and exhorted to fight vigorously in
the common cause. The case would have been far
worse but for a few patriotic men, with Peter Schuyler
at their head, who understood the character of these
Indians, and labored strenuously to keep them in
what was called their allegiance.

The proud and fierce confederates had suffered
greatly in the late war. Their numbers had been
reduced about one half, and they now counted little
more than twelve hundred warriors. They had

learned a bitter and humiliating lesson, and their arrogance had changed to distrust and alarm. Though hating the French, they had learned to respect their military activity and prowess, and to look askance on the Dutch and English, who rarely struck a blow in their defence, and suffered their hereditary enemy to waste their fields and burn their towns. The English called the Five Nations British subjects, on which the French taunted them with being British slaves, and told them that the King of England had ordered the governor of New York to poison them. This invention had great effect. The Iroquois capital, Onondaga, was filled with wild rumors. The credulous savages were tossed among doubts, suspicions, and fears. Some were in terror of poison, and some of witchcraft. They believed that the rival European nations had leagued to destroy them and divide their lands, and that they were bewitched by sorcerers, both French and English.[1]

After the Peace of Ryswick, and even before it, the French governor kept agents among them. Some of these were soldiers, like Joncaire, Maricourt, or Longueuil, and some were Jesuits, like Bruyas, Lamberville, or Vaillant. The Jesuits showed their usual ability and skill in their difficult and perilous task. The Indians derived various advantages from their presence, which they regarded also as a flattering attention; while the English, jealous of their influence, made feeble attempts to counteract it by

[1] *N. Y. Col. Docs.*, iv. 658.

sending Protestant clergymen to Onondaga. "But," writes Lord Bellomont, "it is next to impossible to prevail with the ministers to live among the Indians. They [the Indians] are so nasty as never to wash their hands, or the utensils they dress their victuals with."[1] Even had their zeal been proof to these afflictions, the ministers would have been no match for their astute opponents. In vain Bellomont assured the Indians that the Jesuits were "the greatest lyars and impostors in the world."[2] In vain he offered a hundred dollars for every one of them whom they should deliver into his hands. They would promise to expel them; but their minds were divided, and they stood in fear of one another. While one party distrusted and disliked the priests, another was begging the governor of Canada to send more. Others took a practical view of the question. "If the English sell goods cheaper than the French, we will have ministers; if the French sell them cheaper than the English, we will have priests." Others, again, wanted neither Jesuits nor ministers, "because both of you [English and French] have made us drunk with the noise of your praying."[3]

The aims of the propagandists on both sides were secular. The French wished to keep the Five Nations neutral in the event of another war; the

---

[1] *Bellomont to the Lords of Trade,* 17 *October,* 1700.

[2] *Conference of Bellomont with the Indians,* 26 *August,* 1700.

[3] *Journal of Bleeker and Schuyler on their visit to Onondaga, August, September,* 1701.

English wished to spur them to active hostility; but while the former pursued their purpose with energy and skill, the efforts of the latter were intermittent and generally feeble.

"The Nations," writes Schuyler, "are full of factions." There was a French party and an English party in every town, especially in Onondaga, the centre of intrigue. French influence was strongest at the western end of the confederacy, among the Senecas, where the French officer Joncaire, an Iroquois by adoption, had won many to France; and it was weakest at the eastern end, among the Mohawks, who were nearest to the English settlements. Here the Jesuits had labored long and strenuously in the work of conversion, and from time to time they had led their numerous proselytes to remove to Canada, where they settled at St. Louis, or Caughnawaga, on the right bank of the St. Lawrence, a little above Montreal, where their descendants still remain. It is said that at the beginning of the eighteenth century two-thirds of the Mohawks had thus been persuaded to cast their lot with the French, and from enemies to become friends and allies. Some of the Oneidas and a few of the other Iroquois nations joined them and strengthened the new mission settlement; and the Caughnawagas afterwards played an important part between the rival European colonies.

The "Far Indians," or "Upper Nations," as the French called them, consisted of the tribes of the

Great Lakes and adjacent regions, Ottawas, Pottawattamies, Sacs, Foxes, Sioux, and many more. It
was from these that Canada drew the furs by which
she lived. Most of them were nominal friends and
allies of the French, who in the interest of trade
strove to keep these wild-cats from tearing one another's throats, and who were in constant alarm lest
they should again come to blows with their old enemies, the Five Nations, in which case they would call
on Canada for help, thus imperilling those pacific
relations with the Iroquois confederacy which the
French were laboring constantly to secure.

In regard to the "Far Indians," the French, the
English, and the Five Iroquois Nations all had dis-
tinct and opposing interests. The French wished to
engross their furs, either by inducing the Indians
to bring them down to Montreal, or by sending
traders into their country to buy them. The English, with a similar object, wished to divert the "Far
Indians" from Montreal and draw them to Albany;
but this did not suit the purpose of the Five Nations,
who, being sharp politicians and keen traders, as well
as bold and enterprising warriors, wished to act as
middle-men between the beaver-hunting tribes and
the Albany merchants, well knowing that good profit
might thus accrue. In this state of affairs the converted Iroquois settled at Caughnawaga played a
peculiar part. In the province of New York, goods
for the Indian trade were of excellent quality and
comparatively abundant and cheap; while among the

French, especially in time of war, they were often scarce and dear. The Caughnawagas accordingly, whom neither the English nor the French dared offend, used their position to carry on a contraband trade between New York and Canada. By way of Lake Champlain and the Hudson they brought to Albany furs from the country of the "Far Indians," and exchanged them for guns, blankets, cloths, knives, beads, and the like. These they carried to Canada and sold to the French traders, who in this way, and often in this alone, supplied themselves with the goods necessary for bartering furs from the "Far Indians." This lawless trade of the Caughnawagas went on even in time of war; and opposed as it was to every principle of Canadian policy, it was generally connived at by the French authorities as the only means of obtaining the goods necessary for keeping their Indian allies in good humor.

It was injurious to English interests; but the fur-traders of Albany and also the commissioners charged with Indian affairs, being Dutchmen converted by force into British subjects, were, with a few eminent exceptions, cool in their devotion to the British Crown; while the merchants of the port of New York, from whom the fur-traders drew their supplies, thought more of their own profits than of the public good. The trade with Canada through the Caughnawagas not only gave aid and comfort to the enemy, but continually admitted spies into the colony, from whom the governor of Canada gained information touching English movements and designs.

The Dutch traders of Albany and the importing merchants who supplied them with Indian goods had a strong interest in preventing active hostilities with Canada, which would have spoiled their trade. So, too, and for similar reasons, had influential persons in Canada. The French authorities, moreover, thought it impolitic to harass the frontiers of New York by war parties, since the Five Nations might come to the aid of their Dutch and English allies, and so break the peaceful relations which the French were anxious to maintain with them. Thus it happened that, during the first six or seven years of the eighteenth century, there was a virtual truce between Canada and New York, and the whole burden of the war fell upon New England, or rather upon Massachusetts, with its outlying district of Maine and its small and weak neighbor, New Hampshire.[1]

---

[1] The foregoing chapter rests on numerous documents in the Public Record Office, Archives de la Marine, Archives Nationales, *N. Y. Colonial Documents*, vols. iv. v. ix., and the *Second and Third Series of the Correspondance Officielle* at Ottawa.

CHAPTER II.

1694–1704.

DETROIT.

Michilimackinac. — La Mothe-Cadillac: his Disputes with the Jesuits. — Opposing Views. — Plans of Cadillac: his Memorial to the Court; his Opponents. — Detroit founded. The New Company. — Detroit changes Hands. — Strange Act of the Five Nations.

In the few years of doubtful peace that preceded Queen Anne's War, an enterprise was begun, which, nowise in accord with the wishes and expectations of those engaged in it, was destined to produce as its last result an American city.

Antoine de La Mothe-Cadillac commanded at Michilimackinac, whither Frontenac had sent him in 1694. This old mission of the Jesuits, where they had gathered the remnants of the lake tribes dispersed by the Iroquois at the middle of the seventeenth century, now savored little of its apostolic beginnings. It was the centre of the western fur-trade and the favorite haunt of the *coureurs de bois*. Brandy and squaws abounded, and according to the Jesuit Carheil, the spot where Marquette had labored was now a witness of scenes the most unedifying.[1]

[1] See "Old Régime in Canada," ii. 119.

At Michilimackinac was seen a curious survival of
Huron-Iroquois customs.   The villages of the Hurons
and Ottawas, which were side by side, separated only
by a fence, were surrounded by a common enclosure
of triple palisades, which, with the addition of loopholes for musketry, were precisely like those seen by
Cartier at Hochelaga, and by Champlain in the
Onondaga country.   The dwellings which these
defences enclosed were also after the old Huron-
Iroquois pattern, — those long arched structures
covered with bark which Brébeuf found by the
shores of Matchedash Bay, and Jogues on the banks
of the Mohawk.   Besides the Indians, there was a
French colony at the place, chiefly of fur-traders,
lodged in log-cabins, roofed with cedar bark, and
forming a street along the shore close to the palisaded villages of the Hurons and Ottawas.   The
fort, known as Fort Buade, stood at the head of
the little bay.[1]

The Hurons and Ottawas were thorough savages,
though the Hurons retained the forms of Roman
Catholic Christianity.   This tribe, writes Cadillac,
"are reduced to a very small number; and it is well
for us that they are, for they are ill-disposed and
mischievous, with a turn for intrigue and a capacity
for large undertakings.   Luckily, their power is not
great; but as they cannot play the lion, they play the
fox, and do their best to make trouble between us
and our allies."

1 *Relation de La Mothe-Cadillac,* in Margry, v. 75.

La Mothe-Cadillac[1] was a captain in the colony troops, and an admirer of the late governor, Frontenac, to whose policy he adhered, and whose prejudices he shared. He was amply gifted with the kind of intelligence that consists in quick observation, sharpened by an inveterate spirit of sarcasm, was energetic, enterprising, well instructed, and a bold and sometimes a visionary schemer, with a restless spirit, a nimble and biting wit, a Gascon impetuosity of temperament, and as much devotion as an officer of the King was forced to profess, coupled with small love of priests and an aversion to Jesuits.[2] Carheil and Marest, missionaries of that order at Michilimackinac, were objects of his especial antipathy, which they fully returned. The two priests were impatient of a military commandant to whose authority they were in some small measure subjected; and

---

[1] He wrote his name as above. It is often written La Motte, which has the advantage of conveying the pronunciation unequivocally to an unaccustomed English ear. La Mothe-Cadillac came of a good family of Languedoc. His father, Jean de La Mothe, seigneur de Cadillac et de Launay, or Laumet, was a counsellor in the Parliament of Toulouse. The date of young Cadillac's birth is uncertain. The register of his marriage places it in 1661, and that of his death in 1657. Another record, cited by Farmer in his *History of Detroit*, makes it 1658. In 1703 he himself declared that he was forty-seven years old. After serving as lieutenant in the regiment of Clairembault, he went to Canada about the year 1683. He became skilled in managing Indians, made himself well acquainted with the coasts of New England, and strongly urged an attack by sea on New York and Boston, as the only sure means of securing French ascendency. He was always in opposition to the clerical party.

[2] See *La Mothe-Cadillac à* ——, 3 *Août*, 1695.

they imputed to him the disorders which he did not, and perhaps could not, prevent. They were opposed also to the traffic in brandy, which was favored by Cadillac on the usual ground that it attracted the Indians, and so prevented the English from getting control of the fur-trade, — an argument which he reinforced by sanitary considerations based on the supposed unwholesomeness of the fish and smoked meat which formed the chief diet of Michilimackinac. "A little brandy after the meal," he says, with the solemnity of the learned Purgon, "seems necessary to cook the bilious meats and the crudities they leave in the stomach."[1]

Cadillac calls Carheil, superior of the mission, the most passionate and domineering man he ever knew, and further declares that the Jesuit tried to provoke him to acts of violence, in order to make matter of accusation against him. If this was Carheil's aim, he was near succeeding. Once, in a dispute with the commandant on the brandy-trade, he upbraided him sharply for permitting it; to which Cadillac replied that he only obeyed the orders of the court. The Jesuit rejoined that he ought to obey God, and not man, — "on which," says the commandant, "I told him that his talk smelt of sedition a hundred yards off, and begged that he would amend it. He told me that I gave myself airs that did not belong to me, holding his fist before my nose at the same time. I confess I almost forgot that he was a priest, and

[1] *La Mothe-Cadillac à ——, 3 Août, 1695.*

felt for a moment like knocking his jaw out of joint; but, thank God, I contented myself with taking him by the arm, pushing him out, and ordering him not to come back." [1]

Such being the relations of the commandant and the Father Superior, it is not surprising to find the one complaining that he cannot get absolved from his sins, and the other painting the morals and manners of Michilimackinac in the blackest colors.

I have spoken elsewhere of the two opposing policies that divided Canada, — the policies of concentration and of expansion, on the one hand leaving the west to the keeping of the Jesuits, and confining the population to the borders of the St. Lawrence; on the other, the occupation of the interior of the continent by posts of war and trade.[2] Through the force of events the latter view had prevailed; yet while the military chiefs of Canada could not but favor it, the Jesuits were unwilling to accept it, and various interests in the colony still opposed it openly or secretly. Frontenac had been its strongest champion, and Cadillac followed in his steps. It seemed

---

[1] "Il me dit que je me donnois des airs qui ne m'appartenoient pas, en me portant le poing au nez. Je vous avoue, Monsieur, que je pensai oublier qu'il étoit prêtre, et que je vis le moment où j'allois luy démonter la mâchoire; mais, Dieu merci, je me contentai de le prendre par le bras et de le pousser dehors, avec ordre de n'y plus rentrer." Margry, v. (author's edition), Introduction, civ. This introduction, with other editorial matter, is omitted in the edition of M. Margry's valuable collection, printed under a vote of the American Congress.

[2] See "Count Frontenac," ii. 198.

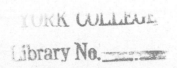
YORK COLLEGE.

Library No.

to him that the time had come for securing the west for France.

The strait — *détroit* — which connects Lake Huron with Lake Erie was the most important of all the western passes. It was the key of the three upper lakes, with the vast countries watered by their tributaries, and it gave Canada her readiest access to the valley of the Mississippi. If the French held it, the English would be shut out from the northwest; if, as seemed likely, the English should seize it, the Canadian fur-trade would be ruined.[1] The possession of it by the French would be a constant curb and menace to the Five Nations, as well as a barrier between those still formidable tribes and the western Indians, allies of Canada; and when the intended French establishment at the mouth of the Mississippi should be made, Detroit would be an indispensable link of communication between Canada and Louisiana.

Denonville had recognized the importance of the position, and it was by his orders that Greysolon Du Lhut, in 1686, had occupied it for a time, and built a picket fort near the site of Fort Gratiot.[2]

It would be idle to imagine that the motives of Cadillac were wholly patriotic. Fur-trading interests were deeply involved in his plans, and bitter opposition was certain. The fur-trade, in its nature, was a constant breeder of discord. The people of Montreal

[1] Robert Livingston urged the occupation of Detroit as early as 1700. *N. Y. Col. Docs.*, iv. 650.

[2] *Denonville à Du Lhut, 6 Juin*, 1686. Count Frontenac, i. 133.

would have the tribes come down every summer from the west and northwest and hold a fair under the palisades of their town. It is said that more than four hundred French families lived wholly or in part by this home trade, and therefore regarded with deep jealousy the establishment of interior posts, which would forestall it. Again, every new western post would draw away trade from those already established, and every trading license granted to a company or an individual would rouse the animosity of those who had been licensed before. The prosperity of Detroit would be the ruin of Michilimackinac, and those whose interests centred at the latter post angrily opposed the scheme of Cadillac.

He laid his plans before Count de Maurepas by a characteristic memorial, apparently written in 1699. In this he proposed to gather all the tribes of the lakes at Detroit, civilize them and teach them French, "insomuch that from pagans they would become children of the Church, and therefore good subjects of the King." They will form, he continues, a considerable settlement, "strong enough to bring the English and the Iroquois to reason, or, with help from Montreal, to destroy both of them." Detroit, he adds, should be the seat of trade, which should not be permitted in the countries beyond it. By this regulation the intolerable glut of beaver-skins, which spoils the market, may be prevented. This proposed restriction of the beaver-trade to Detroit was enough in itself to raise a tempest against the whole scheme.

"Cadillac well knows that he has enemies," pursues the memorial, "but he keeps on his way without turning or stopping for the noise of the puppies who bark after him."[1]

Among the essential features of his plan was a well-garrisoned fort, and a church, served not by Jesuits alone, but also by Récollet friars and priests of the Missions Étrangères. The idea of this ecclesiastical partnership was odious to the Jesuits, who felt that the west was their proper field, and that only they had a right there. Another part of Cadillac's proposal pleased them no better. This was his plan of civilizing the Indians and teaching them to speak French; for it was the reproach of the Jesuit missions that they left the savage a savage still, and asked little of him but the practice of certain rites and the passive acceptance of dogmas to him incomprehensible.

"It is essential," says the memorial, "that in this matter of teaching the Indians our language the missionaries should act in good faith, and that his Majesty should have the goodness to impose his strictest orders upon them; for which there are several good reasons. The first and most stringent is that when members of religious orders or other ecclesiastics undertake anything, they never let it go. The second is that by not teaching French to

---

[1] "Sans se destourner et sans s'arrester au bruit des jappereaux qui crient après luy." — *Mémoire de La Mothe-Cadillac adressé au Comte de Maurepas.*

the Indians they make themselves necessary [as interpreters] to the King and the governor. The third is that if all Indians spoke French, all kinds of ecclesiastics would be able to instruct them. This might cause them [the Jesuits] to lose some of the presents they get; for though these Reverend Fathers come here only for the glory of God, yet the one thing does not prevent the other," — meaning that God and Mammon may be served at once. "Nobody can deny that the priests own three quarters of Canada. From St. Paul's Bay to Quebec, there is nothing but the seigniory of Beauport that belongs to a private person. All the rest, which is the best part, belongs to the Jesuits or other ecclesiastics. The Upper Town of Quebec is composed of six or seven superb palaces belonging to Hospital Nuns, Ursulines, Jesuits, Récollets, Seminary priests, and the bishop. There may be some forty private houses, and even these pay rent to the ecclesiastics, which shows that *the one thing does not prevent the other.*" From this it will be seen that, in the words of one of his enemies, Cadillac "was not quite in the odor of sanctity."

"One may as well knock one's head against a wall," concludes the memorial, "as hope to convert the Indians in any other way [than that of civilizing them]; for thus far all the fruits of the missions consist in the baptism of infants who die before reaching the age of reason."[1] This was not literally true,

---

[1] *Mémoire adressé au Comte de Maurepas,* in Margry, v. 138.

though the results of the Jesuit missions in the
west had been meagre and transient to a surprising degree.

Cadillac's plan of a settlement at Detroit was not
at first received with favor by Callières, the governor;
while the intendant Champigny, a fast friend of the
Jesuits, strongly opposed it. By their order the
chief inhabitants of Quebec met at the Château St.
Louis, — Callières, Champigny, and Cadillac himself
being present. There was a heated debate on the
beaver-trade, after which the intendant commanded
silence, explained the projects of Cadillac, and proceeded to oppose them. His first point was that the
natives should not be taught French, because the
Indian girls brought up at the Ursuline Convent led
looser lives than the young squaws who had received
no instruction, while it was much the same with the
boys brought up at the Seminary.

"M. de Champigny," returned the sarcastic Cadillac, "does great honor to the Ursulines and the
Seminary. It is true that some Indian women who
have learned our language have lived viciously; but
that is because their teachers were too stiff with
them, and tried to make them nuns." [1]

Champigny's position, as stated by his adversary,
was that "all intimacy of the Indians with the French
is dangerous and corrupting to their morals," and
that their only safety lies in keeping them at a distance from the settlements. This was the view of

[1] La Mothe-Cadillac, *Rapport au Ministre*, 1700, in Margry, v. 157

the Jesuits, and there is much to be said in its favor; but it remains not the less true that conversion must go hand in hand with civilization, or it is a failure and a fraud.

Cadillac was not satisfied with the results of the meeting at the Château St. Louis, and he wrote to the minister: "You can never hope that this business will succeed if it is discussed here on the spot. Canada is a country of cabals and intrigues, and it is impossible to reconcile so many different interests." [1] He sailed for France, apparently in the autumn of 1699, to urge his scheme at court. Here he had an interview with the colonial minister, Ponchartrain, to whom he represented the military and political expediency of his proposed establishment; [2] and in a letter which seems to be addressed to La Touche, chief clerk in the Department of Marine and Colonies, he promised that the execution of his plan would insure the safety of Canada and the ruin of the British colonies. [3] He asked for fifty soldiers and fifty Canadians to begin the work, to be followed in the next year by twenty or thirty families and by two hundred picked men of various trades, sent out at the King's charge, along with priests of several communities, and nuns to attend the sick and teach the Indian girls. "I cannot tell you," continues Cadillac,

[1] *Rapport au Ministre*, 1700.

[2] Cadillac's report of this interview is given in Sheldon, *Early History of Michigan*, 85–91.

[3] *La Mothe-Cadillac à un premier commis*, 18 *Octobre*, 1700, in Margry, v. 166.

"the efforts my enemies have made to deprive me of the honor of executing my project; but so soon as M. de Ponchartrain decides in its favor, the whole country will applaud it."

Ponchartrain accepted the plan, and Cadillac returned to Canada commissioned to execute it. Early in June, 1701, he left La Chine with a hundred men in twenty-five canoes loaded with provisions, goods, munitions, and tools. He was accompanied by Alphonse de Tonty, brother of Henri de Tonty, the companion of La Salle, and by two half-pay lieutenants, Dugué and Chacornacle, together with a Jesuit and a Récollet.[1] Following the difficult route of the Ottawa and Lake Huron, they reached their destination on the twenty-fourth of July, and built a picket fort sixty yards square, which by order of the governor they named Fort Ponchartrain.[2] It stood near the west bank of the strait, about forty paces from the water.[3] Thus was planted the germ of the city of Detroit.

Cadillac sent back Chacornacle with the report of what he had done, and a description of the country written in a strain of swelling and gushing rhetoric in singular contrast with his usual sarcastic utterances. "None but enemies of the truth," his letter concludes, "are enemies of this establishment, so

[1] *Callières au Ministre,* 4 *Octobre,* 1701. *Autre lettre du même, sans date,* in Margry, v. 187, 190.

[2] *Callières et Champigny au Ministre, sans date.*

[3] *Relation du Destroit* (by the Jesuit who accompanied the expedition).

necessary to the glory of the King, the progress of
religion, and the destruction of the throne of Baal."[1]

What he had, perhaps, still more at heart was
making money out of it by the fur-trade. By command of the King a radical change had lately been
made in this chief commerce of Canada, and the
entire control of it had been placed in the hands of a
company in which all Canadians might take shares.
But as the risks were great and the conditions ill-
defined, the number of subscribers was not much
above one hundred and fifty; and the rest of the
colony found themselves shut out from the trade, —
to the ruin of some, and the injury of all.[2]

All trade in furs was restricted to Detroit and
Fort Frontenac, both of which were granted to the
company, subject to be resumed by the King at his
pleasure.[3] The company was to repay the eighty
thousand francs which the expedition to Detroit had
cost; and to this were added various other burdens.
The King, however, was to maintain the garrison.

All the affairs of the company were placed in the
hands of seven directors, who began immediately to
complain that their burdens were too heavy, and to
beg for more privileges; while an outcry against the
privileges already granted rose from those who had
not taken shares in the enterprise. Both in the com-

---

[1] *Description de la Rivière du Détroit, jointe à la lettre de MM. de
Callières et de Champigny,* 8 *Octobre,* 1701.

[2] *Callières au Ministre,* 9 *Novembre,* 1700.

[3] *Traité fait avec la Compagnie de la Colonie de Canada,* 31
Octobre, 1701.

pany and out of it there was nothing but discontent.
None were worse pleased than the two Jesuits Carheil
and Marest, who saw their flocks at Michilimackinac,
both Hurons and Ottawas, lured away to a new home
at Detroit. Cadillac took a peculiar satisfaction in
depriving Carheil of his converts, and in 1703 we
find him writing to the minister Ponchartrain, that
only twenty-five Hurons are left at Michilimackinac;
and "I hope," he adds, "that in the autumn I shall
pluck this last feather from his wing; and I am convinced that this obstinate priest will die in his parish
without one parishioner to bury him." [1]

If the Indians came to Detroit, the French would
not come. Cadillac had asked for five or six families
as the modest beginning of a settlement; but not one
had appeared. The Indians, too, were angry because
the company asked too much for its goods; while the
company complained that a forbidden trade, fatal to
its interests, went on through all the region of the
upper lakes. It was easy to ordain a monopoly, but
impossible to enforce it. The prospects of the new
establishment were deplorable; and Cadillac lost no
time in presenting his views of the situation to the
court. "Detroit is good, or it is bad," he writes to

---

[1] *Lamothe-Cadillac à Ponchartrain*, 31 *Aoust*, 1703 (Margry, v.
301). On Cadillac's relations with the Jesuits, see *Conseils tenus par
Lamothe-Cadillac avec les Sauvages* (Margry, v. 253–300); also a
curious collection of Jesuit letters sent by Cadillac to the minister,
with copious annotations of his own. He excepts from his strictures
Father Engelran, who, he says, incurred the ill-will of the other
Jesuits by favoring the establishment of Detroit, and he also has
a word of commendation for Father Germain.

Ponchartrain. "If it is good, it ought to be sustained, without allowing the people of Canada to deliberate any more about it. If it is bad, the court ought to make up its mind concerning it as soon as may be. I have said what I think. I have explained the situation. You have felt the need of Detroit, and its utility for the glory of God, the progress of religion, and the good of the colony. Nothing is left me to do but to imitate the governor of the Holy City, — take water, and wash my hands of it." His aim now appears. He says that if Detroit were made a separate government, and he were put at the head of it, its prospects would improve. "You may well believe that the company cares for nothing but to make a profit out of it. It only wants to have a storehouse and clerks; no officers, no troops, no inhabitants. Take this business in hand, Monseigneur, and I promise that in two years your Detroit shall be established of itself." He then informs the minister that as the company complain of losing money, he has told them that if they will make over their rights to him, he will pay them back all their past outlays. "I promise you," he informs Ponchartrain, "that if they accept my proposal and you approve it, I will make our Detroit flourish. Judge if it is agreeable to me to have to answer for my actions to five or six merchants [the directors of the company], who not long ago were blacking their masters' boots." He is scarcely more reserved as to the Jesuits. "I do what I can to make them my

friends, but, impiety apart, one had better sin against
God than against them; for in that case one gets
one's pardon, whereas in the other the offence is
never forgiven in this world, and perhaps never
would be in the other, if their credit were as great
there as it is here."[1]

The letters of Cadillac to the court are unique.
No governor of New France, not even the audacious
Frontenac, ever wrote to a minister of Louis XIV.
with such off-hand freedom of language as this singular personage, — a mere captain in the colony troops;
and to a more stable and balanced character it would
have been impossible.

Cadillac's proposal was accepted. The company
was required to abandon Detroit to him on his paying them the expenses they had incurred. Their
monopoly was transferred to him; but as far as concerned beaver-skins, his trade was limited to twenty
thousand francs a year. The governor was ordered
to give him as many soldiers as he might want, permit as many persons to settle at Detroit as might
choose to do so, and provide missionaries.[2] The
minister exhorted him to quarrel no more with the
Jesuits, or anybody else, to banish blasphemy and

---

[1] *La Mothe-Cadillac à Ponchartrain*, 31 *Août*, 1703. "Toute
impiété à part, il vaudroit mieux pescher contre Dieu que contre
eux, parce que d'un costé on en reçoit son pardon, et de l'autre,
l'offense, mesme prétendue, n'est jamais remise dans ce monde, et
ne le seroit peut-estre jamais dans l'autre, si leur crédit y estoit
aussi grand qu'il est dans ce pays."

[2] *Ponchartrain à La Mothe-Cadillac*, 14 *Juin*, 1704.

bad morals from the post, and not to offend the Five Nations.

The promised era of prosperity did not come. Detroit lingered on in a weak and troubled infancy, disturbed, as we shall see, by startling incidents. Its occupation by the French produced a noteworthy result. The Five Nations, filled with jealousy and alarm, appealed to the King of England for protection, and, the better to insure it, conveyed the whole country from Lake Ontario northward to Lake Superior, and westward as far as Chicago, "unto our souveraigne Lord King William the Third" and his heirs and successors forever. This territory is described in the deed as being about eight hundred miles long and four hundred wide, and was claimed by the Five Nations as theirs by right of conquest.[1] It of course included Detroit itself. The conveyance was drawn by the English authorities at Albany in a form to suit their purposes, and included terms of subjection and sovereignty which the signers could understand but imperfectly, if at all. The Five Nations gave away their land to no purpose. The French remained in undisturbed possession of Detroit. The English made no attempt to enforce their title, but they put the deed on file, and used it long after as the base of their claim to the region of the Lakes.

---

[1] *Deed from the Five Nations to the King of their Beaver Hunting Ground,* in *N. Y. Col. Docs.,* iv. 908. It is signed by the totems of sachems of all the Nations.

CHAPTER III.

1703–1713.

QUEEN ANNE'S WAR.

FOR untold ages Maine had been one unbroken forest, and it was so still. Only along the rocky seaboard or on the lower waters of one or two great rivers a few rough settlements had gnawed slight indentations into this wilderness of woods; and a little farther inland some dismal clearing around a blockhouse or stockade let in the sunlight to a soil that had lain in shadow time out of mind. This waste of savage vegetation survives, in some part, to this day, with the same prodigality of vital force, the same struggle for existence and mutual havoc that mark all organized beings, from men to mushrooms. Young seedlings in millions spring every summer from the black mould, rich with the decay of those that had preceded them, crowding, choking, and

killing one another, perishing by their very abundance, — all but a scattered few, stronger than the
rest, or more fortunate in position, which survive by
blighting those about them.   They in turn, as they
grow, interlock their boughs, and repeat in a season
or two the same process of mutual suffocation.   The
forest is full of lean saplings dead or dying with
vainly stretching towards the light.   Not one infant
tree in a thousand lives to maturity; yet these survivors form an innumerable host, pressed together in
struggling confusion, squeezed out of symmetry and
robbed of normal development, as men are said to be
in the level sameness of democratic society.   Seen
from above, their mingled tops spread in a sea of
verdure basking in light; seen from below, all is
shadow, through which spots of timid sunshine steal
down among legions of lank, mossy trunks, toad-
stools and rank ferns, protruding roots, matted bushes,
and rotting carcasses of fallen trees.   A generation
ago one might find here and there the rugged trunk
of some great pine lifting its verdant spire above
the undistinguished myriads of the forest.   The
woods of Maine had their aristocracy; but the axe
of the woodman has laid them low, and these lords
of the wilderness are seen no more.

   The life and light of this grim solitude were in its
countless streams and lakes, from little brooks steal-
ing clear and cold under the alders, full of the small
fry of trout, to the mighty arteries of the Penobscot
and the Kennebec; from the great reservoir of

Moosehead to a thousand nameless ponds shining in the hollow places of the forest.

It had and still has its beast of prey, — wolves, savage, cowardly, and mean; bears, gentle and mild compared to their grisly relatives of the Far West, vegetarians when they can do no better, and not without something grotesque and quaint in manners and behavior ; sometimes, though rarely, the strong and sullen wolverine; frequently the lynx; and now and then the fierce and agile cougar.

The human denizens of this wilderness were no less fierce, and far more dangerous. These were the various tribes and sub-tribes of the Abenakis, whose villages were on the Saco, the Kennebec, the Penobscot, and the other great watercourses. Most of them had been converted by the Jesuits, and, as we have seen already, some had been persuaded to remove to Canada, like the converted Iroquois of Caughnawaga.[1] The rest remained in their native haunts, where, under the direction of their missionaries, they could be used to keep the English settlements in check.

We know how busily they plied their tomahawks in William and Mary's War, and what havoc they made among the scattered settlements of the border.[2] Another war with France was declared on the fourth of May, 1702, on which the Abenakis again assumed a threatening attitude. In June of the next year Dudley, governor of Massachusetts, called the chiefs of the various bands to a council at Casco. Here

[1] Count Frontenac, i. 231.   [2] *Ibid.*, chaps. xi. xvi. xvii.

presently appeared the Norridgewocks from the
Kennebec, the Penobscots and Androscoggins from
the rivers that bear their names, the Penacooks from
the Merrimac, and the Pequawkets from the Saco,
all well armed, and daubed with ceremonial paint.
The principal among them, gathered under a large
tent, were addressed by Dudley in a conciliatory
speech. Their orator replied that they wanted nothing but peace, and that their thoughts were as far
from war as the sun was from the earth, — words
which they duly confirmed by a belt of wampum.[1]
Presents were distributed among them and received
with apparent satisfaction, while two of their principal chiefs, known as Captain Samuel and Captain
Bomazeen, declared that several French missionaries
had lately come among them to excite them against
the English, but that they were "firm as mountains,"
and would remain so "as long as the sun and moon
endured." They ended the meeting with dancing,
singing, and whoops of joy, followed by a volley of
musketry, answered by another from the English.
It was discovered, however, that the Indians had

---

[1] Penhallow, *History of the Wars of New England with the Eastern
Indians*, 16 (ed. 1859). Penhallow was present at the council. In
Judge Sewall's clumsy abstract of the proceedings (*Diary of Sewall*,
ii. 85) the Indians are represented as professing neutrality. The
governor and intendant of Canada write that the Abenakis had
begun a treaty of neutrality with the English, but that as "les
Jésuites observoient les sauvages, le traité ne fut pas conclu."
They add that Rale, Jesuit missionary at Norridgewock, informs
them that his Indians were ready to lift the hatchet against the
English. *Vaudreuil et Beauharnois au Ministre*, 1703.

loaded their guns with ball, intending, as the English believed, to murder Dudley and his attendants if they could have done so without danger to their chiefs, whom the governor had prudently kept about him. It was afterwards found, if we may believe a highly respectable member of the party, that two hundred French and Indians were on their way, "resolved to seize the governor, council, and gentlemen, and then to sacrifice the inhabitants at pleasure;" but when they arrived, the English officials had been gone three days.[1]

The French governor, Vaudreuil, says that about this time some of the Abenakis were killed or maltreated by Englishmen. It may have been so: desperadoes, drunk or sober, were not rare along the frontier; but Vaudreuil gives no particulars, and the only English outrage that appears on record at the time was the act of a gang of vagabonds who plundered the house of the younger Saint-Castin, where the town of Castine now stands. He was Abenaki by his mother; but he was absent when the attack took place, and the marauders seem to have shed no blood. Nevertheless, within six weeks after

---

[1] Penhallow, 17, 18 (ed. 1859). There was a previous meeting of conciliation between the English and the Abenakis in 1702. The Jesuit Bigot says that the Indians assured him that they had scornfully repelled the overtures of the English, and told them that they would always stand fast by the French. (*Relation des Abenakis*, 1702.) This is not likely. The Indians probably lied both to the Jesuit and to the English, telling to each what they knew would be most acceptable.

the Treaty of Casco, every unprotected farmhouse in Maine was in a blaze.

The settlements of Maine, confined to the south-western corner of what is now the State of Maine, extended along the coast in a feeble and broken line from Kittery to Casco. Ten years of murderous warfare had almost ruined them. East of the village of Wells little was left except one or two forts and the so-called "garrisons," which were private houses pierced with loopholes and having an upper story projecting over the lower, so that the defenders could fire down on assailants battering the door or piling fagots against the walls. A few were fenced with palisades, as was the case with the house of Joseph Storer at the east end of Wells, where an overwhelming force of French and Indians had been gallantly repulsed in the summer of 1692.[1] These fortified houses were, however, very rarely attacked, except by surprise and treachery. In case of alarm such of the inhabitants as found time took refuge in them with their families, and left their dwellings to the flames; for the first thought of the settler was to put his women and children beyond reach of the scalping-knife. There were several of these asylums in different parts of Wells; and without them the place must have been abandoned. In the little settlement of York, farther westward, there were five of them, which had saved a part of the inhabitants when the rest were surprised and massacred.

[1] See "Count Frontenac," ii. 129.

Wells was a long, straggling settlement, consisting at the beginning of William and Mary's War of about eighty houses and log-cabins,[1] strung at intervals along the north side of the rough track, known as the King's Road, which ran parallel to the sea. Behind the houses were rude, half-cleared pastures, and behind these again, the primeval forest. The cultivated land was on the south side of the road; in front of the houses, and beyond it, spread great salt-marshes, bordering the sea and haunted by innumerable game-birds.

The settlements of Maine were a dependency of Massachusetts, — a position that did not please their inhabitants, but which they accepted because they needed the help of their Puritan neighbors, from whom they differed widely both in their qualities and in their faults. The Indian wars that checked their growth had kept them in a condition more than half barbarous. They were a hard-working and hard-drinking race; for though tea and coffee were scarcely known, the land flowed with New England rum, which was ranked among the necessaries of life. The better sort could read and write in a bungling way; but many were wholly illiterate, and it was not till long after Queen Anne's War that the remoter settlements established schools, taught by poor students from Harvard or less competent instructors, and held at first in private houses or under sheds. The church at Wells had been burned by the Indians; and

---

[1] Bourne, *History of Wells and Kennebunk.*

though the settlers were beggared by the war, they voted in town-meeting to build another. The new temple, begun in 1699, was a plain wooden structure thirty feet square. For want of money the windows long remained unglazed, the walls without plaster, and the floor without seats; yet services were duly held here under direction of the minister, Samuel Emery, to whom they paid £45 a year, half in provincial currency, and half in farm-produce and fire-wood.

In spite of these efforts to maintain public worship, they were far from being a religious community; nor were they a peaceful one. Gossip and scandal ran riot; social jealousies abounded; and under what seemed entire democratic equality, the lazy, drunken, and shiftless envied the industrious and thrifty. Wells was infested, moreover, by several "frightfully turbulent women," as the chronicle styles them, from whose rabid tongues the minister himself did not always escape; and once, in its earlier days, the town had been indicted for not providing a ducking-stool to correct these breeders of discord.

Judicial officers were sometimes informally chosen by popular vote, and sometimes appointed by the governor of Massachusetts from among the inhabitants. As they knew no law, they gave judgment according to their own ideas of justice, and their sentences were oftener wanting in wisdom than in severity. Until after 1700 the county courts met by beat of drum at some of the primitive inns or taverns with which the frontier abounded.

At Wells and other outlying and endangered hamlets life was still exceedingly rude. The log-cabins of the least thrifty were no better furnished than Indian wigwams. The house of Edmond Little-field, reputed the richest man in Wells, consisted of two bedrooms and a kitchen, which last served a great variety of uses, and was supplied with a table, a pewter pot, a frying-pan, and a skillet; but no chairs, cups, saucers, knives, forks, or spoons. In each of the two bedrooms there was a bed, a blanket, and a chest. Another village notable — Ensign John Barrett — was better provided, being the possessor of two beds, two chests and a box, four pewter dishes, four earthen pots, two iron pots, seven trays, two buckets, some pieces of wooden-ware, a skillet, and a frying-pan. In the inventory of the patriarchal Francis Littlefield, who died in 1712, we find the exceptional items of one looking-glass, two old chairs, and two old books. Such of the family as had no bed slept on hay or straw, and no provision for the toilet is recorded.[1]

On the tenth of August, 1703, these rugged borderers were about their usual callings, unconscious of danger, — the women at their household work, the men in the fields or on the more distant salt-marshes. The wife of Thomas Wells had reached the time of her confinement, and her husband had gone for a

---

[1] The above particulars are drawn from the *History of Wells and Kennebunk*, by the late Edward E. Bourne, of Wells, — a work of admirable thoroughness, fidelity, and candor.

nurse. Some miles east of Wells's cabin lived
Stephen Harding, — hunter, blacksmith, and tavern-
keeper, a sturdy, good-natured man, who loved the
woods, and whose frequent hunting trips sometimes
led him nearly to the White Mountains. Distant
gunshots were heard from the westward, and his
quick eye presently discovered Indians approaching,
on which he told his frightened wife to go with their
infant to a certain oak-tree beyond the creek while he
waited to learn whether the strangers were friends or
foes.

That morning several parties of Indians had stolen
out of the dismal woods behind the houses and farms
of Wells, and approached different dwellings of the
far-extended settlement at about the same time.
They entered the cabin of Thomas Wells, where his
wife lay in the pains of childbirth, and murdered her
and her two small children. At the same time they
killed Joseph Sayer, a neighbor of Wells, with all
his family.

Meanwhile Stephen Harding, having sent his wife
and child to a safe distance, returned to his blacksmith's shop, and, seeing nobody, gave a defiant
whoop; on which four Indians sprang at him from
the bushes. He escaped through a back-door of the
shop, eluded his pursuers, and found his wife and
child in a cornfield, where the woman had fainted
with fright. They spent the night in the woods,
and on the next day, after a circuit of nine miles,
reached the palisaded house of Joseph Storer.

They found the inmates in distress and agitation. Storer's daughter Mary, a girl of eighteen, was missing. The Indians had caught her, and afterwards carried her prisoner to Canada. Samuel Hill and his family were captured, and the younger children butchered. But it is useless to record the names and fate of the sufferers. Thirty-nine in all, chiefly women and children, were killed or carried off, and then the Indians disappeared as quickly and silently as they had come, leaving many of the houses in flames.

This raid upon Wells was only part of a combined attack on all the settlements from that place to Casco. Those eastward of Wells had been, as we have seen, abandoned in the last war, excepting the forts and fortified houses; but the inhabitants, reassured, no doubt, by the Treaty of Casco, had begun to return. On this same day, the tenth of August, they were startled from their security. A band of Indians mixed with Frenchmen fell upon the settlements about the stone fort near the Falls of the Saco, killed eleven persons, captured twenty-four, and vainly attacked the fort itself. Others surprised the settlers at a place called Spurwink, and killed or captured twenty-two. Others, again, destroyed the huts of the fishermen at Cape Porpoise, and attacked the fortified house at Winter Harbor, the inmates of which, after a brave resistance, were forced to capitulate. The settlers at Scarborough were also in a fortified house, where they made a long and obstinate defence till help at last arrived. Nine families were settled at Purpooduck Point, near the present city of Portland. They had no place of refuge, and the men being, no doubt, fishermen, were all absent, when the Indians burst into the hamlet, butchered twenty-five women and children, and carried off eight.

The fort at Casco, or Falmouth, was held by Major March, with thirty-six men. He had no thought of danger, when three well-known chiefs from Norridge-wock appeared with a white flag, and asked for an interview. As they seemed to be alone and unarmed, he went to meet them, followed by two or three soldiers and accompanied by two old men named Phippeny and Kent, inhabitants of the place. They had hardly reached the spot when the three chiefs drew hatchets from under a kind of mantle which they wore and sprang upon them, while other Indians, ambushed near by, leaped up and joined in the attack. The two old men were killed at once; but March, who was noted for strength and agility, wrenched a hatchet from one of his assailants, and kept them all at bay till Sergeant Hook came to his aid with a file of men and drove them off.

They soon reappeared, burned the deserted cabins in the neighborhood, and beset the garrison in numbers that continually increased, till in a few days the entire force that had been busied in ravaging the scattered settlements was gathered around the place. It consisted of about five hundred Indians of several tribes, and a few Frenchmen under an officer named Beaubassin. Being elated with past successes, they laid siege to the fort, sheltering themselves under a steep bank by the water-side and burrowing their way towards the rampart. March could not dislodge them, and they continued their approaches till the third day, when Captain Southack, with the Massachusetts armed vessel known as the "Province Galley," sailed into the harbor, recaptured three small vessels that the Indians had taken along the coast, and destroyed a great number of their canoes, on which they gave up their enterprise and disappeared.[1]

Such was the beginning of Queen Anne's War. These attacks were due less to the Abenakis than to the French who set them on. "Monsieur de Vaudreuil," writes the Jesuit historian Charlevoix, "formed a party of these savages, to whom he joined some Frenchmen under the direction of the Sieur de Beaubassin, when they effected some ravages of no great consequence; they killed, however, about three hundred men." This last statement is doubly incorrect. The whole number of persons killed and carried off during the August attacks did not much

---

[1] On these attacks on the frontier of Maine, Penhallow, who well knew the country and the people, is the best authority. Niles, in his *Indian and French Wars*, copies him without acknowledgment, but not without blunders. As regards the attack on Wells, what particulars we have are mainly due to the research of the indefatigable Bourne. Compare Belknap, i. 330 ; Folsom, *History of Saco and Biddeford*, 198; *Coll. Maine Hist. Soc.*, iii. 140, 348; Williamson, *History of Maine*, ii. 42. Beaubassin is called "Bobasser" in most of the English accounts.

exceed one hundred and sixty; [1] and these were of both sexes and all ages, from octogenarians to new-born infants. The able-bodied men among them were few, as most of the attacks were made upon unprotected houses in the absence of the head of the family; and the only fortified place captured was the garrison-house at Winter Harbor, which surrendered on terms of capitulation. The instruments of this ignoble warfare and the revolting atrocities that accompanied it were all, or nearly all, converted Indians of the missions. Charlevoix has no word of disapproval for it, and seems to regard its partial success as a gratifying one so far as it went.

One of the objects was, no doubt, to check the progress of the English settlements; but, pursues Charlevoix, "the essential point was to commit the Abenakis in such a manner that they could not draw back." [2] This object was constantly kept in view. The French claimed at this time that the territory of Acadia reached as far westward as the Kennebec, which therefore formed, in their view, the boundary between the rival nations, and they trusted in the Abenakis to defend this assumed line of demarcation. But the Abenakis sorely needed English guns, knives, hatchets, and kettles, and nothing but the utmost vigilance could prevent them from coming to terms with those who could supply their necessities.   Hence

---

[1] The careful and well-informed Belknap puts it at only 130 *History of New Hampshire*, i. 331.

[2] Charlevoix, ii. 289, 290 (quarto edition).

the policy of the French authorities on the frontier
of New England was the opposite of their policy on
the frontier of New York. They left the latter
undisturbed, lest by attacking the Dutch and English
settlers they should stir up the Five Nations to attack
Canada; while, on the other hand, they constantly
spurred the Abenakis against New England, in order
to avert the dreaded event of their making peace
with her.

The attack on Wells, Casco, and the intervening
settlements was followed by murders and depreda-
tions that lasted through the autumn and extended
along two hundred miles of frontier. Thirty Indians
attacked the village of Hampton, killed the Widow
Mussey, a famous Quakeress, and then fled to escape
pursuit. At Black Point nineteen men going to
their work in the meadows were ambushed by two
hundred Indians, and all but one were shot or captured. The fort was next attacked. It was garrisoned by eight men under Lieutenant Wyatt, who
stood their ground for some time, and then escaped
by means of a sloop in the harbor. At York the wife
and children of Arthur Brandon were killed, and the
Widow Parsons and her daughter carried off. At
Berwick the Indians attacked the fortified house of
Andrew Neal, but were repulsed with the loss of nine
killed and many wounded, for which they revenged
themselves by burning alive Joseph Ring, a prisoner
whom they had taken. Early in February a small
party of them hovered about the fortified house of

Joseph Bradley at Haverhill, till, seeing the gate open and nobody on the watch, they rushed in.   The woman of the house was boiling soap, and in her desperation she snatched up the kettle and threw the contents over them with such effect that one of them, it is said, was scalded to death.   The man who should have been on the watch was killed, and several persons were captured, including the woman. It was the second time that she had been a prisoner in Indian hands.   Half starved and bearing a heavy load, she followed her captors in their hasty retreat towards Canada.   After a time she was safely delivered of an infant in the midst of the winter forest; but the child pined for want of sustenance, and the Indians hastened its death by throwing hot coals into its mouth when it cried.   The astonishing vitality of the woman carried her to the end of the frightful journey.   A Frenchman bought her from the Indians, and she was finally ransomed by her husband.

By far the most dangerous and harassing attacks were those of small parties skulking under the edge of the forest, or lying hidden for days together, watching their opportunity to murder unawares, and vanishing when they had done so.   Against such an enemy there was no defence.   The Massachusetts government sent a troop of horse to Portsmouth, and another to Wells.   These had the advantage of rapid movement in case of alarm along the roads and forest-paths from settlement to settlement; but once in the woods, their horses were worse than useless, and they

could only fight on foot.   Fighting, however, was
rarely possible; for on reaching the scene of action
they found nothing but mangled corpses and burning
houses.

The best defence was to take the offensive.   In
September Governor Dudley sent three hundred and
sixty men to the upper Saco, the haunt of the
Pequawket tribe; but the place was deserted.   Major,
now Colonel, March soon after repeated the attempt,
killing six Indians, and capturing as many more.
The General Court offered £40 for every Indian
scalp, and one Captain Tyng, in consequence, surprised an Indian village in midwinter and brought
back five of these disgusting trophies.   In the spring
of 1704 word came from Albany that a band of
French Indians had built a fort and planted corn at
Coos meadows, high up the river Connecticut.   On
this, one Caleb Lyman with five friendly Indians,
probably Mohegans, set out from Northampton, and
after a long march through the forest, surprised,
under cover of a thunderstorm, a wigwam containing
nine warriors, — bound, no doubt, against the frontier.
They killed seven of them; and this was all that was
done at present in the way of reprisal or prevention.[1]

The murders and burnings along the borders were
destined to continue with little variety and little
interruption during ten years.   It was a repetition
of what the pedantic Cotton Mather calls *Decennium
luctuosum*, or the "woful decade" of William and

[1] Penhallow, *Wars of New England with the Eastern Indians.*

Mary's War.   The wonder is that the outlying settlements were not abandoned.   These ghastly, insidious,
and ever-present dangers demanded a more obstinate
courage than the hottest battle in the open field.

One curious frontier incident may be mentioned
here, though it did not happen till towards the end
of the war.   In spite of poverty, danger, and tribulation, marrying and giving in marriage did not cease
among the sturdy borderers; and on a day in September there was a notable wedding feast at the
palisaded house of John Wheelwright, one of the
chief men of Wells.   Elisha Plaisted was to espouse
Wheelwright's daughter Hannah, and many guests
were assembled, some from Portsmouth, and even
beyond it.   Probably most of them came in sail-
boats; for the way by land was full of peril, especially
on the road from York, which ran through dense
woods, where Indians often waylaid the traveller.   The bridegroom's father was present with the
rest.   It was a concourse of men in homespun, and
women and girls in such improvised finery as their
poor resources could supply; possibly, in default of
better, some wore nightgowns, more or less disguised,
over their daily dress, as happened on similar occasions half a century later among the frontiersmen of
West Virginia.[1]   After an evening of rough merri-
ment and gymnastic dancing, the guests lay down to
sleep under the roof of their host or in adjacent barns
and sheds.   When morning came, and they were

[1] Doddridge, *Notes on Western Virginia and Pennsylvania.*

preparing to depart, it was found that two horses were missing; and not doubting that they had strayed away, three young men — Sergeant Tucker, Joshua Downing, and Isaac Cole — went to find them. In a few minutes several gunshots were heard. The three young men did not return. Downing ànd Cole were killed, and Tucker was wounded and made prisoner.

Believing that, as usual, the attack came from some small scalping-party, Elisha Plaisted and eight or ten more threw themselves on the horses that stood saddled before the house, and galloped across the fields in the direction of the firing; while others ran to cut off the enemy's retreat. A volley was presently heard, and several of the party were seen running back towards the house. Elisha Plaisted and his companions had fallen into an ambuscade of two hundred Indians. One or more of them were shot, and the unfortunate bridegroom was captured. The distress of his young wife, who was but eighteen, may be imagined.

Two companies of armed men in the pay of Massachusetts were then in Wells, and some of them had come to the wedding. Seventy marksmen went to meet the Indians, who ensconced themselves in the edge of the forest, whence they could not be dislodged. There was some desultory firing, and one of the combatants was killed on each side, after which the whites gave up the attack, and Lieutenant Banks went forward with a flag of truce, in the hope of ransoming the prisoners. He was met by six chiefs, among whom were two noted Indians of his acquaintance, Bomazeen and Captain Nathaniel. They well knew that the living Plaisted was worth more than his scalp; and though they would not come to terms at once, they promised to meet the English at Richmond's Island in a few days and give up both him and Tucker on payment of a sufficient ransom. The flag of truce was respected, and Banks came back safe, bringing a hasty note to the elder Plaisted from his captive son. This note now lies before me, and it runs thus, in the dutiful formality of the olden time: —

SIR, — I am in the hands of a great many Indians, with which there is six captains. They say that what they will have for me is 50 pounds, and thirty pounds for Tucker, my fellow prisoner, in good goods, as broadcloth, some provisions, some tobacco pipes, Pomisstone [pumice-stone], stockings, and a little of all things. If you will, come to Richmond's Island in 5 days at farthest, for here is 200 Indians, and they belong to Canada.

If you do not come in 5 days, you will not see me, for Captain Nathaniel the Indian will not stay no longer, for the Canada Indians is not willing for to sell me. Pray, Sir, don't fail, for they have given me one day, for the days were but 4 at first. Give my kind love to my dear wife. This from your dutiful son till death,

ELISHA PLAISTED.

The alarm being spread and a sufficient number of men mustered, they set out to attack the enemy

CHAPTER IV.

1704–1740.

DEERFIELD.

ABOUT midwinter the governor of Canada sent
another large war-party against the New England
border. The object of attack was an unoffending
hamlet, that from its position could never be a menace
to the French, and the destruction of which could
profit them nothing. The aim of the enterprise was
not military, but political. "I have sent no war-
party towards Albany," writes Vaudreuil, "because
we must do nothing that might cause a rupture
between us and the Iroquois; but we must keep
things astir in the direction of Boston, or else the
Abenakis will declare for the English." In short,
the object was fully to commit these savages to hostil-

ity against New England, and convince them at the same time that the French would back their quarrel.[1]

The party consisted, according to French accounts, of fifty Canadians and two hundred Abenakis and Caughnawagas, — the latter of whom, while trading constantly with Albany, were rarely averse to a raid against Massachusetts or New Hampshire.[2] The command was given to the younger Hertel de Rouville, who was accompanied by four of his brothers. They began their march in the depth of winter, journeyed nearly three hundred miles on snow-shoes through the forest, and approached their destination on the afternoon of the twenty-eighth of February, 1704. It was the village of Deerfield, which then formed the extreme northwestern frontier of Massachusetts, — its feeble neighbor, the infant settlement of North-field, a little higher up the Connecticut, having been abandoned during the last war. Rouville halted his followers at a place now called Petty's Plain, two miles from the village; and here, under the shelter of a pine forest, they all lay hidden, shivering with cold, — for they dared not make fires, — and hungry as wolves, for their provisions were spent. Though their numbers, by the lowest account, were nearly

[1] *Vaudreuil au Ministre*, 14 *Novembre*, 1703; *Ibid.*, 3 *Avril*, 1704; *Vaudreuil et Beauharnois au Ministre*, 17 *Novembre*, 1704. French writers say that the English surprised and killed some of the Abenakis, who thereupon asked help from Canada. This perhaps refers to the expeditions of Colonel March and Captain Tyng, who, after the bloody attacks upon the settlements of Maine, made reprisal upon Abenaki camps.

[2] English accounts make the whole number 342.

HERTEL DE ROUVILLE.

equal to the whole population of Deerfield, — men, women, and children, — they had no thought of an open attack, but trusted to darkness and surprise for an easy victory.

Deerfield stood on a plateau above the river meadows, and the houses — forty-one in all — were chiefly along the road towards the villages of Hadley and Hatfield, a few miles distant. In the middle of the place, on a rising ground called Meeting-house Hill, was a small square wooden meeting-house. This, with about fifteen private houses, besides barns and sheds, was enclosed by a fence of palisades eight feet high, flanked by "mounts," or blockhouses, at two or more of the corners. The four sides of this palisaded enclosure, which was called the fort, measured in all no less than two hundred and two rods, and within it lived some of the principal inhabitants of the village, of which it formed the centre or citadel. Chief among its inmates was John Williams, the minister, a man of character and education, who, after graduating at Harvard, had come to Deerfield when it was still suffering under the ruinous effects of King Philip's War, and entered on his ministry with a salary of sixty pounds in depreciated New England currency, payable, not in money, but in wheat, Indian-corn, and pork.[1] His parishioners built him a house, he married, and had now eight children, one of whom was absent with friends at

---

[1] Stephen W. Williams, *Biographical Memoir of Rev. John Williams.*

Hadley.[1] His next neighbor was Benoni Stebbins, sergeant in the county militia, who lived a few rods from the meeting-house. About fifty yards distant, and near the northwest angle of the enclosure, stood the house of Ensign John Sheldon, a framed building, one of the largest in the village, and, like that of Stebbins, made bullet-proof by a layer of bricks between the outer and inner sheathing, while its small windows and its projecting upper story also helped to make it defensible.

The space enclosed by the palisade, though much too large for effective defence, served in time of alarm as an asylum for the inhabitants outside, whose houses were scattered, — some on the north towards the hidden enemy, and some on the south towards Hadley and Hatfield. Among those on the south side was that of the militia captain, Jonathan Wells, which had a palisade of its own, and, like the so-called fort, served as an asylum for the neighbors.

These private fortified houses were sometimes built by the owners alone, though more often they were the joint work of the owners and of the inhabitants, to whose safety they contributed. The palisade fence that enclosed the central part of the village was made under a vote of the town, each inhabitant being required to do his share; and as they were greatly impoverished by the last war, the General Court of the province remitted for a time a part of

[1] *Account of y[e] destruction at Deref[d], February 29, 1703/4.*

their taxes in consideration of a work which aided the general defence.[1]

Down to the Peace of Ryswick the neighborhood had been constantly infested by scalping-parties, and once the village had been attacked by a considerable force of French and Indians, who were beaten off. Of late there had been warnings of fresh disturbance. Lord Cornbury, governor of New York, wrote that he had heard through spies that Deerfield was again to be attacked, and a message to the same effect came from Peter Schuyler, who had received intimations of the danger from Mohawks lately on a visit to their Caughnawaga relatives. During the autumn the alarm was so great that the people took refuge within the palisades, and the houses of the enclosure were crowded with them; but the panic had now subsided, and many, though not all, had returned to their homes. They were reassured by the presence of twenty volunteers from the villages below, whom, on application from the minister, Williams, the General Court had sent as a garrison to Deerfield, where they were lodged in the houses of the villagers. On the night when Hertel de Rouville and his band lay hidden among the pines there were in all the settlement a little less than three hundred souls, of whom two hundred and sixty-eight were inhabitants, twenty were yeomen soldiers of the garrison, two were visi-

---

[1] Papers in the Archives of Massachusetts. Among these, a letter of Rev. John Williams to the governor, 21 October, 1703, states that the palisade is rotten, and must be rebuilt.

tors from Hatfield, and three were negro slaves. They were of all ages, — from the Widow Allison, in her eighty-fifth year, to the infant son of Deacon French, aged four weeks.[1]

Heavy snows had lately fallen and buried the clearings, the meadow, and the frozen river to the depth of full three feet. On the northwestern side the drifts were piled nearly to the top of the palisade fence, so that it was no longer an obstruction to an active enemy.

As the afternoon waned, the sights and sounds of the little border hamlet were, no doubt, like those of any other rustic New England village at the end of a winter day, — an ox-sledge creaking on the frosty snow as it brought in the last load of firewood, boys in homespun snowballing one another in the village street, farmers feeding their horses and cattle in the barns, a matron drawing a pail of water with the help of one of those long well-sweeps still used in some remote districts, or a girl bringing a pail of milk from the cow-shed. In the houses, where one room served as kitchen, dining-room, and parlor, the housewife cooked the evening meal, children sat at their bowls of mush and milk, and the men of the family, their day's work over, gathered about the fire, while perhaps some village coquette sat in

---

[1] The names of nearly all the inhabitants are preserved, and even the ages of most of them have been ascertained, through the indefatigable research of Mr. George Sheldon, of Deerfield, among contemporary records. The house of Thomas French, the town clerk, was not destroyed, and his papers were saved.

the corner with fingers busy at the spinning-wheel, and ears intent on the stammered wooings of her rustic lover. Deerfield kept early hours, and it is likely that by nine o'clock all were in their beds. There was a patrol inside the palisade, but there was little discipline among these extemporized soldiers; the watchers grew careless as the frosty night went on; and it is said that towards morning they, like the villagers, betook themselves to their beds.

Rouville and his men, savage with hunger, lay shivering under the pines till about two hours before dawn; then, leaving their packs and their snow-shoes behind, they moved cautiously towards their prey. There was a crust on the snow strong enough to bear their weight, though not to prevent a rustling noise as it crunched under the feet of so many men. It is said that from time to time Rouville commanded a halt, in order that the sentinels, if such there were, might mistake the distant sound for rising and fall- ing gusts of wind. In any case, no alarm was given till they had mounted the palisade and dropped silently into the unconscious village. Then with one accord they screeched the war-whoop, and assailed the doors of the houses with axes and hatchets.

The hideous din startled the minister, Williams, from his sleep. Half-wakened, he sprang out of bed, and saw dimly a crowd of savages bursting through the shattered door. He shouted to two soldiers who were lodged in the house; and then, with more valor than discretion, snatched a pistol that hung at the head of the bed, cocked it, and snapped it at the breast of the foremost Indian, who proved to be a Caughnawaga chief. It missed fire, or Williams would, no doubt, have been killed on the spot. Amid the screams of his terrified children, three of the party seized him and bound him fast; for they came well provided with cords, since prisoners had a market value. Nevertheless, in the first fury of their attack they dragged to the door and murdered two of the children and a negro woman called Parthena, who was probably their nurse. In an upper room lodged a young man named Stoddard, who had time to snatch a cloak, throw himself out of the window, climb the palisade, and escape in the darkness. Half-naked as he was, he made his way over the snow to Hatfield, binding his bare feet with strips torn from the cloak.

They kept Williams shivering in his shirt for an hour while a frightful uproar of yells, shrieks, and gunshots sounded from without. At length they permitted him, his wife, and five remaining children to dress themselves. Meanwhile the Indians and their allies burst into most of the houses, killed such of the men as resisted, butchered some of the women and children, and seized and bound the rest. Some of the villagers escaped in the confusion, like Stoddard, and either fled half dead with cold towards Hatfield, or sought refuge in the fortified house of Jonathan Wells.

The house of Stebbins, the minister's next neigh-

bor, had not been attacked so soon as the rest, and
the inmates had a little time for preparation. They
consisted of Stebbins himself, with his wife and
five children, David Hoyt, Joseph Catlin, Benjamin
Church, a namesake of the old Indian fighter of
Philip's War, and three other men, — probably
refugees who had brought their wives and families
within the palisaded enclosure for safety. Thus the
house contained seven men, four or five women, and
a considerable number of children. Though the
walls were bullet-proof, it was not built for defence.
The men, however, were well supplied with guns,
powder, and lead, and they seem to have found some
means of barricading the windows. When the enemy
tried to break in, they drove them back with loss.
On this, the French and Indians gathered in great
numbers before the house, showered bullets upon it,
and tried to set it on fire. They were again repulsed,
with the loss of several killed and wounded; among
the former a Caughnawaga chief, and among the
latter a French officer. Still the firing continued.
If the assailants had made a resolute assault, the
defenders must have been overpowered; but to risk
lives in open attack was contrary to every maxim of
forest warfare. The women in the house behaved
with great courage, and moulded bullets, which the
men shot at the enemy. Stebbins was killed outright, and Church was wounded, as was also the
wife of David Hoyt. At length most of the French
and Indians, disgusted with the obstinacy of the

defence, turned their attention to other quarters; though some kept up their fire under cover of the meeting-house and another building within easy range of gunshot.

This building was the house of Ensign John Sheldon, already mentioned. The Indians had had some difficulty in mastering it; for the door being of thick oak plank, studded with nails of wrought iron and well barred, they could not break it open. After a time, however, they hacked a hole in it, through which they fired and killed Mrs. Sheldon as she sat on the edge of a bed in a lower room. Her husband, a man of great resolution, seems to have been absent. Their son John, with Hannah his wife, jumped from an upper chamber window. The young woman sprained her ankle in the fall, and lay helpless, but begged her husband to run to Hatfield for aid, which he did, while she remained a prisoner. The Indians soon got in at a back door, seized Mercy Sheldon, a little girl of two years, and dashed out her brains on the door-stone. Her two brothers and her sister Mary, a girl of sixteen, were captured. The house was used for a short time as a depot for prisoners, and here also was brought the French officer wounded in the attack on the Stebbins house. A family tradition relates that as he lay in great torment he begged for water, and that it was brought him by one of the prisoners, Mrs. John Catlin, whose husband, son, and infant grandson had been killed, and who, nevertheless, did all in her power to relieve the sufferings of the wounded man. Probably it was in recognition of this charity that when the other prisoners were led away, Mrs. Catlin was left behind. She died of grief a few weeks later.

The sun was scarcely an hour high when the miserable drove of captives was conducted across the river to the foot of a mountain or high hill. Williams and his family were soon compelled to follow, and his house was set on fire. As they led him off he saw that other houses within the palisade were burning, and that all were in the power of the enemy except that of his neighbor Stebbins, where the gallant defenders still kept their assailants at bay. Having collected all their prisoners, the main body of the French and Indians began to withdraw towards the pine forest, where they had left their packs and snow-shoes, and to prepare for a retreat before the country should be roused, first murdering in cold blood Marah Carter, a little girl of five years, whom they probably thought unequal to the march. Several parties, however, still lingered in the village, firing on the Stebbins house, killing cattle, hogs, and sheep, and gathering such plunder as the place afforded.

Early in the attack, and while it was yet dark, the light of burning houses, reflected from the fields of snow, had been seen at Hatfield, Hadley, and Northampton. The alarm was sounded through the slumbering hamlets, and parties of men mounted on farm-horses, with saddles or without, hastened to the rescue, not doubting that the fires were kindled by

Indians. When the sun was about two hours high, between thirty and forty of them were gathered at the fortified house of Jonathan Wells, at the southern end of the village. The houses of this neighborhood were still standing, and seem not to have been attacked, — the stubborn defence of the Stebbins house having apparently prevented the enemy from pushing much beyond the palisaded enclosure. The house of Wells was full of refugee families. A few Deerfield men here joined the horsemen from the lower towns, as also did four or five of the yeoman soldiers who had escaped the fate of most of their comrades. The horsemen left their horses within Wells's fence; he himself took the lead, and the whole party rushed in together at the southern gate of the palisaded enclosure, drove out the plunderers, and retook a part of their plunder. The assailants of the Stebbins house, after firing at it for three hours, were put to flight, and those of its male occupants who were still alive joined their countrymen, while the women and children ran back for harborage to the house of Wells.

Wells and his men, now upwards of fifty, drove the flying enemy more than a mile across the river meadows, and ran in headlong pursuit over the crusted snow, killing a considerable number. In the eagerness of the chase many threw off their overcoats, and even their jackets. Wells saw the danger, and vainly called on them to stop. Their blood was up, and most of them were young and inexperienced.

Meanwhile the firing at the village had been heard by Rouville's main body, who had already begun their retreat northward. They turned back to support their comrades, and hid themselves under the bank of the river till the pursuers drew near, when they gave them a close volley and rushed upon them with the war-whoop. Some of the English were shot down, and the rest driven back. There was no panic. "We retreated," says Wells, "facing about and firing." When they reached the palisade they made a final stand, covering by their fire such of their comrades as had fallen within range of musket-shot, and thus saving them from the scalping-knife. The French did not try to dislodge them. Nine of them had been killed, several were wounded, and one was captured.[1]

The number of English carried off prisoners was one hundred and eleven, and the number killed was according to one list forty-seven, and according to

[1] On the thirty-first of May, 1704, Jonathan Wells and Ebenezer Wright petitioned the General Court for compensation for the losses of those who drove the enemy out of Deerfield and chased them into the meadow. The petition, which was granted, gives an account of the affair, followed by a list of all the men engaged. They number fifty-seven, including the nine who were killed. A list of the plunder retaken from the enemy, consisting of guns, blankets, hatchets, etc., is also added. Several other petitions for the relief of men wounded at the same time are preserved in the archives of Massachusetts. In 1736 the survivors of the party, with the representatives of those who had died, petitioned the General Court for allotments of land, in recognition of their services. This petition also was granted. It is accompanied by a narrative written by Wells. These and other papers on the same subject have been recently printed by Mr. George Sheldon, of Deerfield.

another fifty-three, the latter including some who were smothered in the cellars of their burning houses. The names, and in most cases the ages, of both captives and slain are preserved. Those who escaped with life and freedom were, by the best account, one hundred and thirty-seven. An official tabular statement, drawn up on the spot, sets the number of houses burned at seventeen. The house of the town clerk, Thomas French, escaped, as before mentioned, and the town records, with other papers in his charge, were saved. The meeting-house also was left standing. The house of Sheldon was hastily set on fire by the French and Indians when their rear was driven out of the village by Wells and his men; but the fire was extinguished, and "the Old Indian House," as it was called, stood till the year 1849. Its door, deeply scarred with hatchets, and with a hole cut near the middle, is still preserved in the Memorial Hall at Deerfield.[1]

Vaudreuil wrote to the minister, Ponchartrain, that the French lost two or three killed, and twenty or twenty-one wounded, Rouville himself being among the latter. This cannot include the Indians, since there is proof that the enemy left behind a considerable number of their dead. Wherever resistance

---

[1] After the old house was demolished, this door was purchased by my friend Dr. Daniel Denison Slade, and given by him to the town of Deerfield, on condition that it should be carefully preserved. For an engraving of "the Old Indian House," see Hoyt, *Indian Wars* (ed. 1824).

was possible, it had been of the most prompt and determined character.[1]

Long before noon the French and Indians were on their northward march with their train of captives. More armed men came up from the settlements below, and by midnight about eighty were gathered at the ruined village. Couriers had been sent to rouse the country, and before evening of the next day (the first of March) the force at Deerfield was increased to two hundred and fifty; but a thaw and a warm rain had set in, and as few of the men had snow-shoes, pursuit was out of the question. Even could the agile savages and their allies have been overtaken, the probable consequence would have been the murdering of the captives to prevent their escape.

In spite of the foul blow dealt upon it, Deerfield was not abandoned. Such of its men as were left were taken as soldiers into the pay of the province, while the women and children were sent to the villages below. A small garrison was also stationed at the spot, under command of Captain Jonathan Wells, and thus the village held its ground till the storm of war should pass over.[2]

---

[1] Governor Dudley, writing to Lord —— on 21 April, 1704, says that thirty dead bodies of the enemy were found in the village and on the meadow. Williams, the minister, says that they did not seem inclined to rejoice over their success, and continued for several days to bury members of their party who died of wounds on the return march. He adds that he learned in Canada that they lost more than forty, though Vaudreuil assured him that they lost but eleven.

[2] On the attack of Deerfield, see Williams, *The Redeemed Cap-*

We have seen that the minister, Williams, with his wife and family, were led from their burning

tive *Returning to Zion.* This is the narrative of the minister, John Williams. *Account of the Captivity of Stephen Williams, written by himself.* This is the narrative of one of the minister's sons, eleven years old when captured. It is printed in the Appendix to the *Biographical Memoir of Rev. John Williams* (Hartford, 1837) ; *An account of yᵉ destruction at Derefd. febʳ. 29, 1703/4,* in *Proceedings of the Mass. Hist. Soc.,* 1867, p. 478. This valuable document was found among the papers of Fitz-John Winthrop, governor of Connecticut. The authorities of that province, on hearing of the catastrophe at Deerfield, promptly sent an armed force to its relief, which, however, could not arrive till long after the enemy were gone. The paper in question seems to be the official report of one of the Connecticut officers. After recounting what had taken place, he gives a tabular list of the captives, the slain, and those who escaped, with the estimated losses in property of each inhabitant. The list of captives is not quite complete. Compare the lists given by Stephen Williams at the end of his narrative. The town records of Hatfield give various particulars concerning the attack on its unfortunate neighbor, as do the letters of Colonel Samuel Partridge, commanding the militia of the county. Hoyt, *Antiquarian Researches,* gives a valuable account of it. The careful and unwearied research of Mr. George Sheldon, the lineal descendant of Ensign John Sheldon, among all sources, public or private, manuscript or in print, that could throw light on the subject cannot be too strongly commended, and I am indebted to him for much valued information.

Penhallow's short account is inexact, and many of the more recent narratives are not only exaggerated, but sometimes absurdly incorrect.

The French notices of the affair are short, and give few particulars. Vaudreuil in one letter sets the number of prisoners at one hundred and fifty, and increases it in another to two hundred and fifty. Ramesay, governor of Montreal, who hated Hertel de Rouville, and bore no love to Vaudreuil, says that fifty-six women and children were murdered on the way to Canada, — which is a gross exaggeration. (*Ramesay au Ministre,* 14 *Novembre,* 1704.) The account by Dr. Ethier in the *Revue Canadienne* of 1874 is drawn entirely from the *Redeemed Captive* of Williams, with running comments by the Canadian writer, but no new information. The

house across the river to the foot of the mountain, where the crowd of terrified and disconsolate captives — friends, neighbors, and relatives — were already gathered. Here they presently saw the fight in the meadow, and were told that if their countrymen attempted a rescue, they should all be put to death. "After this," writes Williams, "we went up the mountain, and saw the smoke of the fires in town, and beheld the awful desolation of Deerfield; and before we marched any farther they killed a sucking child of the English."

The French and Indians marched that afternoon only four or five miles, — to Greenfield meadows, — where they stopped to encamp, dug away the snow, laid spruce-boughs on the ground for beds, and bound fast such of the prisoners as seemed able to escape. The Indians then held a carousal on some liquor they had found in the village, and in their drunken rage murdered a negro man belonging to Williams. In spite of their precautions, Joseph Alexander, one of the prisoners, escaped during the night, at which they were greatly incensed; and Rouville ordered Williams to tell his companions in misfortune that if any more of them ran off, the rest should be burned alive.[1]

The prisoners were the property of those who had

comments chiefly consist in praise of Williams for truth when he speaks favorably of the Canadians, and charges of lying when he speaks otherwise.

[1] John Williams, *The Redeemed Captive*. Compare Stephen Williams, *Account of the Captivity*, etc.

taken them. Williams had two masters, one of the three who had seized him having been shot in the attack on the house of Stebbins. His principal owner was a surly fellow who would not let him speak to the other prisoners; but as he was presently chosen to guard the rear, the minister was left in the hands of his other master, who allowed him to walk beside his wife and help her on the way. Having borne a child a few weeks before, she was in no condition for such a march, and felt that her hour was near. Williams speaks of her in the strongest terms of affection. She made no complaint, and accepted her fate with resignation. "We discoursed," he says, "of the happiness of those who had God for a father and friend, as also that it was our reasonable duty quietly to submit to his will." Her thoughts were for her remaining children, whom she commended to her husband's care. Their intercourse was short. The Indian who had gone to the rear of the train soon returned, separated them, ordered Williams to the front, "and so made me take a last farewell of my dear wife, the desire of my eyes and companion in many mercies and afflictions." They came soon after to Green River, a stream then about knee-deep, and so swift that the water had not frozen. After wading it with difficulty, they climbed a snow-covered hill beyond. The minister, with strength almost spent, was permitted to rest a few moments at the top; and as the other prisoners passed by in turn, he questioned each for news of his wife. He was not left long in suspense. She had fallen from weakness in fording the stream, but gained her feet again, and, drenched in the icy current, struggled to the farther bank, when the savage who owned her, finding that she could not climb the hill, killed her with one stroke of his hatchet. Her body was left on the snow till a few of her townsmen, who had followed the trail, found it a day or two after, carried it back to Deerfield, and buried it in the churchyard.

On the next day the Indians killed an infant and a little girl of eleven years; on the day following, Friday, they tomahawked a woman, and on Saturday four others. This apparent cruelty was in fact a kind of mercy. The victims could not keep up with the party, and the death-blow saved them from a lonely and lingering death from cold and starvation. Some of the children, when spent with the march, were carried on the backs of their owners, — partly, perhaps, through kindness, and partly because every child had its price.

On the fourth day of the march they came to the mouth of West River, which enters the Connecticut a little above the present town of Brattleboro'. Some of the Indians were discontented with the distribution of the captives, alleging that others had got more than their share; on which the whole troop were mustered together, and some changes of ownership were agreed upon. At this place dog-trains and sledges had been left, and these served to carry their wounded, as well as some of the captive children.

Williams was stripped of the better part of his clothes, and others given him instead, so full of vermin that they were a torment to him through all the journey. The march now continued with pitiless speed up the frozen Connecticut, where the recent thaw had covered the ice with slush and water ankle-deep.

On Sunday they made a halt, and the minister was permitted to preach a sermon from the text, "Hear, all people, and behold my sorrow: my virgins and my young men are gone into captivity." Then amid the ice, the snow, the forest, and the savages, his forlorn flock joined their voices in a psalm.[1] On Monday guns were heard from the rear, and the Indians and their allies, in great alarm, bound their prisoners fast, and prepared for battle. It proved, however, that the guns had been fired at wild geese by some of their own number; on which they recovered their spirits, fired a volley for joy, and boasted that the English could not overtake them.[2] More women fainted by the way and died under the hatchet, — some with pious resignation, some with despairing apathy, some with a desperate joy.

Two hundred miles of wilderness still lay between them and the Canadian settlements. It was a waste without a house or even a wigwam, except here and there the bark shed of some savage hunter. At the

---

[1] The small stream at the mouth of which Williams is supposed to have preached is still called Williams River.

[2] Stephen Williams, *Account of the Captivity*, etc. His father also notices the incident.

mouth of White River, the party divided into small
bands, — no doubt in order to subsist by hunting, for
provisions were fast failing. The Williams family
were separated. Stephen was carried up the Connecticut; Samuel and Eunice, with two younger
children, were carried off in various directions; while
the wretched father, along with two small children
of one of his parishioners, was compelled to follow
his Indian masters up the valley of White River.
One of the children — a little girl — was killed on the
next morning by her Caughnawaga owner, who was
unable to carry her.[1] On the next Sunday the minister was left in camp with one Indian and the surviving child, — a boy of nine, — while the rest of the
party were hunting. "My spirit," he says, "was
almost overwhelmed within me." But he found
comfort in the text, "Leave thy fatherless children,
I will preserve them alive." Nor was his hope
deceived. His youngest surviving child, — a boy of
four, — though harshly treated by his owners, was
carried on their shoulders or dragged on a sledge to
the end of the journey. His youngest daughter —
seven years old — was treated with great kindness
throughout. Samuel and Eunice suffered much
from hunger, but were dragged on sledges when too
faint to walk. Stephen nearly starved to death; but
after eight months in the forest, he safely reached
Chambly with his Indian masters.

[1] The name Macquas (Mohawks) is always given to the Caughnawagas by the elder Williams.

Of the whole band of captives, only about half ever again saw friends and home. Seventeen broke down on the way and were killed; while David Hoyt and Jacob Hix died of starvation at Coos Meadows, on the upper Connecticut. During the entire march, no woman seems to have been subjected to violence; and this holds true, with rare exceptions, in all the Indian wars of New England. This remarkable forbearance towards female prisoners, so different from the practice of many western tribes, was probably due to a form of superstition, aided perhaps by the influence of the missionaries.[1] It is to be observed, however, that the heathen savages of King Philip's War, who had never seen a Jesuit, were no less forbearing in this respect.

The hunters of Williams's party killed five moose, the flesh of which, smoked and dried, was carried on their backs and that of the prisoner whom they had provided with snow-shoes. Thus burdened, the minister toiled on, following his masters along the frozen current of White River till, crossing the snowy backs of the Green Mountains, they struck the headwaters of the stream then called French River, now the Winooski, or Onion. Being in great fear of a thaw, they pushed on with double speed. Williams was not used to snow-shoes, and they gave him those painful cramps of the legs and ankles called in Canada *mal à la raquette*. One morning at dawn he was

---

[1] The Iroquois are well known to have had superstitions in connection with sexual abstinence.

waked by his chief master and ordered to get up, say his prayers, and eat his breakfast, for they must make a long march that day.   The minister was in despair. "After prayer," he says, "I arose from my knees; but my feet were so tender, swollen, bruised, and full of pain that I could scarce stand upon them without holding on the wigwam.   And when the Indians said, ' You must run to-day,' I answered I could not run.   My master, pointing to his hatchet, said to me, ' Then I must dash out your brains and take your scalp.' "   The Indian proved better than his word, and Williams was suffered to struggle on as he could. "God wonderfully supported me," he writes, "and my strength was restored and renewed to admiration." He thinks that he walked that day forty miles on the snow.   Following the Winooski to its mouth, the party reached Lake Champlain a little north of the present city of Burlington.   Here the swollen feet of the prisoner were tortured by the rough ice, till snow began to fall and cover it with a soft carpet.   Bending under his load, and powdered by the falling flakes, he toiled on till, at noon of a Saturday, lean, tired, and ragged, he and his masters reached the French outpost of Chambly, twelve or fifteen miles from Montreal.

Here the unhappy wayfarer was treated with great kindness both by the officers of the fort and by the inhabitants, one of the chief among whom lodged him in his house and welcomed him to his table. After a short stay at Chambly, Williams and his

masters set out in a canoe for Sorel. On the way a
Frenchwoman came down to the bank of the river
and invited the party to her house, telling the minister that she herself had once been a prisoner among
the Indians, and knew how to feel for him. She
seated him at a table, spread a table-cloth, and placed
food before him, while the Indians, to their great
indignation, were supplied with a meal in the chimney-
corner. Similar kindness was shown by the inhabitants along the way till the party reached their
destination, the Abenaki village of St. Francis, to
which his masters belonged. Here there was a fort,
in which lived two Jesuits, directors of the mission,
and here Williams found several English children,
captured the summer before during the raid on the
settlements of Maine, and already transformed into
little Indians both in dress and behavior. At the
gate of the fort one of the Jesuits met him, and
asked him to go into the church and give thanks to
God for sparing his life, to which he replied that he
would give thanks in some other place. The priest
then commanded him to go, which he refused to do.
When on the next day the bell rang for mass, one
of his Indian masters seized him and dragged him
into the church, where he got behind the door, and
watched the service from his retreat with extreme
disapprobation. One of the Jesuits telling him that
he would go to hell for not accepting the apostolic
traditions, and trusting only in the Bible, he replied
that he was glad to know that Christ was to be his

judge, and not they. His chief master, who was a
zealot in his way, and as much bound to the rites and
forms of the Church as he had been before his conversion to his "medicines," or practices of heathen
superstition, one day ordered him to make the sign
of the cross, and on his refusal, tried to force him.
But as the minister was tough and muscular, the
Indian could not guide his hand. Then, pulling out
a crucifix that hung at his neck, he told Williams
in broken English to kiss it; and being again refused,
he brandished his hatchet over him and threatened to
knock out his brains. This failing of the desired
effect, he threw down the hatchet and said he would
first bite out the minister's finger-nails, — a form of
torture then in vogue among the northern Indians,
both converts and heathen. Williams offered him a
hand and invited him to begin; on which he gave the
thumb-nail a gripe with his teeth, and then let it go,
saying, "No good minister, bad as the devil." The
failure seems to have discouraged him, for he made
no further attempt to convert the intractable heretic.

The direct and simple narrative of Williams is
plainly the work of an honest and courageous man.
He was the most important capture of the year; and
the governor, hearing that he was at St. Francis,
despatched a canoe to request the Jesuits of the mission to send him to Montreal. Thither, therefore,
his masters carried him, expecting, no doubt, a good
price for their prisoner. Vaudreuil, in fact, bought
him, exchanged his tattered clothes for good ones,

lodged him in his house, and, in the words of
Williams, "was in all respects relating to my out-
ward man courteous and charitable to admiration."
He sent for two of the minister's children who were
in the town, bought his eldest daughter from the
Indians, and promised to do what he could to get
the others out of their hands. His youngest son was
bought by a lady of the place, and his eldest by a
merchant. His youngest daughter, Eunice, then
seven or eight years old, was at the mission of St.
Louis, or Caughnawaga. Vaudreuil sent a priest to
conduct Williams thither and try to ransom the
child. But the Jesuits of the mission flatly refused
to let him speak to or see her. Williams says that
Vaudreuil was very angry at hearing of this; and a
few days after, he went himself to Caughnawaga
with the minister. This time the Jesuits, whose
authority within their mission seemed almost to over-
ride that of the governor himself, yielded so far as to
permit the father to see his child, on condition that
he spoke to no other English prisoner. He talked
with her for an hour, exhorting her never to forget
her catechism, which she had learned by rote.
Vaudreuil and his wife afterwards did all in their
power to procure her ransom; but the Indians, or the
missionaries in their name, would not let her go.
"She is there still," writes Williams two years later,
"and has forgotten to speak English." What grieved
him still more, Eunice had forgotten her catechism.

While he was at Montreal, his movements were

continually watched, lest he should speak to other
prisoners and prevent their conversion. He thinks
these precautions were due to the priests, whose constant endeavor it was to turn the captives, or at least
the younger and more manageable among them, into
Catholics and Canadians. The governor's kindness
towards him never failed, though he told him that he
should not be set free till the English gave up one
Captain Baptiste, a noted sea-rover whom they had
captured some time before.

He was soon after sent down the river to Quebec
along with the superior of the Jesuits. Here he
lodged seven weeks with a member of the council,
who treated him kindly, but told him that if he did
not avoid intercourse with the other English prisoners
he would be sent farther away. He saw much of the
Jesuits, who courteously asked him to dine; though
he says that one of them afterwards made some Latin
verses about him, in which he was likened to a captive wolf. Another Jesuit told him that when the
mission Indians set out on their raid against Deerfield, he charged them to baptize all children before
killing them, — such, he said, was his desire for the
salvation even of his enemies. To murdering the
children after they were baptized, he appears to have
made no objection. Williams says that in their
dread lest he should prevent the conversion of the
other prisoners, the missionaries promised him a
pension from the King and free intercourse with his
children and neighbors if he would embrace the

VOL. I. — 6

Catholic faith and remain in Canada; to which he answered that he would do so without reward if he thought their religion was true, but as he believed the contrary, "the offer of the whole world would tempt him no more than a blackberry."

To prevent him more effectually from perverting the minds of his captive countrymen, and fortifying them in their heresy, he was sent to Château Richer, a little below Quebec, and lodged with the parish priest, who was very kind to him. "I am persuaded," he writes, "that he abhorred their sending down the heathen to commit outrages against the English, saying it is more like committing murders than carrying on war."

He was sorely tried by the incessant efforts to convert the prisoners. "Sometimes they would tell me my children, sometimes my neighbors, were turned to be of their religion. Some made it their work to allure poor souls by flatteries and great promises; some threatened, some offered abuse to such as refused to go to church and be present at mass; and some they industriously contrived to get married among them. I understood they would tell the English that I was turned, that they might gain them to change their religion. These their endeavors to seduce to popery were very exercising to me."

After a time he was permitted to return to Quebec, where he met an English Franciscan, who, he says, had been sent from France to aid in converting the prisoners. Lest the minister should counteract the efforts of the friar, the priests had him sent back to Château Richer; "but," he observes, "God showed his dislike of such a persecuting spirit; for the very next day the Seminary, a very famous building, was most of it burnt down, by a joiner letting a coal of fire drop among the shavings."[1]

The heaviest of all his tribulations now fell upon him. His son Samuel, about sixteen years old, had been kept at Montreal under the tutelage of Father Meriel, a priest of St. Sulpice. The boy afterwards declared that he was promised great rewards if he would make the sign of the cross, and severe punishment if he would not. Proving obstinate, he was whipped till at last he made the sign; after which he was told to go to mass, and on his refusal, four stout boys of the school were ordered to drag him in. Williams presently received a letter in Samuel's handwriting, though dictated, as the father believed, by his priestly tutors. In this was recounted, with many edifying particulars, the deathbed conversion of two New England women; and to the minister's unspeakable grief and horror, the messenger who brought the letter told him that the boy himself had turned Catholic. "I have heard the news," he wrote to his recreant son, "with the most distressing, afflicting, sorrowful spirit. Oh, I pity you, I mourn over you day and night. Oh, I pity your weakness that,

---

[1] Williams remarks that the Seminary had also been burned three years before. This was the fire of November, 1701. See "Old Régime in Canada," ii. 187.

through the craftiness of man, you are turned from the simplicity of the gospel." Though his correspondence was strictly watched, he managed to convey to the boy a long exposition, from his own pen, of the infallible truth of Calvinistic orthodoxy, and the damnable errors of Rome. This, or something else, had its effect. Samuel returned to the creed of his fathers; and being at last exchanged, went home to Deerfield, where he was chosen town-clerk in 1713, and where he soon after died.[1]

Williams gives many particulars of the efforts of the priests to convert the prisoners, and his account, like the rest of his story, bears the marks of truth. There was a treble motive for conversion: it recruited the Church, weakened the enemy, and strengthened Canada, since few of the converts would peril their souls by returning to their heretic relatives. The means of conversion varied. They were gentle when gentleness seemed likely to answer the purpose. Little girls and young women were placed in convents, where it is safe to assume that they were treated with the most tender kindness by the sisterhood, who fully believed that to gain them to the faith was to snatch them from perdition. But when they or their brothers proved obdurate, different means were used. Threats of hell were varied by threats of a whipping, which, according to Williams, were often put into execution. Parents were rigorously severed from their families; though one Lalande,

[1] Note of Mr. George Sheldon.

who had been sent to watch the elder prisoners, reported that they would persist in trying to see their children, till some of them were killed in the attempt. "Here," writes Williams, "might be a history in itself of the trials and sufferings of many of our children, who, after separation from grown persons, have been made to do as they would have them. I mourned when I thought with myself that I had one child with the Maquas [Caughnawagas], a second turned papist, and a little child of six years of age in danger to be instructed in popery, and knew full well that all endeavors would be used to prevent my seeing or speaking with them." He also says that he and others were told that if they would turn Catholic their children should be restored to them; and among other devices, some of his parishioners were assured that their pastor himself had seen the error of his ways and bowed in submission to Holy Church.

In midwinter, not quite a year after their capture, the prisoners were visited by a gleam of hope. John Sheldon, accompanied by young John Wells, of Deerfield, and Captain Livingston, of Albany, came to Montreal with letters from Governor Dudley, proposing an exchange. Sheldon's wife and infant child, his brother-in-law, and his son-in-law had been killed. Four of his children, with his daughter-in-law, Hannah, — the same who had sprained her ankle in leaping from her chamber window, — besides others of his near relatives and connections, were prisoners in Canada; and so also was the mother of young Wells. In the last December, Sheldon and Wells had gone to Boston and begged to be sent as envoys to the French governor. The petition was readily granted, and Livingston, who chanced to be in the town, was engaged to accompany them. After a snow-shoe journey of extreme hardship they reached their destination, and were received with courtesy by Vaudreuil. But difficulties arose. The French, and above all the clergy, were unwilling to part with captives, many of whom they hoped to transform into Canadians by conversion and adoption. Many also were in the hands of the Indians, who demanded payment for them, — which Dudley had always refused, declaring that he would not "set up an Algiers trade" by buying them from their pretended owners; and he wrote to Vaudreuil that for his own part he "would never permit a savage to tell him that any Christian prisoner was at his disposal." Vaudreuil had insisted that his Indians could not be compelled to give up their captives, since they were not subjects of France, but only allies, — which, so far as concerned the mission Indians within the colony, was but a pretext. It is true, however, that the French authorities were in such fear of offending even these that they rarely ventured to cross their interests or their passions. Other difficulties were raised, and though the envoys remained in Canada till late in spring, they accomplished little. At last, probably to get rid of their importunities, five prisoners were given up to them, — Sheldon's daughter-in-law, Hannah; Esther Williams, eldest daughter of the minister; a certain Ebenezer Carter; and two others unknown. With these, Sheldon and his companions set out in May on their return; and soon after they were gone, four young men, — Baker, Nims, Kellogg, and Petty, — desperate at being left in captivity, made their escape from Montreal, and reached Deerfield before the end of June, half dead with hunger.

Sheldon and his party were escorted homeward by eight soldiers under Courtemanche, an officer of distinction, whose orders were to "make himself acquainted with the country." He fell ill at Boston, where he was treated with much kindness, and on his recovery was sent home by sea, along with Captain Vetch and Samuel Hill, charged to open a fresh negotiation. With these, at the request of Courtemanche, went young William Dudley, son of the governor.[1]

They were received at Quebec with a courtesy qualified by extreme caution, lest they should spy out the secrets of the land. The mission was not very successful, though the elder Dudley had now a good number of French prisoners in his hands, captured in Acadia or on the adjacent seas. A few only of the English were released, including the boy,

---

[1] The elder Dudley speaks with great warmth of Courtemanche, who, on his part, seems equally pleased with his entertainers. Young Dudley was a boy of eighteen. "Il a du mérite," says Vaudreuil. *Dudley to Vaudreuil*, 4 *July*, 1705; *Vaudreuil au Ministre.* 19 *Octobre*, 1705.

Stephen Williams, whom Vaudreuil had bought for forty crowns from his Indian master.

In the following winter John Sheldon made another journey on foot to Canada, with larger powers than before. He arrived in March, 1706, and returned with forty-four of his released countrymen, who, says Williams, were chiefly adults permitted to go because there was no hope of converting them. The English governor had by this time seen the necessity of greater concessions, and had even consented to release the noted Captain Baptiste, whom the Boston merchants regarded as a pirate. In the same summer Samuel Appleton and John Bonner, in the brigantine "Hope," brought a considerable number of French prisoners to Quebec, and returned to Boston at the end of October with fifty-seven English, of all ages. For three, at least, of this number money was paid by the English, probably on account of prisoners bought by Frenchmen from the Indians. The minister, Williams, was exchanged for Baptiste, the so-called pirate, and two of his children were also redeemed, though the Caughnawagas, or their missionaries, refused to part with his daughter Eunice. Williams says that the priests made great efforts to induce the prisoners to remain in Canada, tempting some with the prospect of pensions from the King, and frightening others with promises of damnation, joined with predictions of shipwreck on the way home. He thinks that about one hundred were left in Canada, many of whom were children in the hands of the

Indians, who could easily hide them in the woods, and who were known in some cases to have done so. Seven more were redeemed in the following year by the indefatigable Sheldon, on a third visit to Canada.[1]

The exchanged prisoners had been captured at various times and places. Those from Deerfield amounted in all to about sixty, or a little more than half the whole number carried off. Most of the others were dead or converted. Some married Canadians, and others their fellow-captives. The history of some of them can be traced with certainty. Thus, Thomas French, blacksmith and town clerk of Deerfield, and deacon of the church, was captured, with his wife and six children. His wife and infant child were killed on the way to Canada. He and his two eldest children were exchanged and brought home. His daughter Freedom was converted, baptized under the name of Marie Françoise, and married to Jean Daulnay, a Canadian. His daughter Martha was baptized as Marguerite, and married to Jacques Roy, on whose death she married Jean Louis Ménard, by whom she became ancestress of Joseph Plessis, eleventh bishop of Quebec. Elizabeth Corse, eight

[1] In 1878 Miss C. Alice Baker, of Cambridge, Mass., a descendant of Abigail Stebbins, read a paper on John Sheldon before the Memorial Association at Deerfield. It is the result of great research, and contains much original matter, including correspondence between Sheldon and the captives when in Canada, as well as a full and authentic account of his several missions. Mr. George Sheldon has also traced out with great minuteness the history of his ancestor's negotiations.

years old when captured, was baptized under her own name, and married to Jean Dumontel. Abigail Stebbins, baptized as Marguerite, lived many years at Boucherville, wife of Jacques de Noyon, a sergeant in the colony troops. The widow, Sarah Hurst, whose youngest child, Benjamin, had been murdered on the Deerfield meadows, was baptized as Marie Jeanne.[1] Joanna Kellogg, eleven years old when taken, married a Caughnawaga chief, and became, at all points, an Indian squaw.

She was not alone in this strange transformation. Eunice Williams, the namesake of her slaughtered mother, remained in the wigwams of the Caughnawagas, forgot, as we have seen, her English and her catechism, was baptized, and in due time married to an Indian of the tribe, who thenceforward called himself Williams. Thus her hybrid children bore her family name. Her father, who returned to his parish at Deerfield, and her brother Stephen, who became a minister like his parent, never ceased to pray for her return to her country and her faith.

---

[1] The above is drawn mainly from extracts made by Miss Baker from the registers of the Church of Notre Dame at Montreal. Many of the acts of baptism bear the signature of Father Meriel, so often mentioned in the narrative of Williams. Apparently, Meriel spoke English. At least there is a letter in English from him, relating to Eunice Williams, in the Massachusetts Archives, vol. 51. Some of the correspondence beween Dudley and Vaudreuil concerning exchange of prisoners will be found among the Paris documents in the State House at Boston. Copies of these papers were printed at Quebec in 1883–1885, though with many inaccuracies.

Many years after, in 1740, she came with her husband to visit her relatives in Deerfield, dressed as a squaw and wrapped in an Indian blanket. Nothing would induce her to stay, though she was persuaded on one occasion to put on a civilized dress and go to church; after which she impatiently discarded her gown and resumed her blanket. As she was kindly treated by her relatives, and as no attempt was made to detain her against her will, she came again in the next year, bringing two of her half-breed children, and twice afterwards repeated the visit. She and her husband were offered a tract of land if they would settle in New England; but she positively refused, saying that it would endanger her soul. She lived to a great age, a squaw to the last.[1]

One of her grandsons, Eleazer Williams, turned Protestant, was educated at Dartmouth College at the charge of friends in New England, and was for a time missionary to the Indians of Green Bay, in Wisconsin. His character for veracity was not of the best. He deceived the excellent antiquarian, Hoyt, by various inventions touching the attack on Deerfield, and in the latter part of his life tried to pass himself off as the lost Dauphin, son of Louis XVI.[2]

---

[1] Stephen W. Williams, *Memoir of the Rev. John Williams*, 53. *Sermon preached at Mansfield, August* 4, 1741, *on behalf of Mrs. Eunice, the daughter of Rev. John Williams; by Solomon Williams, A.M. Letter of Mrs. Colton, great granddaughter of John Williams* (in appendix to the *Memoir of Rev. John Williams*).

[2] I remember to have seen Eleazer Williams at my father's house

Here it may be observed that the descendants of young captives brought into Canada by the mission Indians during the various wars with the English colonies became a considerable element in the Canadian population. Perhaps the most prominent example is that of the Gill family. In June, 1697, a boy named Samuel Gill, then in his tenth year, was captured by the Abenakis at Salisbury in Massachusetts, carried to St. Francis, and converted. Some years later he married a young English girl, said to have been named James, and to have been captured at Kennebunk.[1] In 1866 the late Abbé Maurault, missionary at St. Francis, computed their descendants

in Boston, when a boy. My impression of him is that of a good-looking and somewhat portly man, showing little trace of Indian blood, and whose features, I was told, resembled those of the Bourbons. Probably this likeness, real or imagined, suggested the imposition he was practising at the time. The story of the "Bell of St. Regis" is probably another of his inventions. It is to the effect that the bell of the church at Deerfield was carried by the Indians to the mission of St. Regis, and that it is there still. But there is reason to believe that there was no church bell at Deerfield, and it is certain that St. Regis did not exist till more than a half-century after Deerfield was attacked. It has been said that the story is true, except that the name of Caughnawaga should be substituted for that of St. Regis; but the evidence for this conjecture is weak. On the legend of the bell, see Le Moine, *Maple Leaves, New Series* (1873), 29; *Proceedings of the Mass. Hist. Soc.*, 1869, 1870, 311; *Hist. Mag.* 2d Series, ix. 401. Hough, *Hist. St. Lawrence and Franklin Counties*, 116, gives the story without criticism.

[1] The earlier editions of this book follow, in regard to Samuel Gill, the statements of Maurault, which are erroneous, as has been proved by the careful and untiring research of Miss C. Alice Baker, to whose kindness I owe the means of correcting them. Papers in the archives of Massachusetts leave no doubt as to the time and place of Samuel Gill's capture.

at nine hundred and fifty-two, in whose veins French, English, and Abenaki blood were mixed in every conceivable proportion. He gives the tables of genealogy in full, and says that two hundred and thirteen of this prolific race still bear the surname of Gill. "If," concludes the worthy priest, "one should trace out all the English families brought into Canada by the Abenakis, one would be astonished at the number of persons who to-day are indebted to these savages for the blessing of being Catholics and the advantage of being Canadians," [1] — an advantage for which French-Canadians are so ungrateful that they migrate to the United States by myriads.

[1] Maurault, *Hist. des Abenakis*, 377. I am indebted to R. A. Ramsay, Esq., of Montreal, for a paper on the Gill family, by Mr. Charles Gill, who confirms the statements of Maurault so far as relates to the genealogies.

John and Zechariah Tarbell, captured when boys at Groton, became Caughnawaga chiefs; and one of them, about 1760, founded the mission of St. Regis. Green, *Groton during the Indian Wars*, 116, 117-120.

CHAPTER V.

1704–1713.

THE TORMENTED FRONTIER.

BORDER RAIDS. — HAVERHILL. — ATTACK AND DEFENCE. — WAR
TO THE KNIFE. — MOTIVES OF THE FRENCH. — PROPOSED NEU-
TRALITY. — JOSEPH DUDLEY. — TOWN AND COUNTRY.

I HAVE told the fate of Deerfield in full, as an
example of the desolating raids which for years swept
the borders of Massachusetts and New Hampshire.
The rest of the miserable story may be passed more
briefly. It is in the main a weary detail of the
murder of one, two, three, or more men, women, or
children waylaid in fields, woods, and lonely roads,
or surprised in solitary cabins. Sometimes the attacks
were on a larger scale. Thus, not long after the
capture of Deerfield, a band of fifty or more Indians
fell at dawn of day on a hamlet of five houses near
Northampton. The alarm was sounded, and they
were pursued. Eight of the prisoners were rescued,
and three escaped; most of the others being knocked
in the head by their captors. At Oyster River the
Indians attacked a loopholed house, in which the
women of the neighboring farms had taken refuge

while the men were at work in the fields. The
women disguised themselves in hats and jackets,
fired from the loopholes, and drove off the assailants.
In 1709 a hundred and eighty French and Indians
again attacked Deerfield, but failed to surprise it,
and were put to flight. At Dover, on a Sunday,
while the people were at church, a scalping-party
approached a fortified house, the garrison of which
consisted of one woman, — Esther Jones, who, on
seeing them, called out to an imaginary force within,
"Here they are! come on! come on!" on which the
Indians disappeared.

Soon after the capture of Deerfield, the French
authorities, being, according to the prisoner Williams,
"wonderfully lifted up with pride," formed a grand
war-party, and assured the minister that they would
catch so many prisoners that they should not know
what to do with them. Beaucour, an officer of great
repute, had chief command, and his force consisted
of between seven and eight hundred men, of whom
about a hundred and twenty were French, and the
rest mission Indians.[1]   They declared that they would
lay waste all the settlements on the Connecticut, —
meaning, it seems, to begin with Hatfield. "This
army," says Williams, "went away in such a boast-
ing, triumphant manner that I had great hopes God
would discover and disappoint their designs." In
fact, their plans came to nought, owing, according
to French accounts, to the fright of the Indians; for

[1] *Vaudreuil et Beauharnois au Ministre,* 17 *Novembre,* 1704.

a soldier having deserted within a day's march of the English settlements, most of them turned back, despairing of a surprise, and the rest broke up into small parties to gather scalps on the outlying farms.[1]

In the summer of 1708 there was a more successful attempt. The converts of all the Canadian missions were mustered at Montreal, where Vaudreuil, by exercising, as he says, "the patience of an angel," soothed their mutual jealousies and persuaded them to go upon a war-party against Newbury, Portsmouth, and other New England villages. Fortunately for the English, the Caughnawagas were only half-hearted towards the enterprise; and through them the watchful Peter Schuyler got hints of it which enabled him, at the eleventh hour, to set the intended victims on their guard. The party consisted of about four hundred, of whom one hundred were French, under twelve young officers and cadets; the whole commanded by Saint-Ours des Chaillons and Hertel de Rouville. For the sake of speed and secrecy, they set out in three bodies, by different routes. The rendezvous was at Lake Winnepesaukee, where they were to be joined by the Norridgewocks, Penobscots, and other eastern Abenakis. The Caughnawagas and Hurons turned back by reason of evil omens and a disease which broke out among them. The rest met on the shores of the lake, — probably at Alton

---

[1] *Vaudreuil et Beauharnois au Ministre,* 17 *Novembre,* 1704; *Vaudreuil au Ministre,* 16 *Novembre,* 1704; *Ramesay au Ministre,* 14 *Novembre,* 1704. Compare Penhallow.

Bay, — where, after waiting in vain for their eastern allies, they resolved to make no attempt on Portsmouth or Newbury, but to turn all their strength upon the smaller village of Haverhill, on the Merrimac. Advancing quickly under cover of night, they made their onslaught at half an hour before dawn, on Sunday, the twenty-ninth of August.

Haverhill consisted of between twenty and thirty dwelling-houses, a meeting-house, and a small picket fort. A body of militia from the lower Massachusetts towns had been hastily distributed along the frontier, on the vague reports of danger sent by Schuyler from Albany; and as the intended point of attack was unknown, the men were of necessity widely scattered. French accounts say that there were thirty of them in the fort at Haverhill, and more in the houses of the villagers; while others still were posted among the distant farms and hamlets.

In spite of darkness and surprise, the assailants met a stiff resistance and a hot and persistent fusillade. Vaudreuil says that they could dislodge the defenders only by setting fire to both houses and fort. In this they were not very successful, as but few of the dwellings were burned. A fire was kindled against the meeting-house, which was saved by one Davis and a few others, who made a dash from behind the adjacent parsonage, drove the Indians off, and put out the flames. Rolfe, the minister, had already been killed while defending his house. His wife and one of his children were butchered; but two

VOL. I. — 7

others — little girls of six and eight years — were saved by the self-devotion of his maid-servant, Hagar, apparently a negress, who dragged them into the cellar and hid them under two inverted tubs, where they crouched, dumb with terror, while the Indians ransacked the place without finding them. English accounts say that the number of persons killed — men, women, and children — was forty-eight; which the French increase to a hundred.

The distant roll of drums was presently heard, warning the people on the scattered farms; on which the assailants made a hasty retreat. Posted near Haverhill were three militia officers, — Turner, Price, and Gardner, — lately arrived from Salem. With such men as they had with them, or could hastily get together, they ambushed themselves at the edge of a piece of woods, in the path of the retiring enemy, to the number, as the French say, of sixty or seventy, which it is safe to diminish by a half. The French and Indians, approaching rapidly, were met by a volley which stopped them for the moment; then, throwing down their packs, they rushed on, and after a sharp skirmish broke through the ambuscade and continued their retreat. Vaudreuil sets their total loss at eight killed and eighteen wounded, — the former including two officers, Verchères and Chambly. He further declares that in the skirmish all the English, except ten or twelve, were killed outright; while the English accounts say that the French and Indians took to the woods, leaving nine of their number dead on the spot, along with their medicine chest and all their packs.[1]

Scarcely a hamlet of the Massachusetts and New Hampshire borders escaped a visit from the nimble enemy. Groton, Lancaster, Exeter, Dover, Kittery, Casco, Kingston, York, Berwick, Wells, Winter Harbor, Brookfield, Amesbury, Marlborough, were all more or less infested, usually by small scalping-parties, hiding in the outskirts, waylaying stragglers, or shooting men at work in the fields, and disappearing as soon as their blow was struck. These swift and intangible persecutors were found a far surer and more effectual means of annoyance than larger bodies. As all the warriors were converts of the Canadian missions, and as prisoners were an article of value, cases of torture were not very common; though now and then, as at Exeter, they would roast some poor wretch alive, or bite off his fingers and sear the stumps with red-hot tobacco pipes.

This system of petty, secret, and transient attack put the impoverished colonies to an immense charge in maintaining a cordon of militia along their northern frontier, — a precaution often as vain as it was costly; for the wily savages, covered by the forest, found little difficulty in dodging the scouting-parties, pouncing on their victims, and escaping. Rewards were offered for scalps; but one writer calculates

---

[1] *Vaudreuil au Ministre,* 5 *Novembre,* 1708; *Vaudreuil et Raudot au Ministre,* 14 *Novembre,* 1708; Hutchinson, ii. 156; *Mass. Hist. Coll. 2d Series,* iv. 129; Sewall, *Diary,* ii. 234. Penhallow.

67396

that, all things considered, it cost Massachusetts a thousand pounds of her currency to kill an Indian.[1]

In 1703–1704 six hundred men were kept ranging the woods all winter without finding a single Indian, the enemy having deserted their usual haunts and sought refuge with the French, to emerge in February for the destruction of Deerfield. In the next summer nineteen hundred men were posted along two hundred miles of frontier.[2] This attitude of passive defence exasperated the young men of Massachusetts, and it is said that five hundred of them begged Dudley for leave to make a raid into Canada, on the characteristic condition of choosing their own officers. The governor consented; but on a message from Peter Schuyler that he had at last got a promise from the Caughnawagas and other mission Indians to attack the New England borders no more, the raid was countermanded, lest it should waken the tempest anew.[3]

What was the object of these murderous attacks,

---

[1] The rewards for scalps were confined to male Indians thought old enough to bear arms, — that is to say, above twelve years. *Act of General Court*, 19 *August*, 1706.

[2] *Dudley to Lord* ———, 21 *April*, 1704. *Address of Council and Assembly to the Queen*, 12 *July*, 1704. The burden on the people was so severe that one writer — not remarkable, however, for exactness of statement — declares that he " is credibly informed that some have been forced to cut open their beds and sell the feathers to pay their taxes." The general poverty did not prevent a contribution in New England for the suffering inhabitants of the Island of St. Christopher.

[3] *Vaudreuil au Ministre*, 12 *Novembre*, 1708. Vaudreuil says that he got his information from prisoners.

which stung the enemy without disabling him, con·
firmed the Indians in their native savagery, and
taught the French to emulate it? In the time of
Frontenac there was a palliating motive for such barbarous warfare. Canada was then prostrate and
stunned under the blows of the Iroquois war. Successful war-parties were needed as a tonic and a
stimulant to rouse the dashed spirits of French and
Indians alike; but the remedy was a dangerous one,
and it drew upon the colony the attack under Sir
William Phips, which was near proving its ruin. At
present there was no such pressing call for butchering women, children, and peaceful farmers. The
motive, such as it was, lay in the fear that the Indian
allies of France might pass over to the English, or
at least stand neutral. These allies were the Christian savages of the missions, who, all told, from the
Caughnawagas to the Micmacs, could hardly have
mustered a thousand warriors. The danger was that
the Caughnawagas, always open to influence from
Albany, might be induced to lay down the hatchet
and persuade the rest to follow their example.
Therefore, as there was for the time a virtual truce
with New York, no pains were spared to commit
them irrevocably to war against New England.
With the Abenaki tribes of Maine and New Hampshire
the need was still more urgent, for they were continually drawn to New England by the cheapness and
excellence of English goods; and the only sure
means to prevent their trading with the enemy was

to incite them to kill him.   Some of these savages
had been settled in Canada, to keep them under
influence and out of temptation; but the rest were
still in their native haunts, where it was thought
best to keep them well watched by their missionaries,
as sentinels and outposts to the colony.

There were those among the French to whom this
barbarous warfare was repugnant.   The minister,
Ponchartrain, by no means a person of tender
scruples, also condemned it for a time.   After the
attack on Wells and other places under Beaubassin
in 1703, he wrote: "It would have been well if this
expedition had not taken place.   I have certain
knowledge that the English want only peace, knowing that war is contrary to the interests of all the
colonies.   Hostilities in Canada have always been
begun by the French." [1]   Afterwards, when these
bloody raids had produced their natural effect and
spurred the sufferers to attempt the ending of their
woes once for all by the conquest of Canada, Ponchartrain changed his mind and encouraged the

---

[1] *Resumé d'une Lettre de MM. de Vaudreuil et de Beauharnois du
15 Novembre*, 1703, *avec les Observations du Ministre.*   Subercase, governor of Acadia, writes on 25 December, 1708, that he hears that a
party of Canadians and Indians have attacked a place on the
Maramet (Merrimac), " et qu'ils y ont égorgé 4 à 500 personnes sans
faire quartier aux femmes ni aux enfans."   This is an exaggerated
report of the affair of Haverhill.   M. de Chevry writes in the mar-
gin of the letter: "Ces actions de cruauté devroient être modé-
rées:" to which Ponchartrain adds: "Bon; les défendre."   His
attitude, however, was uncertain; for as early as 1707 we find him
approving Vaudreuil for directing the missionaries to prompt the
Abenakis to war.   *N. Y. Col. Docs.*, ix. 805.

sending out of war-parties, to keep the English busy at home.

The schemes of a radical cure date from the attack on Deerfield and the murders of the following summer. In the autumn we find Governor Dudley urging the capture of Quebec. "In the last two years," he says, "the Assembly of Massachusetts has spent about £50,000 in defending the Province, whereas three or four of the Queen's ships and fifteen hundred New England men would rid us of the French and make further outlay needless," — a view, it must be admitted, sufficiently sanguine.[1]

But before seeking peace with the sword, Dudley tried less strenuous methods. It may be remembered that in 1705 Captain Vetch and Samuel Hill, together with the governor's young son William, went to Quebec to procure an exchange of prisoners. Their mission had also another object. Vetch carried a letter from Dudley to Vaudreuil, proposing a treaty of neutrality between their respective colonies, and Vaudreuil seems to have welcomed the proposal. Notwithstanding the pacific relations between Canada and New York, he was in constant fear that Dutch and English influence might turn the Five Nations into open enemies of the French; and he therefore declared himself ready to accept the proposals of Dudley, on condition that New York and the other English colonies should be included in the treaty, and that the English should be excluded from fish-

[1] *Dudley to ———, 26 November, 1704.*

ing in the Gulf of St. Lawrence and the Acadian seas. The first condition was difficult, and the second impracticable; for nothing could have induced the people of New England to accept it. Vaudreuil, moreover, would not promise to give up prisoners in the hands of the Indians, but only to do what he could to persuade their owners to give them up. The negotiations dragged on for several years. For the first three or four months Vaudreuil stopped his war-parties; but he let them loose again in the spring, and the New England borders were tormented as before.

The French governor thought that the New England country people, who had to bear the brunt of the war, were ready to accept his terms. The French court approved the plan, though not without distrust; for some enemy of the governor told Ponchartrain that under pretence of negotiations he and Dudley were carrying on trading speculations, — which is certainly a baseless slander.[1] Vaudreuil on his part had strongly suspected Dudley's emissary, Vetch, of illicit trade during his visit to Quebec; and perhaps there was ground for the suspicion. It is certain that Vetch, who had visited the St. Lawrence before, lost no opportunity of studying the river, and looked forward to a time when he could turn his knowledge to practical account.[2]

[1] *Abrégé d'une lettre de M. de Vaudreuil, avec les notes du Ministre,* 19 *Octobre,* 1705.

[2] On the negotiations for neutrality, see the correspondence and other papers in the *Paris Documents* in the Boston State House; also *N. Y. Col. Docs.,* ix. 770, 776, 779, 809; Hutchinson, ii. 141.

Joseph Dudley, governor of Massachusetts and New Hampshire, was the son of a former governor of Massachusetts, — that upright, sturdy, narrow, bigoted old Puritan, Thomas Dudley, in whose pocket was found after his death the notable couplet, —

> " Let men of God in courts and churches watch
>   O'er such as do a toleration hatch."

Such a son of such a father was the marvel of New England. Those who clung to the old traditions and mourned for the old theocracy under the old charter, hated Joseph Dudley as a renegade; and the worshippers of the Puritans have not forgiven him to this day. He had been president of the council under the detested Andros, and when that representative of the Stuarts was overthrown by a popular revolution, both he and Dudley were sent prisoners to England. Here they found a reception different from the expectations and wishes of those who sent them. Dudley became a member of Parliament and lieutenant-governor of the Isle of Wight, and was at length, in the beginning of the reign of Queen Anne, sent back to govern those who had cast him out. Any governor imposed on them by England would have been an offence; but Joseph Dudley was more than they could bear.

He found bitter opposition from the old Puritan party. The two Mathers, father and son, who through policy had at first favored him, soon denounced him with insolent malignity, and the honest

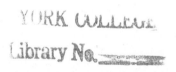
YORK COLLEGE
Library No.

and conscientious Samuel Sewall regarded him with as much asperity as his kindly nature would permit. To the party of religious and political independency he was an abomination, and great efforts were made to get him recalled.   Two pamphlets of the time, one printed in 1707 and the other in the next year, reflect the bitter animosity he excited.[1]   Both seem to be the work of several persons, one of whom, there can be little doubt, was Cotton Mather; for it is not easy to mistake the mingled flippancy and pedantry of his style.   He bore the governor a grudge, for Dudley had chafed him in his inordinate vanity and love of power.

If Dudley loved himself first, he loved his native New England next, and was glad to serve her if he could do so in his own way and without too much sacrifice of his own interests.   He was possessed by a restless ambition, apparently of the cheap kind that prefers the first place in a small community to the second in a large one.   He was skilled in the arts of the politician, and knew how, by attentions, dinners, or commissions in the militia, to influence his Council and Assembly to do his will.   His abilities were beyond question, and his manners easy and graceful; but his instincts were arbitrary.   He stood fast for

---

[1] *A Memorial of the Present Deplorable State of New England,* Boston, 1707.   *The Deplorable State of New England, by Reason of a Covetous and Treacherous Governour and Pusillanimous Counsellors,* London, 1708.   The first of the above is answered by a pamphlet called a *Modest Inquiry*.   All three are reprinted in *Mass. Hist. Coll., 5th Series,* vi.

COTTON MATHER.

prerogative, and even his hereditary Calvinism had strong Episcopal leanings. He was a man of the world in the better as well as the worse sense of the term; was loved and admired by some as much as he was hated by others; and in the words of one of his successors, "had as many virtues as can consist with so great a thirst for honor and power."[1]

His enemies, however, set no bounds to their denunciation. "All the people here are bought and sold betwixt the governour and his son Paul," says one. "It is my belief," says another, probably Cotton Mather, "that he means to help the French and Indians to destroy all they can." And again, "He is a criminal governour. . . . His God is Mammon, his aim is the ruin of his country." The meagreness and uncertainty of his salary, which was granted by yearly votes of the Assembly, gave color to the charge that he abused his official position to improve his income. The worst accusation against him was that of conniving in trade with the French and Indians under pretence of exchanging prisoners. Six prominent men of the colony — Borland, Vetch, Lawson, Rous, Phillips, and Coffin, only three of whom were of New England origin — were brought to trial before the Assembly for trading at Port Royal; and it was said that Dudley, though he had no direct share in the business, found means to make profit from it. All the accused were convicted and fined. The more strenuous of their judges were for

[1] Hutchinson, ii. 194.

sending them to jail, and Rous was to have been sentenced to "sit an hour upon the gallows with a rope about his neck;" but the governor and council objected to these severities, and the Assembly forbore to impose them. The popular indignation against the accused was extreme, and probably not without cause.[1] There was no doubt an illicit trade between Boston and the French of Acadia, who during the war often depended on their enemies for the necessaries of life, since supplies from France, precarious at the best, were made doubly so by New England cruisers. Thus the Acadians and their Indian allies were but too happy to exchange their furs for very modest supplies of tools, utensils, and perhaps, at times, of arms, powder, and lead.[2] What with privateering and illicit trade, it was clear that the war was a source of profit to some of the chief persons in Boston. That place, moreover, felt itself tolerably safe from attack, while the borders were stung from end to end as by a swarm of wasps; and

---

[1] The agent of Massachusetts at London, speaking of the three chief offenders, says that they were neither "of English extraction, nor natives of the place, and two of them were very new comers." Jeremiah Dummer, *Letter to a Noble Lord concerning the late Expedition to Canada.*

[2] The French naval captain Bonaventure says that the Acadians were forced to depend on Boston traders, who sometimes plundered them, and sometimes sold them supplies. (*Bonaventure au Ministre,* 30 *Novembre,* 1705.) Colonel Quary, Judge of Admiralty at New York, writes: "There hath been and still is, as I am informed, a Trade carried on with Port Royal by some of the topping men of that government [Boston], under colour of sending and receiving Flaggs of truce." — *Quary to the Lords of Trade,* 10 *January,* 1708.

thus the country conceived the idea that the town was fattening at its expense. Vaudreuil reports to the minister that the people of New England want to avenge themselves by an attack on Canada, but that their chief men are for a policy of defence. This was far from being wholly true; but the notion that the rural population bore a grudge against Boston had taken strong hold of the French, who even believed that if the town were attacked, the country would not move hand or foot to help it. Perhaps it was well for them that they did not act on the belief, which, as afterwards appeared, was one of their many mistakes touching the character and disposition of their English neighbors.

The sentences on Borland and his five companions were annulled by the Queen and Council, on the ground that the Assembly was not competent to try the case.[1] The passionate charges against Dudley and a petition to the Queen for his removal were equally unavailing. The Assemblies of Massachusetts and New Hampshire, the chief merchants, the officers of militia, and many of the ministers sent addresses to the Queen in praise of the governor's administration;[2] and though his enemies declared that the votes and signatures were obtained by the arts familiar to him, his recall was prevented, and he held his office seven years longer.

[1] *Council Record*, in Hutchinson, ii. 144.

[2] These addresses are appended to *A Modest Inquiry into the Grounds and Occasions of a late Pamphlet intituled a Memorial of the present Deplorable State of New England. London*, 1707.

CHAPTER VI.

1700–1710.

THE OLD RÉGIME IN ACADIA.

THE FISHERY QUESTION. — PRIVATEERS AND PIRATES. — PORT ROYAL. — OFFICIAL GOSSIP. — ABUSE OF BROUILLAN. — COMPLAINTS OF DE GOUTIN. — SUBERCASE AND HIS OFFICERS. — CHURCH AND STATE. — PATERNAL GOVERNMENT.

THE French province of Acadia, answering to the present Nova Scotia and New Brunswick, was a government separate from Canada and subordinate to it. Jacques François de Brouillan, appointed to command it, landed at Chibucto, the site of Halifax, in 1702, and crossed by hills and forests to the Basin of Mines, where he found a small but prosperous settlement. "It seems to me," he wrote to the minister, "that these people live like true republicans, acknowledging neither royal authority nor courts of law."[1] It was merely that their remoteness and isolation made them independent, of necessity, so far as concerned temporal government. When Brouillan reached Port Royal he found a different state of things. The fort and garrison were in bad condition; but the adjacent settlement, primitive as it was, appeared on the whole duly submissive.

[1] *Brouillan au Ministre, 6 Octobre, 1702.*

Possibly it would have been less so if it had been
more prosperous; but the inhabitants had lately been
deprived of fishing, their best resource, by a New
England privateer which had driven their craft from
the neighboring seas; and when the governor sent
Lieutenant Neuvillette in an armed vessel to seize
the interloping stranger, a fight ensued, in which the
lieutenant was killed, and his vessel captured. New
England is said to have had no less than three hundred vessels every year in these waters.[1]   Before the
war a French officer proposed that New England
sailors should be hired to teach the Acadians how to
fish, and the King seems to have approved the plan.[2]
Whether it was adopted or not, New England in
peace or war had a lion's share of the Acadian
fisheries. "It grieves me to the heart," writes
Subercase, Brouillan's successor, "to see Messieurs
les Bastonnais enrich themselves in our domain; for
the base of their commerce is the fish which they
catch off our coasts, and send to all parts of the
world."

When the war broke out, Brouillan's fighting
resources were so small that he was forced to depend
largely for help on sea-rovers of more than doubtful
character.   They came chiefly from the West Indies,
— the old haunt of buccaneers, — and were sometimes
mere pirates, and sometimes semi-piratical privateers

---

[1] *Mémoire de Subercase.*

[2] *Mémoire du Roy au Sieur de Brouillan,* 23 *Mars,* 1700; *La
Ministre à Villebon,* 9 *Avril,* 1700.

commissioned by French West Indian governors
Brouillan's successor writes that their opportunities
are good, since at least a thousand vessels enter
Boston every year.[1] Besides these irregular allies,
the governor usually had at his disposal two French
frigates of thirty and sixty guns, to which was
opposed the Massachusetts navy, consisting of a ship
of fifty-six guns, and the "province galley," of
twenty-two. In 1710 one of these Massachusetts
vessels appeared off the coast escorting a fishing-fleet
of no less than two hundred and fifty sail, some of
which were afterwards captured by French corsairs.
A good number of these last, however, were taken
from time to time by Boston sea-rovers, who, like
their enemies, sometimes bore a close likeness to
pirates. They seized French fishing and trading
vessels, attacked French corsairs, sometimes traded
with the Acadians, and sometimes plundered them.
What with West India rum brought by the French
freebooters, and New England rum brought by the
English, it is reported that one could get drunk in
Acadia for two sous.

Port Royal, now Annapolis, was the seat of government, and the only place of any strength in the
colony. The fort, a sodded earthwork, lately put
into tolerable repair by the joint labor of the soldiers
and inhabitants, stood on the point of land between
the mouth of the river Annapolis and that of the
small stream now called Allen's River, whence it

[1] *Subercase au Ministre,* 3 *Janvier,* 1710.

looked down the long basin, or land-locked bay,
which, framed in hills and forests, had so won the
heart of the Baron de Poutrincourt a century before.[1]
The garrison was small, counting in 1704 only a
hundred and eighty-five soldiers and eight commissioned officers.   At the right of the fort, between it
and the mouth of the Annapolis, was the Acadian
village, consisting of seventy or eighty small houses
of one story and an attic, built of planks, boards, or
logs, simple and rude, but tolerably comfortable.   It
had also a small, new wooden church, to the building of which the inhabitants had contributed eight
hundred francs, while the King paid the rest.   The
inhabitants had no voice whatever in public affairs,
though the colonial minister had granted them the
privilege of travelling in time of peace without pass-
ports.   The ruling class, civil and military, formed
a group apart, living in or near the fort, in complete
independence of public opinion, supposing such to
have existed.   They looked only to their masters at
Versailles; and hence a state of things as curious as
it was lamentable.   The little settlement was a
hot-bed of gossip, backbiting, and slander.   Officials
of every degree were continually trying to undermine
and supplant one another, besieging the minister
with mutual charges.   Brouillan, the governor, was
a frequent object of attack.   He seems to have been
of an irritable temper, aggravated perhaps by an old
unhealed wound in the cheek, which gave him con-

[1] Pioneers of France in the New World, ii. 71.

stant annoyance. One writer declares that Acadia languishes under selfish greed and petty tyranny; that everything was hoped from Brouillan when he first came, but that hope has changed to despair; that he abuses the King's authority to make money, sells wine and brandy at retail, quarrels with officers who are not punctilious enough in saluting him, forces the inhabitants to catch seal and cod for the King, and then cheats them of their pay, and countenances an obnoxious churchwarden whose daughter is his mistress. "The country groans, but dares not utter a word," concludes the accuser, as he closes his indictment.[1]

Brouillan died in the autumn of 1705, on which M. de Goutin. a magistrate who acted as intendant, and was therefore at once the colleague of the late governor and a spy upon him, writes to the minister that "the divine justice has at last taken pity on the good people of this country," but that as it is base to accuse a dead man, he will not say that the public could not help showing their joy at the late governor's departure; and he adds that the deceased was charged with a scandalous connection with the Widow de Freneuse. Nor will he reply, he says, to the governor's complaint to the court about a pretended cabal, of which he, De Goutin, was the head, and which was in reality only three or four honest men, incapable of any kind of deviation, who used to meet in

---

[1] La Touche, *Mémoire sur l'Acadie,* 1702 (adressé à Ponchartrain).

a friendly way, and had given offence by not bowing down before the beast.[1]

Then he changes the subject, and goes on to say that on a certain festal occasion he was invited by Bonaventure, who acted as governor after the death of Brouillan, to share with him the honor of touching off a bonfire before the fort gate; and that this excited such envy, jealousy, and discord that he begs the minister, once for all, to settle the question whether a first magistrate has not the right to the honor of touching off a bonfire jointly with a governor.

De Goutin sometimes discourses of more serious matters. He tells the minister that the inhabitants have plenty of cattle, and more hemp than they can use, but neither pots, scythes, sickles, knives, hatchets, kettles for the Indians, nor salt for themselves. "We should be fortunate if our enemies would continue to supply our necessities and take the beaver-skins with which the colony is gorged;" adding, however, that the Acadians hate the English, and will not trade with them if they can help it.[2]

In the next year the "Bastonnais" were again

---

[1] "Que trois ou quatre amis, honnêtes gens, incapables de gauchir en quoique ce soit, pour n'avoir pas fléché devant la bête, aient été qualifiés de cabalistes." — *De Goutin au Ministre,* 4 *Décembre,* 1705.

[2] *De Goutin au Ministre,* 22 *Décembre,* 1707. In 1705 Bonaventure, in a time of scarcity, sent a vessel to Boston to buy provisions, on pretence of exchanging prisoners. *Bonaventure au Ministre,* 30 *Novembre,* 1705.

bringing supplies, and the Acadians again receiving them. The new governor, Subercase, far from being pleased at this, was much annoyed, or professed to be so, and wrote to Ponchartrain, "Nobody could suffer more than I do at seeing the English so coolly carry on their trade under our very noses." Then he proceeds to the inevitable personalities. "You wish me to write without reserve of the officers here; I have little good to tell you;" and he names two who to the best of his belief have lost their wits, a third who is incorrigibly lazy, and a fourth who is eccentric; adding that he is tolerably well satisfied with the rest, except M. de la Ronde. "You see, Monseigneur, that I am as much in need of a mad-house as of barracks; and what is worse, I am afraid that the *mauvais esprit* of this country will drive me crazy too."[1] "You write to me," he continues, "that you are informed that M. Labat has killed some cattle belonging to the inhabitants. If so, he has expiated his fault by blowing off his thumb by the bursting of his gun while he was firing at a sheep. I am sure that the moon has a good deal to do with his behavior; he always acts very strangely when she is on the wane."

The charge brought against Brouillan in regard to Madame de Freneuse was brought also against Bonaventure in connection with the same lady. "The story," says Subercase, "was pushed as far as

[1] "Ne me fasse à mon tour tourner la cervelle." — *Subercase au Ministre,* 20 *Décembre,* 1708.

hell could desire;"[1] and he partially defends the
accused, declaring that at least his fidelity to the
King is beyond question.

De Goutin had a quarrel with Subercase, and
writes: "I do all that is possible to live on good
terms with him, and to that end I walk as if in the
chamber of a sick prince whose sleep is of the lightest."
As Subercase defends Bonaventure, De Goutin attacks him, and gives particulars concerning him and
Madame de Freneuse which need not be recounted
here.   Then comes a story about a quarrel caused by
some cows belonging to Madame de Freneuse which
got into the garden of Madame de Saint-Vincent, and
were driven out by a soldier who presumed to strike
one of them with a long stick.   "The facts," gravely
adds De Goutin, "have been certified to me as I have
the honor to relate them to your Grandeur."[2]   Then
the minister is treated to a story of one Allein.   "He
insulted Madame de Belleisle at the church door
after high mass, and when her son, a boy of fourteen,
interposed, Allein gave him such a box on the ear
that it drew blood; and I am assured that M. Petit,
the priest, ran to the rescue in his sacerdotal robes."
Subercase, on his side, after complaining that the
price of a certain canoe had been unjustly deducted
from his pay, though he never had the said canoe at
all, protests to Ponchartrain, "there is no country on

[1] "On a poussé la chose aussi loin que l'enfer le pouvait désirer."
— *Subercase au Ministre*, 20 *Décembre*, 1708.
[2] *De Goutin au Ministre*, 29 *Décembre*, 1708.

earth where I would not rather live than in this, by reason of the ill-disposed persons who inhabit it." [1]

There was the usual friction between the temporal and the spiritual powers. "The Church," writes Subercase, "has long claimed the right of commanding here, or at least of sharing authority with the civil rulers." [2] The Church had formerly been represented by the Capuchin friars, and afterwards by the Récollets. Every complaint was of course carried to the minister. In 1700 we find M. de Villieu, who then held a provisional command in the colony, accusing the ecclesiastics of illicit trade with the English. [3] Bonaventure reports to Ponchartrain that Père Félix, chaplain of the fort, asked that the gate might be opened, in order that he might carry the sacraments to a sick man, his real object being to marry Captain Duvivier to a young woman named Marie Muis de Poubomcoup, — contrary, as the governor thought, to the good of the service. He therefore forbade the match; on which the priests told him that when they had made up their minds to do anything, nobody had power to turn them from it; and the chaplain presently added that he cared no more for the governor than for the mud on his shoes. [4] He carried his point, and married Duvivier in spite of the commander.

Every king's ship from Acadia brought to Ponchartrain letters full of matters like these. In one

---

[1] *Subercase au Ministre*, 20 *Décembre*, 1708.   [2] *Ibid.*

[3] *Villieu au Ministre*, 20 *Octobre*, 1700.

[4] " Il répondit qu'il se soucioit de moi comme de la boue de ses souliers." — *Bonaventure au Ministre*, 30 *Novembre*, 1705.

year, 1703, he got at least fourteen such.   If half of
what Saint-Simon tells us of him is true, it is not to
be supposed that he gave himself much trouble concerning them.   This does not make it the less astonishing that in the midst of a great and disastrous war
a minister of State should be expected to waste time
on matters worthy of a knot of old gossips babbling
round a tea-table.   That pompous spectre which calls
itself the Dignity of History would scorn to take note
of them; yet they are highly instructive, for the
morbid anatomy of this little colony has a scientific
value as exhibiting, all the more vividly for the nar-
rowness of the field, the workings of an unmitigated
paternalism acting from across the Atlantic.   The
King's servants in Acadia pestered his minister at
Versailles with their pettiest squabbles, while Marlborough and Eugene were threatening his throne
with destruction.[1]   The same system prevailed in
Canada; but as there the field was broader and the
men often larger, the effects are less whimsically
vivid than they appear under the Acadian micro-
scope.   The two provinces, however, were ruled
alike; and about this time the Canadian Intendant
Raudot was writing to Ponchartrain in a strain
worthy of De Goutin, Subercase, or Bonaventure.[2]

[1] These letters of Acadian officials are in the Archives du
Ministère de la Marine et des Colonies at Paris.   Copies of some of
them will be found in the 3d series of the *Correspondance Officielle*
at Ottawa.

[2] *Raudot au Ministre*, 20 *Septembre*, 1709.   The copy before me
covers 108 folio pages, filled with gossiping personalities.

CHAPTER VII.

1704–1710.

ACADIA CHANGES HANDS.

Reprisal for Deerfield. — Major Benjamin Church: his Ravages at Grand-Pré. — Port Royal Expedition. — Futile Proceedings. — A Discreditable Affair. — French Successes in Newfoundland. — Schemes of Samuel Vetch. — A Grand Enterprise. — Nicholson's Advance. — An Infected Camp. — Ministerial Promises broken. — A New Scheme. — Port Royal attacked. — Acadia conquered.

When war-parties from Canada struck the English borders, reprisal was difficult against those who had provoked it. Canada was made almost inaccessible by a hundred leagues of pathless forest, prowled by her Indian allies, who were sure to give the alarm of an approaching foe; while, on the other hand, the New Englanders could easily reach Acadia by their familiar element, the sea; and hence that unfortunate colony often made vicarious atonement for the sins of her northern sister. It was from French privateers and fishing-vessels on the Acadian seas that Massachusetts drew most of the prisoners whom she exchanged for her own people held captive in Canada.

Major Benjamin Church, the noted Indian fighter of King Philip's War, was at Tiverton in Rhode Island when he heard of Hertel de Rouville's attack on Deerfield. Boiling with rage, he mounted his horse and rode to Boston to propose a stroke of retaliation. Church was energetic, impetuous, and bull-headed, sixty-five years old, and grown so fat that when pushing through the woods on the trail of Indians, he kept a stout sergeant by him to hoist him over fallen trees. Governor Dudley approved his scheme, and appointed him to command the expedition, with the rank of colonel. Church repaired to his native Duxbury; and here, as well as in Plymouth and other neighboring settlements, the militia were called out, and the veteran readily persuaded a sufficient number to volunteer under him. With the Indians of Cape Cod he found more difficulty, they being, as his son observes, "a people that need much treating, especially with drink." At last, however, some of them were induced to join him. Church now returned to Boston, and begged that an attack on Port Royal might be included in his instructions, — which was refused, on the ground that a plan to that effect had been laid before the Queen, and that nothing could be done till her answer was received. The governor's enemies seized the occasion to say that he wished Port Royal to remain French, in order to make money by trading with it.

The whole force, including Indians and sailors,

amounted to about seven hundred men; they sailed
to Matinicus in brigs and sloops, the province galley,
and two British frigates.   From Matinicus most of
the sailing-vessels were sent to Mount Desert to wait
orders, while the main body rowed eastward in
whale-boats.   Touching at Saint-Castin's fort, where
the town of Castine now stands, they killed or
captured everybody they found there.   Receiving
false information that there was a large war-party
on the west side of Passamaquoddy Bay, they hastened to the place, reached it in the night, and
pushed into the woods in hope of surprising the
enemy.   The movement was difficult; and Church's
men, being little better than a mob, disregarded his
commands, and fell into disorder.   He raged and
stormed; and presently, in the darkness and confusion, descrying a hut or cabin on the farther side of
a small brook, with a crowd gathered about it, he
demanded what was the matter, and was told that
there were Frenchmen inside who would not come
out.   "Then knock them in the head," shouted the
choleric old man; and he was obeyed.   It was said
that the victims belonged to a party of Canadians
captured just before, under a promise of life.   Afterwards, when Church returned to Boston, there was
an outcry of indignation against him for this butch-
ery.   In any case, however, he could have known
nothing of the alleged promise of quarter.

To hunt Indians with an endless forest behind
them was like chasing shadows.   The Acadians

were surer game. Church sailed with a part of his force up the Bay of Fundy, and landed at Grand Pré, — a place destined to a dismal notoriety half a century later. The inhabitants of this and the neighboring settlements made some slight resistance, and killed a lieutenant named Baker, and one soldier, after which they fled; when Church, first causing the houses to be examined, to make sure that nobody was left in them, ordered them to be set on fire. The dikes were then broken, and the tide let in upon the growing crops.[1] In spite of these harsh proceedings, he fell far short in his retaliation for the barbarities at Deerfield, since he restrained his Indians and permitted no woman or child to be hurt, — at the same time telling his prisoners that if any other New England village were treated as Deerfield had been, he would come back with a thousand Indians and leave them free to do what they pleased. With this bluster, he left the unfortunate peasants in the extremity of terror, after carrying off as many of them as were needed for purposes of exchange. A small detachment was sent to Beaubassin, where it committed similar havoc.

Church now steered for Port Royal, which he had been forbidden to attack. The two frigates and the

---

[1] Church, *Entertaining Passages.* "Un habitant des Mines a dit que les ennemis avaient été dans toutes les rivières, qu'il n'y restait plus que quatre habitations en entier, le restant ayant été brulé." — *Expéditions faites par les Anglois,* 1704. " Qu'ils avaient . . . brulé toutes les maisons à la reserve du haut des rivières."—Labat, *Invasion des Anglois,* 1704.

transports had by this time rejoined him, and in spite of Dudley's orders to make no attempt on the French fort, the British and provincial officers met in council to consider whether to do so.   With one voice they decided in the negative, since they had only four hundred men available for landing, while the French garrison was no doubt much stronger, having had ample time to call the inhabitants to its aid.   Church, therefore, after trying the virtue of a bombastic summons to surrender, and destroying a few houses, sailed back to Boston.   It was a miserable retaliation for a barbarous outrage; as the guilty were out of reach, the invaders turned their ire on the innocent.[1]

If Port Royal in French hands was a source of illicit gain to some persons in Boston, it was also an occasion of loss by the privateers and corsairs it sent out to prey on trading and fishing vessels, while at the same time it was a standing menace as the possible naval base for one of those armaments against the New England capital which were often threatened, though never carried into effect.   Hence, in 1707 the New England colonists made, in their bungling way, a serious attempt to get possession of it.

Dudley's enemies raised the old cry that at heart

[1] On this affair, Thomas Church, *Entertaining Passages* (1716). The writer was the son of Benjamin Church.   Penhallow; Belknap, i. 266 ; *Dudley to* ———, 21 *April*, 1704 ; Hutchinson, ii. 132 ; *Deplorable State of New England ; Entreprise des Anglais sur l'Acadie*, 1704 ; *Expéditions faites par les Anglais de la Nouvelle Angleterre*, 1704 ; Labat, *Invasion des Anglois de Baston*, 1704.

he wished Port Royal to remain French, and was
only forced by popular clamor to countenance an
attack upon it. The charge seems a malicious
slander. Early in March he proposed the enterprise
to the General Court; and the question being referred
to a committee, they reported that a thousand soldiers
should be raised, vessels impressed, and her Majesty's
frigate "Deptford," with the province galley, employed to convoy them. An Act was passed accordingly.[1] Two regiments were soon afoot, one uni-
formed in red, and the other in blue; one commanded
by Colonel Francis Wainwright, and the other by
Colonel Winthrop Hilton. Rhode Island sent eighty
more men, and New Hampshire sixty, while Connecticut would do nothing. The expedition sailed
on the thirteenth of May, and included one thousand
and seventy-six soldiers, with about four hundred and
fifty sailors.

The soldiers were nearly all volunteers from the
rural militia, and their training and discipline were
such as they had acquired in the uncouth frolics and
plentiful New England rum of the periodical "muster
days." There chanced to be one officer who knew
more or less of the work in hand. This was the
English engineer Rednap, sent out to look after
the fortifications of New York and New England.
The commander-in-chief was Colonel John March, of

---

[1] *Report of a Committee to consider his Excellency's Speech,* 12 *March,*
1707. *Resolve for an Expedition against Port Royal* (Massachusetts
Archives).

Newbury, who had popular qualities, had seen frontier service, and was personally brave, but totally unfit for his present position. Most of the officers were civilians from country towns, — Ipswich, Topsfield, Lynn, Salem, Dorchester, Taunton, or Weymouth.[1] In the province galley went, as secretary of the expedition, that intelligent youth, William Dudley, son of the governor.

New England has been blamed for not employing trained officers to command her levies; but with the exception of Rednap, and possibly of Captain Samuel Vetch, there were none in the country, nor were they wanted. In their stubborn and jealous independence, the sons of the Puritans would have resented their presence. The provincial officers were, without exception, civilians. British regular officers, good, bad, or indifferent, were apt to put on airs of superiority which galled the democratic susceptibilities of the natives, who, rather than endure a standing military force imposed by the mother-country, preferred to suffer if they must, and fight their own battles in their own crude way. Even for irregular warfare they were at a disadvantage; Canadian feudalism developed good partisan leaders, which was rarely the case with New England democracy. Colonel John March was a tyro set over a crowd of ploughboys, fishermen, and mechanics, officered by tradesmen, farmers, blacksmiths, village

[1] *Autobiography of Rev. John Barnard,* one of the five chaplains of the expedition.

magnates, and deacons of the church, — for the characters of deacon and militia officer were often joined in one. These improvised soldiers commonly did well in small numbers, and very ill in large ones.

Early in June the expedition sailed into Port Royal Basin, and Lieutenant-Colonel Appleton, with three hundred and fifty men, landed on the north shore, four or five miles below the fort, marched up to the mouth of the Annapolis, and was there met by an ambushed body of French, who, being outnumbered, presently took to their boats and retreated to the fort. Meanwhile, March, with seven hundred and fifty men, landed on the south shore and pushed on to the meadows of Allen's River, which they were crossing in battle array when a fire blazed out upon them from a bushy hill on the farther bank, where about two hundred French lay in ambush under Subercase, the governor. March and his men crossed the stream, and after a skirmish that did little harm to either side, the French gave way. The English then advanced to a hill known as the Lion Rampant, within cannon-shot of the fort, and here began to intrench themselves, stretching their lines right and left towards the Annapolis on the one hand, and Allen's River on the other, so as to form a semicircle before the fort, where all the inhabitants had by this time taken refuge.

Soon all was confusion in the New England camp, — the consequence of March's incapacity for a large command, and the greenness and ignorance of both himself and his subordinates.   There were conflicting opinions, wranglings, and disputes.   The men, losing all confidence in their officers, became unmanageable. "The devil was at work among us," writes one of those present.   The engineer, Rednap, the only one of them who knew anything of the work in hand, began to mark out the batteries; but he soon lost temper, and declared that "it was not for him to venture his reputation with such ungovernable and undisciplined men and inconstant officers."[1]   He refused to bring up the cannon, saying that it could not be done under the fire of the fort; and the naval captains were of the same opinion.

One of the chaplains, Rev. John Barnard, being of a martial turn and full of zeal, took it upon himself to make a plan of the fort; and to that end, after providing himself with pen, ink, paper, and a horse-pistol, took his seat at a convenient spot; but his task was scarcely begun when it was ended by a cannon-ball that struck the ground beside him, peppered him with gravel, and caused his prompt retreat.[2]

French deserters reported that there were five hundred men in the fort, with forty-two heavy cannon, and that four or five hundred more were expected every day.   This increased the general bewilderment of the besiegers.   There was a council of war.   Rednap declared that it would be useless

---

[1] *A Boston Gentleman to his Friend,* 13 *June,* 1707 (Mass. Archives).
[2] *Autobiography of Rev. John Barnard.*

to persist; and after hot debate and contradiction, it was resolved to decamp. Three days after, there was another council, which voted to bring up the cannon and open fire, in spite of Rednap and the naval captains; but in the next evening a third council resolved again to raise the siege as hopeless. This disgusted the rank and file, who were a little soothed by an order to destroy the storehouse and other buildings outside the fort; and, ill led as they were, they did the work thoroughly. "Never did men act more boldly," says the witness before quoted; "they threatened the enemy to his nose, and would have taken the fort if the officers had shown any spirit. They found it hard to bring them off. At the end we broke up with the confusion of Babel, and went about our business like fools." [1]

The baffled invaders sailed crestfallen to Casco Bay, and a vessel was sent to carry news of the miscarriage to Dudley, who, vexed and incensed, ordered another attempt. March was in a state of helpless indecision, increased by a bad cold; but the governor would not recall him, and chose instead the lamentable expedient of sending three members of the provincial council to advise and direct him. Two of them had commissions in the militia; the third, John Leverett, was a learned bachelor of divinity, formerly a tutor in Harvard College, and soon after

---

[1] *A Boston Gentleman to his Friend,* 13 *June* (old style), 1707. The final attack here alluded to took place on the night of the **sixteenth** of June (new style).

its president, — capable, no doubt, of preaching Calvinistic sermons to the students, but totally unfit to command men or conduct a siege.

Young William Dudley was writing meanwhile to his father how jealousies and quarrels were rife among the officers, how their conduct bred disorder and desertion among the soldiers, and how Colonel March and others behaved as if they had nothing to do but make themselves popular.[1] Many of the officers seem, in fact, to have been small politicians in search of notoriety, with an eye to votes or appointments. Captain Stuckley, of the British frigate, wrote to the governor in great discontent about the "nonsensical malice" of Lieutenant-Colonel Appleton, and adds, "I don't see what good I can do by lying here, where I am almost murdered by mosquitoes."[2]

The three commissioners came at last, with a reinforcement of another frigate and a hundred recruits, which did not supply losses, as the soldiers had deserted by scores. In great ill-humor, the expedition sailed back to Port Royal, where it was found that reinforcements had also reached the French, including a strongly manned privateer from Martinique. The New England men landed, and there was some sharp skirmishing in an orchard. Chaplain Barnard took part in the fray. "A shot brushed my wig," he says, "but I was mercifully preserved.

[1] *William Dudley to Governor Dudley*, 24 *June*, 1707.
[2] *Stuckley to Dudley*, 28 *June*, 1707.

We soon drove them out of the orchard, killed a few of them, desperately wounded the privateer captain, and after that we all embarked and returned to Boston as fast as we could." This summary statement is imperfect, for there was a good deal of skirmishing from the thirteenth August to the twentieth, when the invaders sailed for home. March was hooted as he walked Boston streets, and children ran after him crying, "Wooden sword!" There was an attempt at a court-martial; but so many officers were accused, on one ground or another, that hardly enough were left to try them, and the matter was dropped. With one remarkable exception, the New England militia reaped scant laurels on their various expeditions eastward; but of all their shortcomings, this was the most discreditable.[1]

Meanwhile events worthy of note were passing in Newfoundland. That island was divided between the two conflicting powers, — the chief station of the French being at Placentia, and that of the English at St. John. In January, 1705, Subercase, who soon

---

[1] A considerable number of letters and official papers on this expedition will be found in the 51st and 71st volumes of the Massachusetts Archives. See also Hutchinson, ii. 151, and Belknap, i. 273. The curious narrative of the chaplain, Barnard, is in *Mass. Hist. Coll.*, 3d *Series*, v. 189–196. The account in the *Deplorable State of New England* is meant solely to injure Dudley. The chief French accounts are *Entreprise des Anglois contre l'Acadie, 26 Juin,* 1707 ; *Subercase au Ministre, même date; Labat au Ministre, 6 Juillet,* 1707 ; *Relation* appended to Dièreville, *Voyage de l'Acadie.* The last is extremely loose and fanciful. Subercase puts the English force at three thousand men, whereas the official returns show it to have been, soldiers and sailors, about half this number.

after became governor of Acadia, marched with four
hundred and fifty soldiers, Canadians, and buccaneers, aided by a band of Indians, against St.
John, — a fishing-village defended by two forts, the
smaller, known as the castle, held by twelve men,
and the larger, called Fort William, by forty men
under Captain Moody.   The latter was attacked by
the French, who were beaten off; on which they
burned the unprotected houses and fishing-huts with
a brutality equal to that of Church in Acadia, and
followed up the exploit by destroying the hamlet at
Ferryland and all the defenceless hovels and fish-
stages along the shore towards Trinity Bay and
Bonavista.[1]

Four years later, the Sieur de Saint-Ovide, a
nephew of Brouillan, late governor at Port Royal,
struck a more creditable blow.   He set out from Placentia on the thirteenth of December, 1708, with one
hundred and sixty-four men, and on the first of
January approached Fort William two hours before
day, found the gate leading to the covered way open,
entered with a band of volunteers, rapidly crossed
the ditch, planted ladders against the wall, and
leaped into the fort, then, as he declares, garrisoned
by a hundred men.   His main body followed close.
The English were taken unawares; their commander,

---

[1] Penhallow puts the French force at five hundred and fifty.
Jeremiah Dummer, *Letter to a Noble Lord concerning the late Expedition to Canada,* says that the havoc committed occasioned a total
loss of £80,000.

who showed great courage, was struck down by
three shots, and after some sharp fighting the place
was in the hands of the assailants. The small fort
at the mouth of the harbor capitulated on the second
day, and the palisaded village of the inhabitants,
which, if we are to believe Saint-Ovide, contained
nearly six hundred men, made little resistance. St.
John became for the moment a French possession;
but Costebelle, governor at Placentia, despaired of
holding it, and it was abandoned in the following
summer.[1]

About this time a scheme was formed for the
permanent riddance of New England from war-
parties by the conquest of Canada.[2] The prime
mover in it was Samuel Vetch, whom we have seen
as an emissary to Quebec for the exchange of prisoners, and also as one of the notables fined for illicit
trade with the French. He came of a respectable
Scotch family. His grandfather, his father, three of
his uncles, and one of his brothers were Covenanting
ministers, who had suffered some persecution under
Charles II. He himself was destined for the ministry; but his inclinations being in no way clerical, he

[1] *Saint-Ovide au Ministre*, 20 *Janvier*, 1709; *Ibid.*, 6 *Septembre*,
1709; *Rapport de Costebelle*, 26 *Février*, 1709. Costebelle makes the
French force one hundred and seventy-five.

[2] Some of the French officials in Acadia foresaw aggressive
action on the part of the English in consequence of the massacre
at Haverhill. " Le coup que les Canadiens viennent de faire, où
Mars, plus féroce qu'en Europe, a donné carrière à sa rage, me fait
appréhender une représaille." — *De Goutin au Ministre*, 29 *Décembre*,
1708.

and his brother William got commissions in the army, and took an active part in the war that ended with the Peace of Ryswick.

In the next year the two brothers sailed for the Isthmus of Panama as captains in the band of adventurers embarked in the disastrous enterprise known as the Darien Scheme. William Vetch died at sea, and Samuel repaired to New York, where he married a daughter of Robert Livingston, one of the chief men of the colony, and engaged largely in the Canadian trade. From New York he went to Boston, where we find him when the War of the Spanish Succession began. During his several visits to Canada he had carefully studied the St. Lawrence and its shores, and boasted that he knew them better than the Canadians themselves.[1] He was impetuous, sanguine, energetic, and headstrong, astute withal, and full of ambition. A more vigorous agent for the execution of the proposed plan of conquest could not have been desired. The General Court of Massachusetts, contrary to its instinct and its past practice, resolved, in view of the greatness of the stake, to ask this time for help from the mother-country, and Vetch sailed for England, bearing an address to the Queen, begging for an armament to aid in the reduction of Canada and Acadia. The scheme waxed broader yet in the ardent brain of the agent;

1 Patterson, *Memoir of Hon. Samuel Vetch,* in *Collections of the Nova Scotia Historical Society,* iv. Compare a paper by General James Grant Wilson in *International Review,* November, 1881.

he proposed to add Newfoundland to the other conquests, and when all was done in the North, to sail to the Gulf of Mexico and wrest Pensacola from the Spaniards; by which means, he writes, "Her Majesty shall be sole empress of the vast North American continent." The idea was less visionary than it seems. Energy, helped by reasonable good luck, might easily have made it a reality, so far as concerned the possessions of France.

The court granted all that Vetch asked. On the eleventh of March he sailed for America, fully empowered to carry his plans into execution, and with the assurance that when Canada was conquered, he should be its governor. A squadron bearing five regiments of regular troops was promised. The colonies were to muster their forces in all haste. New York was directed to furnish eight hundred men; New Jersey, two hundred; Pennsylvania, one hundred and fifty; and Connecticut, three hundred and fifty, — the whole to be at Albany by the middle of May, and to advance on Montreal by way of Wood Creek and Lake Champlain, as soon as they should hear that the squadron had reached Boston. Massachusetts, New Hampshire, and Rhode Island were to furnish twelve hundred men, to join the regulars in attacking Quebec by way of the St. Lawrence.[1]

[1] *Instructions to Colonel Vetch*, 1 *March*, 1709 ; *The Earl of Sunderland to Dudley*, 28 *April*, 1709 ; *The Queen to Lord Lovelace*, 1 *March*, 1709 ; *The Earl of Sunderland to Lord Lovelace*, 28 *April*, 1709.

Vetch sailed from Portsmouth in the ship "Dragon," accompanied by Colonel Francis Nicholson, late lieutenant-governor of New York, who was to take an important part in the enterprise. The squadron with the five regiments was to follow without delay. The weather was bad, and the "Dragon," beating for five weeks against headwinds, did not enter Boston harbor till the evening of the twenty-eighth of April. Vetch, chafing with impatience, for every moment was precious, sent off expresses that same night to carry the Queen's letters to the governors of Rhode Island, Connecticut, New Jersey, and Pennsylvania. Dudley and his council met the next morning, and to them Vetch delivered the royal message, which was received, he says, "with the dutiful obedience becoming good subjects, and all the marks of joy and thankfulness." [1] Vetch, Nicholson, and the Massachusetts authorities quickly arranged their plans. An embargo was laid on the shipping; provision was made for raising men and supplies and providing transportation. When all was in train, the two emissaries hired a sloop for New York, and touching by the way at Rhode Island, found it in the throes of the annual election of governor. Yet every warlike preparation was already made, and Vetch and his companion sailed at once for New Haven to meet Saltonstall, the newly elected governor of Connecti-

---

[1] *Journal of Vetch and Nicholson* (Public Record Office). This is in the form of a letter, signed by both, and dated at New York, 29 June, 1709.

taking care to suppress on the record every indication
that the money was meant for military uses.   New
York, on the other hand, raised her full contingent,
and Massachusetts and New Hampshire something
more, being warm in the faith that their borders
would be plagued with war-parties no longer.

It remained for New York to gain the help of the
Five Nations of the Iroquois, to which end Abraham
Schuyler went to Onondaga, well supplied with
presents.   The Iroquois capital was now, as it had
been for years, divided between France and England.
French interests were represented by the two Jesuits,
Mareuil and Jacques Lamberville.   The skilful man--
agement of Schuyler, joined to his gifts and his rum,
presently won over so many to the English party,
and raised such excitement in the town that Lamberville thought it best to set out for Montreal with
news of what was going on.   The intrepid Joncaire,
agent of France among the Senecas, was scandalized
at what he calls the Jesuit's flight, and wrote to the
commandant of Fort Frontenac that its effect on the
Indians was such that he, Joncaire, was in peril of
his life.[1]   Yet he stood his ground, and managed so
well that he held the Senecas firm in their neutrality.
Lamberville's colleague, Mareuil, whose position was
still more critical, was persuaded by Schuyler that
his only safety was in going with him to Albany,
which he did; and on this the Onondagas, excited
by rum, plundered and burned the Jesuit mission-

[1] Joncaire in *N. Y. Col. Docs.*, ix. 838.

house and chapel.[1] Clearly, the two priests at
Onondaga were less hungry for martyrdom than their
murdered brethren Jogues, Brébeuf, Lalemant, and
Charles Garnier; but it is to be remembered that the
Canadian Jesuit of the first half of the seventeenth
century was before all things an apostle, and his
successor of a century later was before all things a
political agent.

As for the Five Nations, that once haughty confederacy, in spite of divisions and waverings, had
conceived the idea that its true policy lay, not in
siding with either of the European rivals, but in
making itself important to both, and courted and
caressed by both. While some of the warriors sang
the war-song at the prompting of Schuyler, they had
been but half-hearted in doing so; and even the
Mohawks, nearest neighbors and best friends of the
English, sent word to their Canadian kindred,
the Caughnawagas, that they took up the hatchet
only because they could not help it.

The attack on Canada by way of the Hudson and
Lake Champlain was to have been commanded by
Lord Lovelace or some officer of his choice; but as
he was dead, Ingoldsby, his successor in the government of the province, jointly with the governors of
several adjacent colonies who had met at New York,
appointed Colonel Nicholson in his stead.[2]   Nichol-

---

[1] Mareuil in *N. Y. Col. Docs.*, ix. 836, text and note.   *Vaudreuil
au Ministre*, 14 *Novembre*, 1709.

[2] " If I had not accepted the command, there would have been

son went to Albany, whence, with about fifteen hundred men, he moved up the Hudson, built a stockade fort opposite Saratoga, and another at the spot known as the Great Carrying Place. This latter he called Fort Nicholson, — a name which it afterwards exchanged for that of Fort Lydius, and later still for that of Fort Edward, which the town that occupies the site owns to this day.[1] Thence he cut a rough roadway through the woods to where Wood Creek, choked with beaver dams, writhed through flat green meadows, walled in by rock and forest. Here he built another fort, which was afterwards rebuilt and named Fort Anne. Wood Creek led to Lake Champlain, and Lake Champlain to Chambly and Montreal, — the objective points of the expedition. All was astir at the camp. Flat-boats and canoes were made, and stores brought up from Albany, till everything was ready for an advance the moment word should come that the British fleet had reached Boston. Vetch, all impatience, went thither to meet it, as if his presence could hasten its arrival.

Reports of Nicholson's march to Wood Creek had reached Canada, and Vaudreuil sent Ramesay, governor of Montreal, with fifteen hundred troops, Canadians, and Indians, to surprise his camp. Ramesay's fleet of canoes had reached Lake Cham-

---

insuperable difficulties" (arising from provincial jealousies). — *Nicholson to Sunderland*, 8 *July*, 1709.

[1] Forts Nicholson, Lydius, and Edward were not the same, but succeeded each other on the same ground.

plain, and was halfway to the mouth of Wood Creek, when his advance party was discovered by English scouts, and the French commander began to fear that he should be surprised in his turn; in fact, some of his Indians were fired upon from an ambuscade. All was now doubt, perplexity, and confusion. Ramesay landed at the narrows of the lake, a little south of the place now called Crown Point. Here, in the dense woods, his Indians fired on some Canadians whom they took for English. This was near producing a panic. "Every tree seemed an enemy," writes an officer present. Ramesay lost himself in the woods, and could not find his army. One Deruisseau, who had gone out as a scout, came back with the report that nine hundred Englishmen were close at hand. Seven English canoes did in fact appear, supported, as the French in their excitement imagined, by a numerous though invisible army in the forest; but being fired upon, and seeing that they were entering a hornet's nest, the English sheered off. Ramesay having at last found his army, and order being gradually restored, a council of war was held, after which the whole force fell back to Chambly, having accomplished nothing.[1]

---

[1] *Mémoire sur le Canada, Année* 1709. This paper, which has been ascribed to the engineer De Léry, is printed in *Collection de Manuscrits relatifs à la Nouvelle France*, i. 615 (Quebec, 1883), printed from the MS. *Paris Documents* in the Boston State House. The writer of the *Mémoire* was with Ramesay's expedition. Also *Ramesay à Vaudreuil*, 19 *Octobre*, 1709, and *Vaudreuil au Ministre*, 14 *Novembre*, 1709. Charlevoix says that Ramesay turned back

Great was the alarm in Canada when it became known that the enemy aimed at nothing less than the conquest of the colony. One La Plaine spread a panic at Quebec by reporting that, forty-five leagues below, he had seen eight or ten ships under sail and heard the sound of cannon. It was afterwards surmised that the supposed ships were points of rocks seen through the mist at low tide, and the cannon the floundering of whales at play.[1] Quebec, however, was all excitement, in expectation of attack. The people of the Lower Town took refuge on the rock above; the men of the neighboring parishes were ordered within the walls; and the women and children, with the cattle and horses, were sent to hiding-places in the forest. There had been no less consternation at Montreal, caused by exaggerated reports of Iroquois hostility and the movements of Nicholson. It was even proposed to abandon Chambly and Fort Frontenac, and concentrate all available force to defend the heart of the colony. "A most bloody war is imminent," wrote Vaudreuil to the minister, Ponchartrain.

Meanwhile, for weeks and months Nicholson's little army lay in the sultry valley of Wood Creek,

because he believed that there were five thousand English at Wood Creek; but Ramesay himself makes their number only one thousand whites and two hundred Indians. He got his information from two Dutchmen caught just after the alarm near Pointe à la Chevelure (Crown Point). He turned back because he had failed to surprise the English, and also, it seems, because there were disagreements among his officers.

[1] *Monseigneur de Saint-Vallier et l'Hôpital Général de Québec*, 203.

waiting those tidings of the arrival of the British
squadron at Boston which were to be its signal of
advance. At length a pestilence broke out. It is
said to have been the work of the Iroquois allies,
who thought that the French were menaced with
ruin, and who, true to their policy of balancing
one European power against the other, poisoned the
waters of the creek by throwing into it, above the
camp, the skins and offal of the animals they had
killed in their hunting. The story may have some
foundation, though it rests only on the authority of
Charlevoix. No contemporary writer mentions it;
and Vaudreuil says that the malady was caused by
the long confinement of the English in their fort.
Indeed, a crowd of men, penned up through the
heats of midsummer in a palisaded camp, ill-ordered
and unclean as the camps of the raw provincials
usually were, and infested with pestiferous swarms
of flies and mosquitoes, could hardly have remained
in health. Whatever its cause, the disease, which
seems to have been a malignant dysentery, made
more havoc than the musket and the sword. A
party of French who came to the spot late in the
autumn, found it filled with innumerable graves.

The British squadron, with the five regiments on
board, was to have reached Boston at the middle of
May. On the twentieth of that month the whole
contingent of Massachusetts, New Hampshire, and
Rhode Island was encamped by Boston harbor, with
transports and stores, ready to embark for Quebec at

ten hours' notice.[1]   When Vetch, after seeing everything in readiness at New York, returned to Boston
on the third of July, he found the New England
levies encamped there still, drilled diligently every
day by officers whom he had brought from England
for the purpose. "The bodies of the men," he
writes to Lord Sunderland, "are in general better
than in Europe, and I hope their courage will prove
so too; so that nothing in human probability can
prevent the success of this glorious enterprise but
the too late arrival of the fleet."[2]   But of the fleet
there was no sign.   "The government here is put to
vast expense," pursues Vetch, "but they cheerfully
pay it, in hopes of being freed from it forever here-
after.   All that they can do now is to fast and pray
for the safe and speedy arrival of the fleet, for which
they have already had two public fast-days kept."

If it should not come in time, he continues, "it
would be the last disappointment to her Majesty's
colonies, who have so heartily complied with her
royal order, and would render them much more
miserable than if such a thing had never been undertaken."   Time passed, and no ships appeared. Vetch
wrote again: "I shall only presume to acquaint your
Lordship how vastly uneasy all her Majesty's loyall
subjects here on this continent are.   Pray God

---

1 *Dudley to Sunderland*, 14 *August*, 1709.

2 *Vetch to Sunderland*, 2 *August*, 1709. The pay of the men was nine
shillings a week, with eightpence a day for provisions; and most of
them had received an enlistment bounty of £12.

hasten the fleet." [1] Dudley, scarcely less impatient, wrote to the same effect. It was all in vain, and the soldiers remained in their camp, monotonously drilling day after day through all the summer and half the autumn. At length, on the eleventh of October, Dudley received a letter from Lord Sunderland, informing him that the promised forces had been sent to Portugal to meet an exigency of the European war. They were to have reached Boston, as we have seen, by the middle of May. Sunderland's notice of the change of destination was not written till the twenty-seventh of July, and was eleven weeks on its way, thus imposing on the colonists a heavy and needless tax in time, money, temper, and, in the case of the expedition against Montreal, health and life.[2] What was left of Nicholson's force had fallen back before Sunderland's letter came, making a scapegoat of the innocent Vetch, cursing him, and wishing him hanged.

In New England the disappointment and vexation were extreme; but, not to lose all the fruits of their efforts, the governors of Massachusetts, Connecticut, New Hampshire, and Rhode Island met and resolved to attack Port Royal if the captains of several British frigates then at New York and Boston would take part in the enterprise. To the disgust of the provincials, the captains, with one exception, refused,

---

[1] *Vetch to Sunderland*, 12 *August*, 1709. Dudley writes with equal urgency two days later.

[2] *Letters of Nicholson, Dudley, and Vetch*, 20 *June* to 24 *Octobe ·*, 1709

on the score of the late season and the want of orders.

A tenacious energy has always been a characteristic of New England, and the hopes of the colonists had been raised too high to be readily abandoned. Port Royal was in their eyes a pestilent nest of privateers and pirates that preyed on the New England fisheries; and on the refusal of the naval commanders to join in an immediate attack, they offered to the court to besiege the place themselves next year, if they could count on the help of four frigates and five hundred soldiers, to be at Boston by the end of March.[1] The Assembly of Massachusetts requested Nicholson, who was on the point of sailing for Europe, to beg her Majesty to help them in an enterprise which would be so advantageous to the Crown, "and which, by the long and expensive war, we are so impoverished and enfeebled as not to be in a capacity to effect."[2]

Nicholson sailed in December, and Peter Schuyler soon followed. New York, having once entered on

[1] *Joint Letter of Nicholson, Dudley, Vetch, and Moody to Sunderland,* 24 *October,* 1709; also *Joint Letter of Dudley, Vetch, and Moody to Sunderland,* 25 *October,* 1709; *Abstracts of Letters and Papers relating to the Attack of Port Royal,* 1709 (Public Record Office); *Address of ye Inhabitants of Boston and Parts adjacent,* 1709. Moody, named above, was the British naval captain who had consented to attack Port Royal.

[2] *Order of Assembly,* 27 *October,* 1709. Massachusetts had spent about £22,000 on her futile expedition of 1707, and, with New Hampshire and Rhode Island, a little more than £46,000 on that of 1709, besides continual outlay in guarding her two hundred miles of frontier, — a heavy expense for the place and time.

MOHAWK CHIEFS. — PLATE I.

the path of war, saw that she must continue in it;
and to impress the Five Nations with the might and
majesty of the Queen, and so dispose them to hold
fast to the British cause, Schuyler took five Mohawk
chiefs with him to England.   One died on the voyage; the rest arrived safe, and their appearance was
the sensation of the hour.   They were clad, at the
Queen's expense, in strange and gay attire, invented
by the costumer of one of the theatres; were lodged
and feasted as the guests of the nation, driven about
London in coaches with liveried servants, conducted
to dockyards, arsenals, and reviews, and saluted with
cannon by ships of war.   The Duke of Shrewsbury
presented them to Queen Anne, — one as emperor of
the Mohawks, and the other three as kings, — and
the Archbishop of Canterbury solemnly gave each of
them a Bible.   Steele and Addison wrote essays about
them, and the Dutch artist Verelst painted their portraits, which were engraved in mezzotint.[1]   Their
presence and the speech made in their name before
the court seem to have had no small effect in drawing attention to the war in America and inclining the
ministry towards the proposals of Nicholson.   These
were accepted, and he sailed for America commis-

[1] See J. R. Bartlett, in *Magazine of American History*, March,
1878, and Schuyler, *Colonial New York*, ii. 34–39. The chiefs returned to America in May on board the " Dragon." An elaborate
pamphlet appeared in London, giving an account of them and their
people. A set of the mezzotint portraits, which are large and well
executed, is in the John Carter Brown collection at Providence.
For photographic reproductions, see Winsor, *Nar. and Crit. Hist.*, v.
107. Compare Smith, *Hist. N. Y.*, i. 204 (1830).

sioned to command the enterprise against Port Royal, with Vetch as adjutant-general.[1]

Colonel Francis Nicholson had held some modest military positions, but never, it is said, seen active service.   In colonial affairs he had played an important part, and in the course of his life governed, at different times, Virginia, New York, Maryland, and Carolina.   He had a robust, practical brain, capable of broad views and large schemes.   One of his plans was a confederacy of the provinces to resist the French, which, to his great indignation, Virginia rejected.   He had Jacobite leanings, and had been an adherent of James II.; but being no idealist, and little apt to let his political principles block the path of his interests, he turned his back on the fallen cause and offered his services to the Revolution. Though no pattern of domestic morals, he seems to have been officially upright, and he wished well to the colonies, saving always the dominant interests of England.   He was bold, ambitious, vehement, and sometimes headstrong and perverse.

Though the English ministry had promised aid, it was long in coming.   The Massachusetts Assembly had asked that the ships should be at Boston before the end of March; but it was past the middle of May before they sailed from Plymouth.   Then, towards midsummer, a strange spasm of martial energy seems to have seized the ministry, for Viscount

---

[1] *Commission of Colonel Francis Nicholson, 18 May, 1710. Instructions to Colonel Nicholson, same date.*

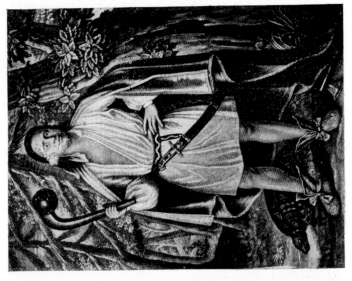

MOHAWK CHIEFS. — PLATE II.

Shannon was ordered to Boston with an additional force, commissioned to take the chief command and attack, not Port Royal, but Quebec.[1] This ill-advised change of plan seems to have been reconsidered; at least, it came to nothing.[2]

Meanwhile, the New England people waited impatiently for the retarded ships. No order had come from England for raising men, and the colonists resolved this time to risk nothing till assured that their labor and money would not be wasted. At last, not in March, but in July, the ships appeared. Then all was astir with preparation. First, the House of Representatives voted thanks to the Queen for her "royal aid." Next, it was proclaimed that no vessel should be permitted to leave the harbor "till the service is provided;" and a committee of the House proceeded to impress fourteen vessels to serve as transports. Then a vote was passed that nine hundred men be raised as the quota of Massachusetts, and a month's pay in advance, together with a coat worth thirty shillings, was promised to volunteers; a committee of three being at the same time appointed to provide the coats. On the next

[1] *Instructions to Richard Viscount Shannon, July,* 1710. A report of the scheme reached Boston. Hutchinson, ii. 164.

[2] The troops, however, were actually embarked. *True State of the Forces commanded by the Right Hon*^ble *The Lord Viscount Shannon, as they were Embark'd the* 14th *of October,* 1710. The total was three thousand two hundred and sixty-five officers and men. Also, *Shannon to Sunderland,* 16 *October,* 1710. The absurdity of the attempt at so late a season is obvious. Yet the fleet lay some weeks more at Portsmouth, waiting for a fair wind.

day appeared a proclamation from the governor announcing the aforesaid "encouragements," calling on last year's soldiers to enlist again, promising that all should return home as soon as Port Royal was taken, and that each might keep as his own forever the Queen's musket that would be furnished him. Now came an order to colonels of militia to muster their regiments on a day named, read the proclamation at the head of each company, and if volunteers did not come forward in sufficient number, to draft as many men as might be wanted, appointing, at the same time, officers to conduct them to the rendezvous at Dorchester or Cambridge; and, by a stringent and unusual enactment, the House ordered that they should be quartered in private houses, with or without the consent of the owners, "any law or usage to the contrary notwithstanding." Sailors were impressed without ceremony to man the transports; and, finally, it was voted that a pipe of wine, twenty sheep, five pigs, and one hundred fowls be presented to the Honorable General Nicholson for his table during the expedition.[1] The above, with slight variation, may serve as an example of the manner in which, for several generations, men were raised in Massachusetts to serve against the French.

Autumn had begun before all was ready. Connecticut, New Hampshire, and Rhode Island sent their contingents; there was a dinner at the Green

---

[1] *Archives of Massachusetts*, vol. lxxi., where the original papers are preserved.

Dragon Tavern in honor of Nicholson, Vetch, and Sir Charles Hobby, the chief officers of the expedition; and on the eighteenth of September the whole put to sea.

On the twenty-fourth the squadron sailed into the narrow entrance of Port Royal, where the tide runs like a mill-stream. One vessel was driven upon the rocks, and twenty-six men were drowned. The others got in safely, and anchored above Goat Island, in sight of the French fort. They consisted of three fourth-rates, — the "Dragon," the "Chester," and the "Falmouth;" two fifth-rates,— the "Lowestoffe" and the "Feversham;" the province galley, one bomb-ketch, twenty-four small transports, two or three hospital ships, a tender, and several sloops carrying timber to make beds for cannon and mortars. The landing force consisted of four hundred British marines, and about fifteen hundred provincials, divided into four battalions.[1] Its unnecessary numbers were due to the belief of Nicholson that the fort had been reinforced and strengthened.

In the afternoon of the twenty-fifth they were all on shore, — Vetch with his two battalions on the north side, and Nicholson with the other two on the south. Vetch marched to his camping-ground, on which, in the words of Nicholson's journal, "the

---

[1] *Nicholson and Vetch to the Secretary of State, 16 September,* 1710; Hutchinson, ii. 164; Penhallow. Massachusetts sent two battalions of four hundred and fifty men each, and Connecticut one battalion of three hundred men, while New Hampshire and Rhode Island united their contingents to form a fourth battalion.

French began to fire pretty thick." On the next morning Nicholson's men moved towards the fort, hacking their way through the woods and crossing the marshes of Allen's River, while the French fired briskly with cannon from the ramparts, and small-arms from the woods, houses, and fences. They were driven back, and the English advance guard intrenched itself within four hundred yards of the works. Several days passed in landing artillery and stores, cannonading from the fort and shelling from the English bomb-ketch, when on the twenty-ninth, Ensign Perelle, with a drummer and a flag of truce, came to Nicholson's tent, bringing a letter from Subercase, who begged him to receive into his camp and under his protection certain ladies of the fort who were distressed by the bursting of the English shells. The conduct of Perelle was irregular, as he had not given notice of his approach by beat of drum and got himself and attendants blindfolded before entering the camp. Therefore Nicholson detained him, sending back an officer of his own with a letter to the effect that he would receive the ladies and lodge them in the same house with the French ensign, "for the queen, my royal mistress, hath not sent me hither to make war against women." Subercase on his part detained the English officer, and wrote to Nicholson, —

SIR, — You have one of my officers, and I have one of yours; so that now we are equal. However, that hinders me not from believing that once you have given me your word, you will keep it very exactly. On that ground I now write to tell you, sir, that to prevent the spilling of both English and French blood, I am ready to hold up both hands for a capitulation that will be honorable to both of us.[1]

In view of which agreement, he adds that he defers sending the ladies to the English camp.

Another day passed, during which the captive officers on both sides were treated with much courtesy. On the next morning, Sunday, October 1, the siege-guns, mortars, and coehorns were in position; and after some firing on both sides, Nicholson sent Colonel Tailor and Captain Abercrombie with a summons to surrender the fort. Subercase replied that he was ready to listen to proposals; the firing stopped, and within twenty-four hours the terms were settled. The garrison were to march out with the honors of war, and to be carried in English ships to Rochelle or Rochefort. The inhabitants within three miles of the fort were to be permitted to remain, if they chose to do so, unmolested, in their homes during two years, on taking an oath of allegiance and fidelity to the Queen.

Two hundred provincials marched to the fort gate and formed in two lines on the right and left. Nicholson advanced between the ranks, with Vetch on one hand and Hobby on the other, followed by all

[1] The contemporary English translation of this letter is printed among the papers appended to *Nicholson's Journal* in *Collections of the Nova Scotia Historical Society,* i.

the field-officers. Subercase came to meet them, and gave up the keys, with a few words of compliment. The French officers and men marched out with shouldered arms, drums beating, and colors flying, saluting the English commander as they passed; then the English troops marched in, raised the union flag, and drank the Queen's health amid a general firing of cannon from the fort and ships. Nicholson changed the name of Port Royal to Annapolis Royal; and Vetch, already commissioned as governor, took command of the new garrison, which consisted of two hundred British marines, and two hundred and fifty provincials who had offered themselves for the service.

The English officers gave a breakfast to the French ladies in the fort. Sir Charles Hobby took in Madame de Bonaventure, and the rest followed in due order of precedence; but as few of the hosts could speak French, and few of the guests could speak English, the entertainment could hardly have been a lively one.

The French officers and men in the fort when it was taken were but two hundred and fifty-eight. Some of the soldiers and many of the armed inhabitants deserted during the siege, which, no doubt, hastened the surrender; for Subercase, a veteran of more than thirty years' service, had borne fair repute as a soldier.

Port Royal had twice before been taken by New England men, — once under Major Sedgwick in 1654, and again under Sir William Phips in the last war; and in each case it had been restored to France by treaty. This time England kept what she had got; and as there was no other place of strength in the province, the capture of Port Royal meant the conquest of Acadia.[1]

[1] In a letter to Ponchartrain, 1 *October*, 1710 (new style), Subercase declares that he has not a sou left, nor any credit. " I have managed to borrow enough to maintain the garrison for the last two years, and have paid what I could by selling all my furniture." Charlevoix's account of the siege has been followed by most writers, both French and English ; but it is extremely incorrect. It was answered by one De Gannes, apparently an officer under Subercase, in a paper called *Observations sur les Erreurs de la Relation du Siège du Port Royal . . . faittes sur de faux mémoires par le révérend Père Charlevoix,* whom De Gannes often contradicts flatly. Thus Charlevoix puts the besieging force at thirty-four hundred men, besides officers and sailors, while De Gannes puts it at fourteen hundred ; and while Charlevoix says that the garrison were famishing, his critic says that they were provisioned for three months. See the valuable notes to Shea's *Charlevoix,* v. 227–232.

The journal of Nicholson was published " by authority " in the *Boston News Letter, November,* 1710, and has been reprinted, with numerous accompanying documents, including the French and English correspondence during the siege, in the *Collections of the Nova Scotia Historical Society,* i.

Vaudreuil, before the siege, sent a reinforcement to Subercase, who, by a strange infatuation, refused it. *N. Y. Col. Docs.,* ix. 853.

CHAPTER VIII.

1710, 1711.

WALKER'S EXPEDITION.

MILITARY aid from Old England to New, promised in one year and actually given in the next, was a fact too novel and surprising to escape the notice either of friends or of foes.

The latter drew strange conclusions from it. Two Irish deserters from an English station in Newfoundland appeared at the French post of Placentia full of stories of British and provincial armaments against Canada. On this, an idea seized the French commandant, Costebelle, and he hastened to make it known to the colonial minister. It was to the effect that the aim of England was not so much to conquer the French colonies as to reduce her own to submission, especially Massachusetts, — a kind of republic which has never willingly accepted a governor from its king.[1] In sending ships and soldiers to the "Bastonnais" under pretence of helping them to conquer their French neighbors, Costebelle is sure that England only means to bring them to a dutiful subjection. "I do not think," he writes on another occasion, "that they are so blind as not to see that they will insensibly be brought under the yoke of the Parliament of Old England; but by the cruelties that the Canadians and Indians exercise in continual incursions upon their lands, I judge that they would rather be delivered from the inhumanity of such neighbors than preserve all the former powers of their little republic."[2] He thinks, however, that the design of England ought to be strongly represented to the Council at Boston, and that M. de la Ronde Denys will be a good man to do it, as he speaks English, has lived in Boston, and has many acquaintances there.[3]

---

[1] *Rapport de Costebelle*, 14 *Octobre*, 1709. *Ibid.*, 3 *Décembre*, 1709.

[2] "Je ne les crois pas assez aveugles pour ne point s'apercevoir qu'insensiblement ils vont subir le joug du parlement de la vieille Angleterre, mais par les cruautés que les Canadiens et sauvages exercent sur leurs terres par des courses continuelles je juge qu'ils aiment encore mieux se délivrer de l'inhumanité de semblables voisins que de conserver toute l'ancienne autorité de leur petite république." — *Costebelle au Ministre*, 3 *Décembre*, 1710. He clung tenaciously to this idea, and wrote again in 1712 that "les cruautés de nos sauvages, qui font horreur à rapporter," would always incline the New England people to peace. They had, however, an opposite effect.

[3] It is more than probable that La Ronde Denys, who had studied the "Bastonnais" with care, first gave the idea to Costebelle.

The minister, Ponchartrain, was struck by Costebelle's suggestion, and wrote both to him and to
Vaudreuil in high approval of it.   To Vaudreuil he
says: "Monsieur de Costebelle has informed me that
the chief object of the armament made by the English
last year was to establish their sovereignty at Boston
and New York, the people of these provinces having
always maintained a sort of republic, governed by
their council, and having been unwilling to receive
absolute governors from the kings of England.   This
destination of the armament seems to me probable,
and it is much to be wished that the Council at
Boston could be informed of the designs of the
English court, and shown how important it is for
that province to remain in the state of a republic.
The King would even approve our helping it to do
so.   If you see any prospect of success, no means
should be spared to secure it.   The matter is of the
greatest importance, but care is essential to employ
persons who have the talents necessary for conducting it, besides great secrecy and prudence, as well as
tried probity and fidelity.   This affair demands your
best attention, and must be conducted with great
care and precaution, in order that no false step may
be taken." [1]

Ponchartrain could not be supposed to know that
while under her old charter Massachusetts, called by

---

1 *Ponchartrain à Vaudreuil*, 10 *Août*, 1710.   *Ponchartrain à Costebelle*,
même date.   These letters are in answer to the reports of Costebelle,
before cited.

him and other Frenchmen the government of Boston,
had chosen her own governor, New York had always
received hers from the court.   What is most curious
in this affair is the attitude of Louis XIV., who
abhorred republics, and yet was prepared to bolster
up one or more of them beyond the Atlantic, —
thinking, no doubt, that they would be too small
and remote to be dangerous.

Costebelle, who had suggested the plan of warning
the Council at Boston, proceeded to unfold his
scheme for executing it.   This was to send La
Ronde Denys to Boston in the spring, under the pretext of treating for an exchange of prisoners, which
would give him an opportunity of insinuating to the
colonists that the forces which the Queen of England
sends to join their own for the conquest of Acadia
and Canada have no object whatever but that of
ravishing from them the liberties they have kept so
firmly and so long, but which would be near ruin if
the Queen should become mistress of New France by
the fortune of war; and that either they must have
sadly fallen from their ancient spirit, or their chiefs
have been corrupted by the Court of London, if they
do not see that they are using their own weapons for
the destruction of their republic.[1]

La Ronde Denys accordingly received his instructions, which authorized him to negotiate with the
" Bastonnais " as with an independent people, and
offer them complete exemption from French hostility

---

[1] *Costebelle à Ponchartrain,* 3 *Décembre,* 1710.

if they would promise to give no more aid to Old
England either in ships or men.   He was told at the
same time to approach the subject with great caution,
and unless he found willing listeners, to pass off the
whole as a pleasantry.[1]   He went to Boston, where
he was detained in consequence of preparations then
on foot for attacking Canada.   He tried to escape;
but his vessel was seized and moored under the guns
of the town, and it is needless to say that his mission
was a failure.

The idea of Costebelle, or rather of La Ronde, —
for it probably originated with him, — was not without foundation; for though there is no reason to
believe that in sending ships and soldiers against the
French, England meant to use them against the
liberties of her own colonies, there can be no doubt
that she thought those liberties excessive and troublesome; and, on the other side, while the people of
Massachusetts were still fondly attached to the land
of their fathers, and still called it "Home," they
were at the same time enamoured of their autonomy,
and jealously watchful against any abridgment of it.

While La Ronde Denys was warning Massachusetts
of the danger of helping England to conquer Canada,

---

[1] *Instruction pour Monsieur de la Ronde, Capitaine d'Infanterie des
Détachements de la Marine*, 1711.   "Le dit sieur de la Ronde pourroit
entrer en négociation et se promettre de faire cesser toutes sortes
d'hostilités du côté du Canada, supposé que les Bastonnais pro-
missent d'en faire de même de leur côté, et qu'ils ne donassent aucun
secours à l'avenir, d'hommes ni de vaisseaux, aux puissances de la
vieille Angleterre et d'Ecosse."

another Frenchman, in a more prophetic spirit, declared that England would make a grave mistake if she helped her colonies to the same end. "There is an antipathy," this writer affirms, "between the English of Europe and those of America, who will not endure troops from England even to guard their forts;" and he goes on to say that if the French colonies should fall, those of England would control the continent from Newfoundland to Florida. "Old England" — such are his words — "will not imagine that these various provinces will then unite, shake off the yoke of the English monarchy, and erect themselves into a democracy."[1]   Forty or fifty years later, several Frenchmen made the same prediction; but at this early day, when the British provinces were so feeble and divided, it is truly a remarkable one.

The anonymous prophet regards the colonies of England, Massachusetts above all, as a standing menace to those of France; and he proposes a drastic remedy against the danger. This is a powerful attack on Boston by land and sea, for which he hopes that God will prepare the way. "When Boston is reduced, we would call together all the chief men of the other towns of New England, who would pay heavy sums to be spared from the flames. As for Boston, it should be pillaged, its workshops,

---

[1] "La vieille Angleterre ne s'imaginera pas que ces diverses Provinces se réuniront, et, secouant le joug de la monarchie Anglaise, s'érigeront en démocratie." — *Mémoire sur la Nouvelle Angleterre,* 1710, 1711. (Archives de la Marine.)

manufactures, shipyards, all its fine establishments
ruined, and its ships sunk." If these gentle means
are used thoroughly, he thinks that New England
will cease to be a dangerous rival for some time,
especially if "Rhodelene" (Rhode Island) is treated
like Boston.[1]

While the correspondent of the French court was
thus consigning New England to destruction, an
attack was preparing against Canada less truculent
but quite as formidable as that which he urged
against Boston. The French colony was threatened
by an armament stronger in proportion to her present
means of defence than that which brought her under
British rule half a century later. But here all comparison ceases; for there was no Pitt to direct and
inspire, and no Wolfe to lead.

The letters of Dudley, the proposals of Vetch, the
representations of Nicholson, the promptings of
Jeremiah Dummer, agent of Massachusetts in England, and the speech made to the Queen by the four
Indians who had been the London sensation of the
last year, had all helped to draw the attention of the

---

[1] "Pour Baston, il faudrait la piller, ruiner ses ateliers, ses
manufactures, tous ses beaux établissements, couler bas ses navires,
. . . ruiner les ateliers de construction de navires." — *Mémoire sur
la Nouvelle Angleterre*, 1710, 1711. The writer was familiar with
Boston and its neighborhood, and had certainly spent some time
there. Possibly he was no other than La Ronde Denys himself,
after the failure of his mission to excite the "Bastonnais" to refuse
co-operation with British armaments. He enlarges with bitterness
on the extent of the fisheries, foreign trade, and ship-building of
New England.

ministry to the New World, and the expediency of driving the French out of it. Other influences conspired to the same end, or in all likelihood little or nothing would have been done. England was tiring of the Continental war, the costs of which threatened ruin. Marlborough was rancorously attacked, and his most stanch supporters the Whigs had given place to the Tories, led by the Lord Treasurer Harley, and the Secretary of State St. John, soon afterwards Lord Bolingbroke. Never was party spirit more bitter; and the new ministry found a congenial ally in the coarse and savage but powerful genius of Swift, who, incensed by real or imagined slights from the late minister, Godolphin, gave all his strength to the winning side.

The prestige of Marlborough's victories was still immense. Harley and St. John dreaded it as their chief danger, and looked eagerly for some means of counteracting it. Such means would be supplied by the conquest of New France. To make America a British continent would be an achievement almost worth Blenheim or Ramillies, and one, too, in which Britain alone would be the gainer; whereas the enemies of Marlborough, with Swift at their head, contended that his greatest triumphs turned more to the profit of Holland or Germany than of England.[1] Moreover, to send a part of his army across the Atlantic would tend to cripple his movements and diminish his fame.

[1] See Swift, *Conduct of the Allies.*

St. John entered with ardor into the scheme.
Seven veteran regiments, five of which were from
the army in Flanders, were ordered to embark. But
in the choice of commanders the judgment of the
ministers was not left free; there were influences
that they could not disregard. The famous Sarah,
Duchess of Marlborough, lately the favorite of the
feeble but wilful queen, had lost her good graces and
given place to Mrs. Masham, one of the women of
her bedchamber. The new favorite had a brother,
John Hill, known about the court as Jack Hill,
whom Marlborough had pronounced good for nothing, but who had been advanced to the rank of
colonel, and then of brigadier, through the influence
of Mrs. Masham; and though his agreeable social
qualities were his best recommendation, he was now
appointed to command the troops on the Canada
expedition. It is not so clear why the naval command was given to Admiral Sir Hovenden Walker,
a man whose incompetence was soon to become
notorious.

Extreme care was taken to hide the destination of
the fleet. Even the Lords of the Admiralty were
kept ignorant of it. Some thought the ships bound
for the West Indies; some for the South Sea.
Nicholson was sent to America with orders to the
several colonies to make ready men and supplies.
He landed at Boston on the eighth of June. The
people of the town, who were nearly all Whigs, were
taken by surprise, expecting no such enterprise on

the part of the Tory ministry; and their perplexity
was not diminished when they were told that the
fleet was at hand, and that they were to supply it
forthwith with provisions for ten weeks.[1] There
was no time to lose. The governors of New York,
Connecticut, and Rhode Island were summoned to
meet at New London, and Dudley and Nicholson
went thither to join them. Here plans were made
for the double attack; for while Walker and Hill
were to sail up the St. Lawrence against Quebec,
Nicholson, as in the former attempt, was to move
against Montreal by way of Lake Champlain. In a
few days the arrangements were made, and the governors hastened back to their respective posts.[2]

When Dudley reached Boston, he saw Nantasket
Roads crowded with transports and ships of war, and
the pastures of Noddle's Island studded with tents.
The fleet had come on the twenty-fourth, having
had what the Admiral calls "by the blessing of God
a favorable and extraordinary passage, being but
seven weeks and two days between Plymouth and
Nantasket."[3]

The Admiral and the General had been welcomed

---

[1] Boston, devoted to fishing, shipbuilding, and foreign trade,
drew most of its provisions from neighboring colonies. (Dummer,
Letter to a Noble Lord.) The people only half believed that the
Tory ministry were sincere in attacking Canada, and suspected that
the sudden demand for provisions, so difficult to meet at once, was
meant to furnish a pretext for throwing the blame of failure upon
Massachusetts. Hutchinson, ii. 173.

[2] *Minutes of Proceedings of the Congress of Governors, June,* 1711.

[3] *Walker to Burchett, Secretary of the Admiralty,* 14 *August,* 1711.

with all honor. The provincial Secretary, with two members of the Council, conducted them to town amid salutes from the batteries of Copp's Hill and Fort Hill, and the Boston militia regiment received them under arms; after which they were feasted at the principal tavern, and accompanied in ceremony to the lodgings provided for them.[1] When the troops were disembarked and the tents pitched, curious townspeople and staring rustics crossed to Noddle's Island, now East Boston, to gaze with wonder on a military pageant the like of which New England had never seen before. Yet their joy at this unlooked-for succor was dashed with deep distrust and jealousy. They dreaded these new and formidable friends, with their imperious demeanor and exacting demands. The British officers, on their part, were no better pleased with the colonists, and one of them, Colonel King, of the artillery, thus gives vent to his feelings: "You'll find in my Journal what Difficultyes we mett with through the Misfortune that the Coloneys were not inform'd of our Coming two Months sooner, and through the Interestedness, ill Nature, and Sowerness of these People, whose Government, Doctrine, and Manners, whose Hypocracy and canting, are insupportable; and no man living but one of Gen'l Hill's good Sense and good Nature could have managed them. But if such a Man mett with nothing he could depend on,

[1] *Abstract of the Journal of the Governor, Council, and Assembly of the Province of the Massachusetts Bay.*

altho' vested with the Queen's Royal Power and
Authority, and Supported by a Number of Troops
sufficient to reduce by force all the Coloneys, 'tis
easy to determine the Respect and Obedience her
Majesty may reasonably expect from them." And
he gives it as his conviction that till all the colonies
are deprived of their charters and brought under one
government, "they will grow more stiff and disobedient every Day."[1]

It will be seen that some coolness on the part of
the Bostonians was not unnatural. But whatever
may have been the popular feeling, the provincial
authorities did their full part towards supplying the
needs of the new-comers; for Dudley, with his strong
Tory leanings, did not share the prevailing jealousy,
and the country members of the Assembly were
anxious before all things to be delivered from war-
parties. The problem was how to raise the men and
furnish the supplies in the least possible time. The
action of the Assembly, far from betraying any slack-
ness, was worthy of a military dictatorship. All
ordinary business was set aside. Bills of credit for
£40,000 were issued to meet the needs of the expedition. It was ordered that the prices of provisions
and other necessaries of the service should stand
fixed at the point where they stood before the
approach of the fleet was known. Sheriffs and con-
stables, jointly with the Queen's officers, were ordered
to search all the town for provisions and liquors, and

[1] *King to Secretary St. John, 25 July, 1711.*

if the owners refused to part with them at the pre-
scribed prices, to break open doors and seize them.
Stringent and much-needed Acts were passed against
harboring deserters. Provincial troops, in greater
number than the ministry had demanded, were
ordered to be raised at once, and quartered upon the
citizens, with or without their consent, at the rate of
eightpence a day for each man.[1] Warrants were
issued for impressing pilots, and also mechanics and
laborers, who, in spite of Puritan scruples, were
required to work on Sundays.

Such measures, if imposed by England, would
have roused the most bitter resentment. Even
when ordered by their own representatives, they
caused a sullen discontent among the colonists, and
greatly increased the popular dislike of their military
visitors. It was certain that when the expedition
sailed and the operation of the new enactments
ceased, prices would rise; and hence the compulsion
to part with goods at low fixed rates was singularly
trying to the commercial temper. It was a busy
season, too, with the farmers, and they showed no
haste to bring their produce to the camp. Though
many of the principal inhabitants bound themselves
by mutual agreement to live on their family stores of
salt provisions, in order that the troops might be
better supplied with fresh, this failed to soothe the

---

[1] The number demanded from Massachusetts was one thousand,
and that raised by her was eleven hundred and sixty. *Dudley to
Walker,* 27 *July,* 1711.

irritation of the British officers, aggravated by frequent desertions, which the colonists favored, and
by the impossibility of finding pilots familiar with
the St. Lawrence.   Some when forced into the service made their escape, to the great indignation of
Walker, who wrote to the governor: "Her Majesty
will resent such actions in a very signal manner; and
when it shall be represented that the people live here
as if there were no king in Israel, but every one does
what seems right in his own eyes, measures will be
taken to put things upon a better foot for the future." [1]
At length, however, every preparation was made,
the supplies were all on board, and after a grand
review of the troops on the fields of Noddle's Island,
the whole force set sail on the thirtieth of July,
the provincials wishing them success, and heartily
rejoicing that they were gone.

The fleet consisted of nine ships of war and two
bomb-ketches, with about sixty transports, store-
ships, hospital-ships, and other vessels, British and
provincial.   They carried the seven British regiments, numbering, with the artillery train, about
fifty-five hundred men, besides six hundred marines
and fifteen hundred provincials; counting, with the
sailors, nearly twelve thousand in all. [2]

---

[1] Walker prints this letter in his Journal.   Colonel King writes
in his own Journal: "The conquest of Canada will naturally lead
the Queen into changing their present disorderly government;"
and he thinks that the conviction of this made the New Englanders
indifferent to the success of the expedition.

[2] The above is drawn from the various lists and tables in

Vetch commanded the provincials, having been brought from Annapolis for that purpose. The great need was of pilots. Every sailor in New England who had seen the St. Lawrence had been pressed into the service, though each and all declared themselves incapable of conducting the fleet to Quebec. Several had no better knowledge of the river than they had picked up when serving as soldiers under Phips twenty-one years before. The best among them was the veteran Captain Bonner, who afterwards amused his old age by making a plan of Boston, greatly prized by connoisseurs in such matters. Vetch had studied the St. Lawrence in his several visits to Quebec, but, like Bonner, he had gone up the river only in sloops or other small craft, and was, moreover, no sailor. One of Walker's ships, the "Chester," sent in advance to cruise in the Gulf, had captured a French vessel commanded by one Paradis, an experienced old voyager, who knew the river well. He took a bribe of five hundred pistoles to act as pilot; but the fleet would perhaps have fared better if he had refused the money. He gave such dismal accounts of the Canadian winter that the Admiral could see nothing but ruin ahead, even if he should safely reach his destination. His tribulation is recorded in his Journal. "That which now chiefly

Walker, *Journal of the Canada Expedition*. The armed ships that entered Boston in June were fifteen in all; but several had been detached for cruising. The number of British transports, store-ships, etc., was forty, the rest being provincial.

wide, and no land had been seen since noon of the day before. There was a strong east wind, with fog. Walker thought that he was not far from the south shore, when in fact he was at least fifty miles from it, and more than half that distance north of his true course. At eight in the evening the Admiral signalled the fleet to bring to, under mizzen and main-topsails, with heads turned southward. At half-past ten, Paddon, the captain of the "Edgar," came to tell him that he saw land which he supposed must be the south shore; on which Walker, in a fatal moment, signalled for the ships to wear and bring to, with heads northward. He then turned into his berth, and was falling asleep, when a military officer, Captain Goddard, of Seymour's regiment, hastily entered, and begged him to come on deck, saying that there were breakers on all sides. Walker, scornful of a landsman, and annoyed at being disturbed, answered impatiently and would not stir. Soon after, Goddard appeared again, and implored him for Heaven's sake to come up and see for himself, or all would be lost. At the same time the Admiral heard a great noise and trampling, on which he turned out of his berth, put on his dressing-gown and slippers, and going in this attire on deck, found a scene of fright and confusion. At first he could see nothing, and shouted to the men to reassure them; but just then the fog opened, the moon shone out, and the breaking surf was plainly visible to leeward. The French pilot, who at first could not be found, now appeared on deck, and declared, to the astonishment of both the Admiral and Captain Paddon, that they were off the north shore.   Paddon, in his perplexity, had ordered an anchor to be let go; Walker directed the cable to be cut, and, making all sail, succeeded in beating to windward and gaining an offing.[1]

The ship that carried Colonel King, of the artillery, had a narrow escape.   King says that she anchored in a driving rain, "with a shoal of rocks on each quarter within a cable's length of us, which we plainly perceived by the waves breaking over them in a very violent manner."   They were saved by a lull in the gale; for if it had continued with the same violence, he pursues, "our anchors could not have held, and the wind and the vast seas which ran, would have broke our ship into ten thousand pieces against the rocks.   All night we heard nothing but ships firing and showing lights, as in the utmost distress."[2]

Vetch, who was on board the little frigate "Despatch," says that he was extremely uneasy at the course taken by Walker on the night of the storm. "I told Colonel Dudley and Captain Perkins, commander of the ' Despatch,' that I wondered what the Flag meant by that course, and why he did not steer west and west-by-south."[3]   The "Despatch" kept well astern, and so escaped the danger.   Vetch heard through the fog guns firing signals of distress; but

---

[1] Walker, *Journal*, 124, 125.   [2] King, *Journal*.
[3] Vetch, *Journal*.

three days passed before he knew how serious the disaster was. The ships of war had all escaped; but eight British transports, one store-ship, and one sutler's sloop were dashed to pieces.[1] "It was lamentable to hear the shrieks of the sinking, drowning, departing souls," writes the New England commissary, Sheaf, who was very near sharing their fate.

The disaster took place at and near a rocky island, with adjacent reefs, lying off the north shore and called Isle aux Œufs. On the second day after it happened, Walker was told by the master of one of the wrecked transports that eight hundred and eighty-four soldiers had been lost, and he gives this hasty estimate in his published Journal; though he says in his Introduction to it that the total loss of officers, soldiers, and sailors was scarcely nine hundred.[2] According to a later and more trustworthy statement, the loss of the troops was twenty-nine officers, six hundred and seventy-six sergeants, corporals, drummers, and private soldiers, and thirty-five women attached to the regiments; that is, a total of seven hundred and forty lives.[3] The loss of the sailors is not given; but it could scarcely have exceeded two hundred.

---

[1] King, *Journal.*

[2] Compare Walker, *Journal,* 45, and *Ibid.,* 127, 128. He elsewhere intimates that his first statement needed correction.

[3] *Report of ye Soldiers, etc., Lost.* (Public Record Office.) This is a tabular statement, giving the names of the commissioned officers and the positions of their subordinates, regiment by regiment. All the French accounts of the losses are exaggerations.

The fleet spent the next two days in standing to and fro between the northern and southern shores, with the exception of some of the smaller vessels employed in bringing off the survivors from the rocks of Isle aux Œufs. The number thus saved was, according to Walker, four hundred and ninety-nine. On the twenty-fifth he went on board the General's ship, the "Windsor," and Hill and he resolved to call a council of war. In fact, Hill had already got his colonels together. Signals were made for the captains of the men-of-war to join them, and the council began.

"Jack Hill," the man about town, placed in high command by the influence of his sister, the Queen's tire-woman, had now an opportunity to justify his appointment and prove his mettle. Many a man of pleasure and fashion, when put to the proof, has revealed the latent hero within him; but Hill was not one of them. Both he and Walker seemed to look for nothing but a pretext for retreat; and when manhood is conspicuously wanting in the leaders, a council of war is rarely disposed to supply it. The pilots were called in and examined, and they all declared themselves imperfectly acquainted with the St. Lawrence, which, as some of the captains observed, they had done from the first. Sir William Phips, with pilots still more ignorant, had safely carried his fleet to Quebec in 1690, as Walker must have known, for he had with him Phips's Journal of the voyage. The expedition had lost about a twelfth part of its soldiers and sailors, besides the transports that carried them; with this exception there was no reason for retreat which might not as well have been put forward when the fleet left Boston. All the war-ships were safe, and the loss of men was not greater than might have happened in a single battle. Hill says that Vetch, when asked if he would pilot the fleet to Quebec, refused to undertake it;[1] but Vetch himself gives his answer as follows: "I told him [the Admiral] I never was bred to sea, nor was it any part of my province; but I would do my best by going ahead and showing them where the difficulty of the river was, which I knew pretty well."[2] The naval captains, however, resolved that by reason of the ignorance of the pilots and the dangerous currents it was impossible to go up to Quebec.[3] So discreditable a backing out from a great enterprise will hardly be found elsewhere in English annals. On the next day Vetch, disappointed and indignant, gave his mind freely to the Admiral. "The late disaster cannot, in my humble opinion, be anyways imputed to the difficulty of the navigation, but to the wrong course we steered, which most unavoidably carried us upon the north shore. Who directed that course you best know; and as our return without any

---

[1] *Hill to Dudley,* 25 *August,* 1711.

[2] Vetch, *Journal.* His statement is confirmed by the report of the council.

[3] *Report of a Consultation of Sea Officers belonging to the Squadron under Command of Sir Hovenden Walker, Kt.,* 25 *August,* 1711. Signed by Walker and eight others.

further attempt would be a vast reflection upon the conduct of this affair, so it would be of very fatal consequence to the interest of the Crown and all the British colonies upon this continent." [1]　His protest was fruitless. The fleet retraced its course to the gulf, and then steered for Spanish River, — now the harbor of Sydney, — in the Island of Cape Breton; the Admiral consoling himself with the reflection that the wreck was a blessing in disguise and a merciful intervention of Providence to save the expedition from the freezing, starvation, and cannibalism which his imagination had conjured up. [2]

The frigate "Sapphire" was sent to Boston with news of the wreck and the retreat, which was at once despatched to Nicholson, who, if he continued his movement on Montreal, would now be left to conquer Canada alone. His force consisted of about twenty-three hundred men, white and red, and when the fatal news reached him he was encamped on Wood Creek, ready to pass Lake Champlain. Captain Butler, a New York officer at the camp, afterwards told Kalm, the Swedish naturalist, that when Nicholson heard what had happened, he was beside himself with rage, tore off his wig, threw it on the ground and stamped upon it, crying out, "Roguery! Treachery!" [3] When his fit was over, he did all that was now left for him to do, — burned the wooden

[1] *Vetch to Walker*, 26 *August*, 1711.

[2] Walker, *Journal, Introduction*, 25.

[3] Kalm, *Travels*, ii. 135.

forts he had built, marched back to Albany, and disbanded his army, after leaving one hundred and fifty men to protect the frontier against scalping-parties.[1]

Canada had been warned of the storm gathering against her. Early in August, Vaudreuil received letters from Costebelle, at Placentia, telling him that English prisoners had reported mighty preparations at Boston against Quebec, and that Montreal was also to be attacked.[2] The colony was ill prepared for the emergency, but no effort was spared to give the enemy a warm reception. The militia were mustered, Indians called together, troops held in readiness, and defences strengthened. The saints were invoked, and the aid of Heaven was implored by masses, processions, and penances, as in New England by a dismal succession of fasts. Mother Juchereau de Saint-Denis tells us how devout Canadians prayed for help from God and the most holy Virgin; "since their glory was involved, seeing that the true religion would quickly perish if the English should prevail." The general alarm produced effects which, though transient, were thought highly commendable while they lasted. The ladies, according to Mother Juchereau, gave up their ornaments, and became more modest and more pious. "Those of Montreal," pursues the worthy nun, "even outdid those of Quebec; for they bound themselves by oath to wear neither ribbons nor lace, to keep

[1] Schuyler, *Colonial New York,* ii. 48.
[2] *Vaudreuil au Ministre,* 25 *Octobre,* 1711.

their throats covered, and to observe various holy
practices for the space of a year." The recluse of
Montreal, Mademoiselle Le Ber, who, by reason of
her morbid seclusion and ascetic life, was accounted
almost a saint, made a flag embroidered with a prayer
to the Virgin, to be borne against the heretical bands
of Nicholson.

When that commander withdrew, his retreat,
though not the cause of it, was quickly known at
Montreal, and the forces gathered there went down
to Quebec to aid in repelling the more formidable
attack by sea. Here all was suspense and expect-
ancy till the middle of October, when the report
came that two large ships had been seen in the river
below. There was great excitement, for they were
supposed to be the van of the British fleet; but alarm
was soon turned to joy by the arrival of the ships,
which proved to be French. On the nineteenth, the
Sieur de la Valterie, who had come from Labrador
in September, and had been sent down the river again
by Vaudreuil to watch for the English fleet, appeared
at Quebec with tidings of joy. He had descended
the St. Lawrence in a canoe, with two Frenchmen
and an Indian, till, landing at Isle aux Œufs on the
first of October, they met two French sailors or
fishermen loaded with plunder, and presently discovered the wrecks of seven English ships, with, as
they declared, fifteen or sixteen hundred dead bodies
on the strand hard by, besides dead horses, sheep,
dogs, and hens, three or four hundred large iron-

hooped casks, a barrel of wine and a barrel and a keg of brandy, cables, anchors, chains, planks, boards, shovels, picks, mattocks, and piles of old iron three feet high.[1]

"The least devout," writes Mother Juchereau, "were touched by the grandeur of the miracle wrought in our behalf, — a marvellous effect of God's love for Canada, which, of all these countries, is the only one that professes the true religion."

Quebec was not ungrateful. A solemn mass was ordered every month during a year, to be followed by the song of Moses after the destruction of Pharaoh and his host.[2] Amazing reports were spread concerning the losses of the English. About three thousand of "these wretches" — so the story ran — died after reaching land, without counting the multitudes drowned in the attempt; and even this did not satisfy divine justice, for God blew up one of the ships by lightning during the storm. Vessels were sent to gather up the spoils of the wreck, and they came back, it was reported, laden with marvellous treasures, including rich clothing, magnificent saddles, plate, silver-hilted swords, and the like; bringing also the gratifying announcement that though the autumn tides had swept away many corpses, more than two thousand still lay on the rocks, naked and in atti-

---

[1] *Déposition de François de Marganne, Sieur de la Valterie; par devant Nous, Paul Dupuy, Ecuyer, Conseiller du Roy, etc., 19 Octobre, 1711.*

[2] *Monseigneur de Saint-Vallier et l'Histoire de l'Hôpital Général de Quebec, 209.*

tudes of despair.[1] These stories, repeated by later
writers, find believers to this day.[2]

When Walker and his ships reached Spanish
River, he called another council of war. The question was whether, having failed to take Quebec, they
should try to take Placentia; and it was resolved
that the short supply of provisions, the impossibility
of getting more from Boston before the first of
November, and the risks of the autumnal storms,
made the attempt impracticable. Accordingly, the
New England transports sailed homeward, and the
British fleet steered for the Thames.

Swift writes on the sixth of October in his Journal
to Stella: "The news of Mr. Hill's miscarriage in
his expedition came to-day, and I went to visit Mrs.
Masham and Mrs. Hill, his two sisters, to condole
with them." A week after, he mentions the arrival
of the general himself; and again on the sixteenth
writes thus: "I was to see Jack Hill this morning,
who made that unfortunate expedition; and there is
still more misfortune, for that ship which was admiral
of his fleet [the "Edgar"] is blown up in the Thames
by an accident and carelessness of some rogue, who

[1] Juchereau, *Histoire de l'Hôtel-Dieu de Québec,* 473–491. La
Ronde Denys says that nearly one thousand men were drowned,
and that about two thousand died of injuries received. *La Ronde
au Ministre,* 30 *Décembre,* 1711.

[2] Some exaggeration was natural enough. Colonel Lee, of the
Rhode Island contingent, says that a day or two after the wreck he
saw "the bodies of twelve or thirteen hundred brave men, with
women and children, lying in heaps." *Lee to Governor Cranston,* 12
September, 1711.

was going, as they think, to steal some gunpowder: five hundred men are lost."

A report of this crowning disaster reached Quebec, and Mother Juchereau does not fail to improve it. According to her, the Admiral, stricken with divine justice, and wrought to desperation, blew up the ship himself, and perished with all on board, except only two men.

There was talk of an examination into the causes of the failure, but nothing was done. Hill, strong in the influence of Mrs. Masham, reaped new honors and offices. Walker, more answerable for the result, and less fortunate in court influence, was removed from command, and his name was stricken from the half-pay list. He did not, however, blow himself up, but left England and emigrated to South Carolina, whence, thinking himself ill-treated by the authorities, he removed to Barbadoes, and died some years later.[1]

[1] Walker's Journal was published in 1720, with an Introduction of forty-eight pages, written in bad temper and bad taste. The Journal contains many documents, printed in full. In the Public Record Office are preserved the Journals of Hill, Vetch, and King. Copies of these, with many other papers on the same subject, from the same source, are before me. Vetch's Journal and his letter to Walker after the wreck are printed in the *Collections of the Nova Scotia Historical Society*, vol. iv.

It appears by the muster-rolls of Massachusetts that what with manning the coast-guard vessels, defending the frontier against Indians, and furnishing her contingent to the Canada expedition, more than one in five of her able-bodied men were in active service in the summer of 1711. Years passed before she recovered from the effects of her financial exhaustion.

CHAPTER IX.

1712–1749.

LOUISBOURG AND ACADIA.

Peace of Utrecht. — Perilous Questions. — Louisbourg founded.
— Annapolis attacked. — Position of the Acadians. —
Weakness of the British Garrison. — Apathy of the
Ministry. — French Intrigue. — Clerical Politicians. —
The Oath of Allegiance. — Acadians refuse it: their Ex-
pulsion proposed; they take the Oath.

The great European war was drawing to an end,
and with it the American war, which was but its
echo. An avalanche of defeat and disaster had
fallen upon the old age of Louis XIV., and France
was burdened with an insupportable load of debt.
The political changes in England came to her relief.
Fifty years later, when the elder Pitt went out of
office and Bute came in, France had cause to be
grateful; for the peace of 1763 was far more favorable to her than it would have been under the imperious war minister. It was the same in 1712. The
Whigs who had fallen from power would have wrung
every advantage from France; the triumphant Tories
were eager to close with her on any terms not so
easy as to excite popular indignation. The result

was the Treaty of Utrecht, which satisfied none of
the allies of England, and gave to France conditions
more favorable than she had herself proposed two
years before.   The fall of Godolphin and the dis-
grace of Marlborough were a godsend to her.

Yet in America Louis XIV. made important concessions.   The Five Nations of the Iroquois were
acknowledged to be British subjects; and this became
in future the preposterous foundation for vast terri-
torial claims of England.   Hudson Bay, Newfoundland, and Acadia, "according to its ancient limits,"
were also given over by France to her successful
rival; though the King parted from Acadia with a
reluctance shown by the great offers he made for
permission to retain it.[1]

But while the Treaty of Utrecht seemed to yield
so much, and yielded so much in fact, it staved off
the settlement of questions absolutely necessary for
future peace.   The limits of Acadia, the boundary
line between Canada and the British colonies, and
the boundary between those colonies and the great
western wilderness claimed by France, were all left
unsettled, since the attempt to settle them would
have rekindled the war.   The peace left the embers
of war still smouldering, sure, when the time should
come, to burst into flame.   The next thirty years
were years of chronic, smothered war, disguised,

---

[1] *Offres de la France; Demandes de l'Angleterre et Réponses de la
France, in Memorials of the English and French Commissaries concerning
the Limits of Acadia.*

but never quite at rest.   The standing subjects of
dispute were three, very different in importance.
First, the question of Acadia: whether the treaty
gave England a vast country, or only a strip of sea-
coast.   Next, that of northern New England and the
Abenaki Indians, many of whom French policy still
left within the borders of Maine, and whom both
powers claimed as subjects or allies.   Last and
greatest was the question whether France or England should hold the valleys of the Mississippi and
the Great Lakes, and with them the virtual control
of the continent.   This was the triple problem that
tormented the northern English colonies for more
than a generation, till it found a solution at last in
the Seven Years' War.

Louis XIV. had deeply at heart the recovery of
Acadia.   Yet the old and infirm King, whose sun was
setting in clouds after half a century of unrivalled
splendor, felt that peace was a controlling necessity, and he wrote as follows to his plenipotentiaries
at Utrecht: "It is so important to prevent the breaking off of the negotiations that the King will give up
both Acadia and Cape Breton, if necessary for peace;
but the plenipotentiaries will yield this point only in
the last extremity, for by this double cession Canada
will become useless, the access to it will be closed,
the fisheries will come to an end, and the French
marine be utterly destroyed." [1]   And he adds that if
the English will restore Acadia, he, the King, will

[1] *Mémoire du Roy à ses Plénipotentiaires,* 20 *Mars,* 1712.

give them, not only St. Christopher, but also the
islands of St. Martin and St. Bartholomew.

The plenipotentiaries replied that the offer was
refused, and that the best they could do without
endangering the peace was to bargain that Cape
Breton should belong to France.[1] On this, the
King bid higher still for the coveted province, and
promised that if Acadia were returned to him, the
fortifications of Placentia should be given up un-
touched, the cannon in the forts of Hudson Bay
abandoned to the English, and the Newfoundland
fisheries debarred to Frenchmen,[2] — a remarkable
concession; for France had fished on the banks of
Newfoundland for two centuries, and they were
invaluable to her as a nursery of sailors.   Even these
offers were rejected, and England would not resign
Acadia.

Cape Breton was left to the French.   This large
island, henceforth called by its owners Isle Royale,
lies east of Acadia, and is separated from it only by
the narrow Strait of Canseau.   From its position, it
commands the chief entrance of the gulf and river
of St. Lawrence.   Some years before, the intendant
Raudot had sent to the court an able paper, in which
he urged its occupation and settlement, chiefly on
commercial and industrial grounds.   The war was
then at its height; the plan was not carried into

---

[1] *Précis de ce qui s'est passé pendant la Négotiation de la Paix
d'Utrecht au Sujet de l'Acadie; Juillet,* 1711–*Mai,* 1712.

[2] *Mémoire du Roy,* 20 *Avril,* 1712.

effect, and Isle Royale was still a wilderness. It was now proposed to occupy it for military and political reasons. One of its many harbors, well fortified and garrisoned, would guard the approaches of Canada, and in the next war furnish a base for attacking New England and recovering Acadia.

After some hesitation the harbor called Port à l'Anglois was chosen for the proposed establishment, to which the name of Louisbourg was given, in honor of the King. It lies near the southeastern point of the island, where an opening in the iron-bound coast, at once easily accessible and easily defended, gives entrance to a deep and sheltered basin, where a fleet of war-ships may find good anchorage. The proposed fortress was to be placed on the tongue of land that lies between this basin and the sea. The place, well chosen from the point of view of the soldier or the fisherman, was unfit for an agricultural colony, its surroundings being barren hills studded with spruce and fir, and broad marshes buried in moss.

In spite of the losses and humiliations of the war, great expectations were formed from the new scheme. Several years earlier, when the proposals of Raudot were before the Marine Council, it was confidently declared that a strong fortress on Cape Breton would make the King master of North America. The details of the establishment were settled in advance. The King was to build the fortifications, supply them with cannon, send out eight companies of soldiers, besides all the usual officers of government, establish a well-endowed hospital, conducted by nuns, as at Quebec, provide Jesuits and Récollets as chaplains, besides Filles de la Congrégation to teach girls, send families to the spot, support them for two years, and furnish a good number of young women to marry the soldiers.[1]

This plan, or something much like it, was carried into effect. Louisbourg was purely and solely the offspring of the Crown and its ally, the Church. In time it grew into a compact fishing town of about four thousand inhabitants, with a strong garrison and a circuit of formidable ramparts and batteries. It became by far the strongest fortress on the Atlantic coast, and so famous as a resort of privateers that it was known as the Dunquerque of America.

What concerns us now is its weak and troubled infancy. It was to be peopled in good part from the two lost provinces of Acadia and Newfoundland, whose inhabitants were to be transported to Louisbourg or other parts of Isle Royale, which would thus be made at once and at the least possible cost a dangerous neighbor to the newly acquired possessions of England. The Micmacs of Acadia, and even some of the Abenakis, were to be included in this scheme of immigration.

In the autumn, the commandant of Plaisance, or Placentia, — the French stronghold in Newfoundland, — received the following mandate from the King: —

[1] *Mémoire sur l'Isle du Cap Breton*, 1709.

MONSIEUR DE COSTEBELLE,— I have caused my orders
to be given you to evacuate the town and forts of Plaisance
and the other places of your government of Newfoundland,
ceded to my dear sister the Queen of Great Britain.   I
have given my orders for the equipment of the vessels
necessary to make the evacuation and transport you, with
the officers, garrison, and inhabitants of Plaisance and
other places of Newfoundland, to my Isle Royale, vulgarly
called Cape Breton; but as the season is so far advanced
that this cannot be done without exposing my troops and
my subjects to perishing from cold and misery, and
placing my vessels in evident peril of wreck, I have judged
it proper to defer the transportation till the next spring.[1]

The inhabitants of Placentia consisted only of
twenty-five or thirty poor fishermen, with their
families,[2] and some of them would gladly have become English subjects and stayed where they were;
but no choice was given them. "Nothing," writes
Costebelle, "can cure them of the error, to which
they obstinately cling, that they are free to stay or
go, as best suits their interest."[3] They and their
fishing-boats were in due time transported to Isle
Royale, where for a while their sufferings were
extreme.

Attempts were made to induce the Indians of
Acadia to move to the new colony; but they refused,
and to compel them was out of the question.   But

---

[1] Le Roy à Costebelle, 29 Septembre, 1713.

[2] Recensement des Habitans de Plaisance et Iles de St. Pierre, rendus
à Louisbourg avec leurs Femmes et Enfans, 5 Novembre, 1714.

[3] Costebelle au Ministre, 19 Juillet, 1713.

by far the most desirable accession to the establishment of Isle Royale would be that of the Acadian
French, who were too numerous to be transported in
the summary manner practised in the case of the
fishermen of Placentia.   It was necessary to persuade
rather than compel them to migrate, and to this end
great reliance was placed on their priests, especially
Fathers Pain and Dominique.   Ponchartrain himself
wrote to the former on the subject.   The priest
declares that he read the letter to his flock, who
answered that they wished to stay in Acadia; and he
adds that the other Acadians were of the same mind,
being unwilling to leave their rich farms and risk
starvation on a wild and barren island.[1] "Nevertheless," he concludes, "we shall fulfil the intentions
of his Majesty by often holding before their eyes
that religion for which they ought to make every
sacrifice."   He and his brother priests kept their
word.   Freedom of worship was pledged on certain conditions to the Acadians by the Treaty of
Utrecht, and no attempt was ever made to deprive
them of it; yet the continual declaration of their
missionaries that their souls were in danger under
English rule was the strongest spur to impel them
to migrate.

The condition of the English in Acadia since it
fell into their hands had been a critical one.   Port
Royal, thenceforth called Annapolis Royal, or simply
Annapolis, had been left, as before mentioned, in

---

[1] *Félix Pain à Costebelle*, 23 *Septembre*, 1713.

charge of Colonel Vetch, with a heterogeneous garrison of four hundred and fifty men.[1]   The Acadians of the *banlieue* — a term defined as covering a space of three miles round the fort — had been included in the capitulation, and had taken an oath of allegiance to Queen Anne, binding so long as they remained in the province.   Some of them worked for the garrison and helped to repair the fort, which was in a ruinous condition.   Meanwhile the Micmac Indians remained fiercely hostile to the English; and in June, 1711, aided by a band of Penobscots, they ambuscaded and killed or captured nearly seventy of them.   This completely changed the attitude of the Acadians. They broke their oath, rose against their new masters, and with their Indian friends, invested the fort to the number of five or six hundred.   Disease, desertion, and the ambuscade had reduced the garrison to about two hundred effective men, and the defences of the place were still in bad condition.[2]   The assailants, on the other hand, had no better leader than the priest, Gaulin, missionary of the Micmacs

---

[1] Vetch was styled " General and Commander-in-chief of all his Majesty's troops in these parts, and Governor of the fort of Annapolis Royal, country of l'Accady and Nova Scotia."   Hence he was the first English governor of Nova Scotia after its conquest in 1710.   He was appointed a second time in 1715, Nicholson having served in the interim.

[2] *Narrative of Paul Mascarene*, addressed to Nicholson.   According to French accounts, a pestilence at Annapolis had carried off three fourths of the garrison.   *Gaulin à*——, 5 *Septembre*, 1711; *Cahouet au Ministre*, 20 *Juillet*, 1711.   In reality a little more than one hundred had died.

and prime mover in the rising. He presently sailed for Placentia to beg for munitions and a commander; but his errand failed, the siege came to nought, and the besiegers dispersed. Vaudreuil, from whom the Acadians had begged help, was about to send it when news of the approach of Walker's fleet forced him to keep all his strength for his own defence.

From this time to the end of the war, the chief difficulties of the governor of Acadia rose, not from the enemy, but from the British authorities at home. For more than two years he, with his starved and tattered garrison, were treated with absolute neglect. He received no orders, instructions, or money.[1] Acadia seemed forgotten by the ministry, till Vetch heard at last that Nicholson was appointed to succeed him.

Now followed the Treaty of Utrecht, the cession of Acadia to England, and the attempt on the part of France to induce the Acadians to remove to Isle Royale. Some of the English officials had once been of opinion that this French Catholic population should be transported to Martinique or some other distant French colony, and its place supplied by Protestant families sent from England or Ireland.[2] Since the English Revolution, Protestantism was bound up with the new political order, and Catholi-

---

[1] Passages from Vetch's letters, in Patterson, *Memoir of Vetch.*

[2] *Vetch to the Earl of Dartmouth,* 22 *January,* 1711; *Memorial of Council of War at Annapolis,* 14 *October,* 1710.

cism with the old. No Catholic could favor the Protestant succession, and hence politics were inseparable from creed. Vetch, who came of a race of hot and stubborn Covenanters, had been one of the most earnest for replacing the Catholic Acadians by Protestants; but after the peace he and others changed their minds. No Protestant colonists appeared, nor was there the smallest sign that the government would give itself the trouble to attract any. It was certain that if the Acadians removed at all, they would go, not to Martinique or any other distant colony, but to the new military establishment of Isle Royale, which would thus become a strong and dangerous neighbor to the feeble British post of Annapolis. Moreover, the labor of the French inhabitants was useful and sometimes necessary to the English garrison, which depended mainly on them for provisions; and if they left the province, they would leave it a desert, with the prospect of long remaining so.

Hence it happened that the English were for a time almost as anxious to keep the Acadians in Acadia as they were forty years later to get them out of it; nor had the Acadians themselves any inclination to leave their homes. But the French authorities needed them at Isle Royale, and made every effort to draw them thither. By the fourteenth article of the Treaty of Utrecht such of them as might choose to leave Acadia were free to do so within the space of a year, carrying with them their personal effects; while a letter of Queen Anne, addressed to Nicholson, then governor of Acadia, permitted the emigrants to sell their lands and houses.

The missionary Félix Pain had reported, as we have seen, that they were, in general, disposed to remain where they were; on which Costebelle, who now commanded at Louisbourg, sent two officers, La Ronde Denys and Pensens, with instructions to set the priests at work to persuade their flocks to move.[1] La Ronde Denys and his colleague repaired to Annapolis, where they promised the inhabitants vessels for their removal, provisions for a year, and freedom from all taxation for ten years. Then, having been well prepared in advance, the heads of families were formed in a circle, and in presence of the English governor, the two French officers, and the priests Justinien, Bonaventure, and Gaulin, they all signed, chiefly with crosses, a paper to the effect that they would live and die subjects of the King of France.[2] A few embarked at once for Isle Royale in the vessel "Marie-Joseph," and the rest were to follow within the year.

This result was due partly to the promises of La Ronde Denys, and still more to a pastoral letter from the Bishop of Quebec, supporting the assurances of the missionaries that the heretics would rob them of the ministrations of the Church. This was not

---

[1] Costebelle, *Instruction au Capitaine de la Ronde*, 1714.
[2] *Écrit des Habitants d'Annapolis Royale*, 25 *Aoust*, 1714; *Mémoire de La Ronde Denys*, 30 *Aoust*, 1714.

all. The Acadians about Annapolis had been alien-
ated by the conduct of the English authorities, which
was not conciliating, and on the part of the governor
was sometimes outrageous.[1] Yet those of the *banlieue*
had no right to complain, since they had made themselves liable to the penalties of treason by first taking
an oath of allegiance to Queen Anne, and then
breaking it by trying to seize her fort.[2]

Governor Nicholson, like his predecessor, was
resolved to keep the Acadians in the province if he
could. This personage, able, energetic, perverse,
headstrong, and unscrupulous, conducted himself,
even towards the English officers and soldiers, in a
manner that seems unaccountable, and that kindled
their utmost indignation.[3] Towards the Acadians
his behavior was still worse. As Costebelle did not
keep his promise to send vessels to bring them to
Isle Royale, they built small ones for themselves,
and the French authorities at Louisbourg sent them
the necessary rigging. Nicholson ordered it back,
forbade the sale of their lands and houses, — a needless stretch of power, as there was nobody to buy, —
and would not let them sell even their personal

---

[1] In 1711, however, the missionary Félix Pain says, " The English
have treated the Acadians with much humanity." — *Père Félix à*
——, 8 *Septembre*, 1711.

[2] This was the oath taken after the capitulation, which bound
those who took it to allegiance so long as they remained in the
province.

[3] " As he used to curse and Damm Governor Vetch and all his
friends, he is now served himself in the same manner." — *Adams to
Steele*, 24 *January*, 1715.

effects, coolly setting at nought both the Treaty of Utrecht and the letter of the Queen.[1]

Nicholson was but a short time at Annapolis, leaving the government, during most of his term, to his deputies, Caulfield and afterwards Doucette, both of whom roundly denounce their principal for his general conduct; while both, in one degree or another, followed his example in preventing so far as they could the emigration of the Acadians. Some of them, however, got away, and twelve or fifteen families who settled at Port Toulouse, on Isle Royale, were near perishing from cold and hunger.[2]

From Annapolis the French agents, La Ronde Denys and Pensens, proceeded to the settlements about Chignecto and the Basin of Mines, — the most populous and prosperous parts of Acadia. Here they were less successful than before. The people were doubtful and vacillating, — ready enough to promise, but slow to perform. While declaring with perfect sincerity their devotion to "our invincible monarch," as they called King Louis, who had just been compelled to surrender their country, they clung tenaciously to the abodes of their fathers. If they had wished to emigrate, the English governor had no power to stop them. From Baye Verte, on the isthmus, they had frequent and easy communi-

---

1 For a great number of extracts from documents on this subject see a paper by Abbé Casgrain in *Canada Français*, i. 411–414; also the documentary supplement of the same publication.

2 *La Ronde Denys au Ministre*, 3 *Décembre*, 1715.

cation with the French at Louisbourg, which the English did not and could not interrupt. They were armed, and they far outnumbered the English garrison; while at a word they could bring to their aid the Micmac warriors, who had been taught to detest the English heretics as foes of God and man. To say that they wished to leave Acadia, but were prevented from doing so by a petty garrison at the other end of the province, so feeble that it could hardly hold Annapolis itself, is an unjust reproach upon a people who, though ignorant and weak of purpose, were not wanting in physical courage. The truth is that from this time to their forced expatriation in 1755, all the Acadians, except those of Annapolis and its immediate neighborhood, were free to go or stay at will. Those of the eastern parts of the province especially, who formed the greater part of the population, were completely their own masters. This was well known to the French authorities. The governor of Louisbourg complains of the apathy of the Acadians.[1] Saint-Ovide declares that they do not want to fulfil the intentions of the King and remove to Isle Royale. Costebelle makes the same complaint; and again, after three years of vain attempts to overcome their reluctance, he writes that every effort has failed to induce them to migrate.

From this time forward the state of affairs in Acadia was a peculiar one. By the Treaty of Utrecht it was a British province, and the nominal sover

[1] *Costebelle au Ministre*, 15 *Janvier*, 1715.

eignty resided at Annapolis, in the keeping of the miserable little fort and the puny garrison, which as late as 1743 consisted of but five companies, counting, when the ranks were full, thirty-one men each.[1] More troops were often asked for, and once or twice were promised; but they were never sent. "This has been hitherto no more than a mock government, its authority never yet having extended beyond cannon-shot of the fort," wrote Governor Philipps in 1720. "It would be more for the honour of the Crown, and profit also, to give back the country to the French, than to be contented with the name only of government."[2]   Philipps repaired the fort, which, as the engineer Mascarene says, "had lain tumbling down" before his arrival; but Annapolis and the whole province remained totally neglected and almost forgotten by England till the middle of the century. At one time the soldiers were in so ragged a plight that Lieutenant-Colonel Armstrong was forced to clothe them at his own expense.[3]

While this seat of British sovereignty remained in unchanging feebleness for more than forty years, the French Acadians were multiplying apace.   Before

[1] *Governor Mascarene to the Secretary of State, 1 December,* 1743. At this time there was also a blockhouse at Canseau, where a few soldiers were stationed. These were then the only British posts in the province. In May, 1727, Philipps wrote to the Lords of Trade. "Everything there [at Annapolis] is wearing the face of ruin and decay," and the ramparts are "lying level with the ground in breaches sufficiently wide for fifty men to enter abreast."

[2] *Philipps to Secretary Craggs, 26 September,* 1720.

[3] *Selections from the Public Documents of Nova Scotia,* 18, *note.*

1749 they were the only white inhabitants of the province, except ten or twelve English families who, about the year 1720, lived under the guns of Annapolis. At the time of the cession the French population seems not to have exceeded two thousand souls, about five hundred of whom lived within the *banlieue* of Annapolis, and were therefore more or less under English control. They were all alike a simple and ignorant peasantry, prosperous in their humble way, and happy when rival masters ceased from troubling, though vexed with incessant quarrels among themselves, arising from the unsettled boundaries of their lands, which had never been properly surveyed. Their mental horizon was of the narrowest, their wants were few, no military service was asked of them by the English authorities, and they paid no taxes to the government. They could even indulge their strong appetite for litigation free of cost; for when, as often happened, they brought their land disputes before the Council at Annapolis, the cases were settled and the litigants paid no fees. Their communication with the English officials was carried on through deputies chosen by themselves, and often as ignorant as their constituents, for a remarkable equality prevailed through this primitive little society.

Except the standing garrison at Annapolis, Acadia was as completely let alone by the British government as Rhode Island or Connecticut. Unfortunately, the traditional British policy of inaction towards her colonies was not applicable in the case of a newly conquered province with a disaffected population and active, enterprising, and martial neighbors bent on recovering what they had lost. Yet it might be supposed that a neglect so invigorating in other cases might have developed among the Acadians habits of self-reliance and faculties of self-care. The reverse took place; for if England neglected Acadia, France did not; and though she had renounced her title to it, she still did her best to master it and make it hers again. The chief instrument of her aggressive policy was the governor of Isle Royale, whose station was the fortress of Louisbourg, and who was charged with the management of Acadian affairs. At all the Acadian settlements he had zealous and efficient agents in the missionary priests, who were sent into the province by the Bishop of Quebec, or in a few cases by their immediate ecclesiastical superiors in Isle Royale.

The Treaty of Utrecht secured freedom of worship to the Acadians under certain conditions. These were that they should accept the sovereignty of the British Crown, and that they and their pastors should keep within the limits of British law.[1] Even supposing that by swearing allegiance to Queen Anne the Acadians had acquired the freedom of

---

[1] "Those who are willing to remain there [in Acadia] and to be subject to the kingdom of Great Britain, are to enjoy the free exercise of their religion according to the usage of the Church of Rome, as far as the laws of Great Britain do allow the same." — *Treaty of Utrecht, 14th article.*

worship which the treaty gave them on condition of
their becoming British subjects, it would have been
an abuse of this freedom to use it for subverting
the power that had granted it.   Yet this is what the
missionaries did.   They were not only priests of the
Roman Church, they were also agents of the King
of France; and from first to last they labored against
the British government in the country that France
had ceded to the British Crown.   So confident were
they, and with so much reason, of the weakness of
their opponents that they openly avowed that their
object was to keep the Acadians faithful to King
Louis.   When two of their number, Saint-Poncy and
Chevereaux, were summoned before the Council at
Annapolis, they answered, with great contempt,
"We are here on the business of the King of France."
They were ordered to leave Acadia.   One of them
stopped among the Indians at Cape Sable; the other,
in defiance of the Council, was sent back to Annapolis
by the Governor of Isle Royale.[1]   Apparently he was
again ordered away; for four years later the French
governor, in expectation of speedy war, sent him to
Chignecto with orders secretly to prepare the Acadians
for an attack on Annapolis.[2]

The political work of the missionaries began with
the cession of the colony, and continued with increas-
ing activity till 1755, kindling the impotent wrath of

[1] *Minutes of Council*, 18 *May*, 1736.   *Governor Armstrong to the
Secretary of State*, 22 *November*, 1736.

[2] *Minutes of Council*, 18 *September*, 1740, in *Nova Scotia Archives*.

the British officials, and drawing forth the bitter complaints of every successive governor. For this world and the next, the priests were fathers of their flocks, generally commanding their attachment, and always their obedience. Except in questions of disputed boundaries, where the Council alone could settle the title, the ecclesiastics took the place of judges and courts of justice, enforcing their decisions by refusal of the sacraments.[1] They often treated the British officials with open scorn. Governor Armstrong writes to the Lords of Trade: "Without some particular directions as to the insolent behavior of those priests, the people will never be brought to obedience, being by them incited to daily acts of rebellion." Another governor complains that they tell the Acadians of the destitution of the soldiers and the ruinous state of the fort, and assure them that the Pretender will soon be King of England, and that Acadia will then return to France.[2] "The bearer, Captain Bennett," writes Armstrong, "can further tell your Grace of the disposition of the French inhabitants of this province, and of the conduct of their missionary priests, who instil hatred into both Indians and French against the English."[3] As to the Indians, Governor Philipps declares that their priests hear a general confession from them twice a year, and give

[1] *Governor Mascarene to Père des Enclaves, 29 June, 1741.*

[2] *Deputy-Governor Doucette to the Secretary of State, 5 November, 1717.*

[3] *Governor Armstrong to the Secretary of State, 30 April, 1727.*

them absolution on condition of always being enemies
of the English.[1] The condition was easy, thanks to
the neglect of the British government, which took
no pains to conciliate the Micmacs, while the French
governor of Isle Royale corresponded secretly with
them and made them yearly presents.

In 1720 Philipps advised the recall of the French
priests, and the sending of others in their place, as
the only means of making British subjects of the
Acadians,[2] who at that time, having constantly
refused the oath of allegiance, were not entitled,
under the treaty, to the exercise of their religion.
Governor, Armstrong wrote sixteen years after: "By
some of the above papers your Grace will be informed
how high the French government carries its preten-
sions over its priests' obedience; and how to prevent
the evil consequences I know not, unless we could
have missionaries from places independent of that
Crown."[3] He expresses a well-grounded doubt
whether the home government will be at the trouble
and expense of such a change, though he adds that
there is not a missionary among either Acadians or
Indians who is not in the pay of France.[4] Gaulin,

[1] *Governor Philipps to Secretary Craggs, 26 September,* 1720.

[2] *Ibid., 26 May,* 1720.

[3] *Armstrong to the Secretary of State, 22 November,* 1736. The dis-
missal of French priests and the substitution of others was again
recommended some time after.

[4] The motives for paying priests for instructing the people of a
province ceded to England are given in a report of the French
Marine Council. The Acadians "ne pourront jamais conserver un
véritable attachement à la religion et *à leur légitime souverain* sans le

missionary of the Micmacs, received a "gratification" of fifteen hundred livres, besides an annual allowance of five hundred, and is described in the order granting it as a "brave man, capable even of leading these savages on an expedition." [1] In 1726 he was brought before the Council at Annapolis charged with incendiary conduct among both Indians and Acadians; but on asking pardon and promising nevermore to busy himself with affairs of government, he was allowed to remain in the province, and even to act as curé of the Mines. [2] No evidence appears that the British authorities ever molested a priest, except when detected in practices alien to his proper functions and injurious to the government. On one occasion when two cures were vacant, one through sedition and the other apparently through illness or death, Lieutenant-Governor Armstrong requested the governor of Isle Royale to send two priests "of known probity" to fill them. [3]

Who were answerable for the anomalous state of affairs in the province, — the *imperium in imperio* where the inner power waxed and strengthened every day, and the outer relatively pined and dwindled? It

secours d'un missionnaire" (*Délibérations du Conseil de Marine*, 23 *Mai*, 1719, in *Le Canada-Français*). The Intendant Bégon highly commends the efforts of the missionaries to keep the Acadians in the French interest (*Bégon au Ministre*, 25 *Septembre*, 1715), and Vaudreuil praises their zeal in the same cause (*Vaudreuil au Ministre*, 31 *Octobre*, 1717).

[1] *Délibérations du Conseil de Marine*, 3 *Mai*, 1718.
[2] *Record of Council at Annapolis*, 11 *and* 24 *October*, 1726.
[3] *Armstrong to Saint-Ovide*, 17 *June*, 1732.

was not mainly the Crown of France nor its agents, secular or clerical.   Their action under the circumstances, though sometimes inexcusable, was natural, and might have been foreseen.   Nor was it the Council at Annapolis, who had little power either for good or evil.   It was mainly the neglect and apathy of the British ministers, who seemed careless as to whether they kept Acadia or lost it, apparently thinking it not worth their notice.

About the middle of the century they wakened from their lethargy, and warned by the signs of the times, sent troops and settlers into the province at the eleventh hour.   France and her agents took alarm, and redoubled their efforts to keep their hold on a country which they had begun to regard as theirs already.   The settlement of the English at Halifax startled the French into those courses of intrigue and violence which were the immediate cause of the removal of the Acadians in 1755.

At the earlier period which we are now considering, the storm was still remote.   The English made no attempt either to settle the province or to secure it by sufficient garrisons; they merely tried to bind the inhabitants by an oath of allegiance which the weakness of the government would constantly tempt them to break.   When George I. came to the throne, Deputy-Governor Caulfield tried to induce the inhabitants to swear allegiance to the new monarch.   The Acadians asked advice of Saint-Ovide, governor at Louisbourg, who sent them elaborate directions how

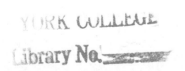
YORK COLLEGE
Library No.

to answer the English demand and remain at the same time faithful children of France. Neither Caulfield nor his successor could carry their point. The Treaty of Utrecht, as we have seen, gave the Acadians a year in which to choose between remaining in the province and becoming British subjects, or leaving it as subjects of the King of France. The year had long ago expired, and most of them were still in Acadia, unwilling to leave it, yet refusing to own King George. In 1720 General Richard Philipps, the governor of the province, set himself to the task of getting the oath taken, while the missionaries and the French officers at Isle Royale strenuously opposed his efforts. He issued a proclamation ordering the Acadians to swear allegiance to the King of England or leave the country, without their property, within four months. In great alarm, they appealed to their priests, and begged the Récollet, Père Justinien, curé of Mines, to ask advice and help from Saint-Ovide, successor of Costebelle at Louisbourg, protesting that they would abandon all rather than renounce their religion and their King.[1] At the same time they prepared for a general emigration by way of the isthmus and Baye Verte, where it would have been impossible to stop them.[2]

---

[1] *The Acadians to Saint-Ovide*, 6 *May*, 1720, in **Public Documents of Nova Scotia**, 25. This letter was evidently written for them, — no doubt by a missionary.

[2] "They can march off at their leisure, by way of the **Baye Verte**, with their effects, without danger of being molested by this garrison, which scarce suffices to secure the Fort." — *Philipps to Secretary Craggs*, 26 *May*, 1720.

Without the influence of their spiritual and temporal advisers, to whom they turned in all their
troubles, it is clear that the Acadians would have
taken the oath and remained in tranquil enjoyment
of their homes; but it was then thought important
to French interests that they should remove either to
Isle Royale or to Isle St. Jean, now Prince Edward's
Island. Hence no means were spared to prevent
them from becoming British subjects, if only in
name; even the Micmacs were enlisted in the good
work, and induced to threaten them with their enmity
if they should fail in allegiance to King Louis.
Philipps feared that the Acadians would rise in arms
if he insisted on the harsh requirements of his proclamation; in which case his position would have been
difficult, as they now outnumbered his garrison about
five to one. Therefore he extended indefinitely the
term of four months, that he had fixed for their final
choice, and continued to urge and persuade, without
gaining a step towards the desired result. In vain
he begged for aid from the British authorities. They
would do nothing for him, but merely observed that
while the French officers and priests had such influence over the Acadians, they would never be good
subjects, and so had better be put out of the country.[1]
This was easier said than done; for at this very time
there were signs that the Acadians and the Micmacs
would unite to put out the English garrison.[2]

---

[1] *The Board of Trade to Philipps,* 28 *December,* 1720.

[2] *Délibérations du Conseil de Marine, Aoust,* 1720. The attempt

Philipps was succeeded by a deputy-governor, Lieutenant-Colonel Armstrong, — a person of ardent impulses and unstable disposition. He applied himself with great zeal and apparent confidence to accomplishing the task in which his principal had failed. In fact, he succeeded in 1726 in persuading the inhabitants about Annapolis to take the oath, with a proviso that they should not be called upon for military service; but the main body of the Acadians stiffly refused. In the next year he sent Ensign Wroth to Mines, Chignecto, and neighboring settlements to renew the attempt on occasion of the accession of George II. The envoy's instructions left much to his discretion or his indiscretion, and he came back with the signatures, or crosses, of the inhabitants attached to an oath so clogged with conditions that it left them free to return to their French allegiance whenever they chose.

Philipps now came back to Acadia to resume his difficult task. And here a surprise meets us. He reported a complete success. The Acadians, as he declared, swore allegiance without reserve to King George; but he does not tell us how they were brought to do so. Compulsion was out of the question. They could have cut to pieces any part of the paltry English garrison that might venture outside

---

against the garrison was probably opposed by the priests, who must have seen the danger that it would rouse the ministry into sending troops to the province, which would have been disastrous to their plans.

the ditches of Annapolis, or they might have left
Acadia, with all their goods and chattels, with no
possibility of stopping them. The taking of the oath
was therefore a voluntary act.

But what was the oath? The words reported by
Philipps were as follows: "I promise and swear sincerely, on the faith of a Christian, that I will be entirely faithful, and will truly obey his Majesty King
George the Second, whom I recognize as sovereign
lord of Acadia or Nova Scotia. So help me God."
To this the Acadians affixed their crosses, or, in exceptional cases, their names. Recently, however,
evidence has appeared that, so far at least as regards
the Acadians on and near Mines Basin, the effect of
the oath was qualified by a promise on the part of
Philipps that they should not be required to take up
arms against either French or Indians, — they on
their part promising never to take up arms against
the English. This statement is made by Gaudalie,
curé of the parish of Mines, and Noiville, priest at
Pigiquid, or Pisiquid, now Windsor.[1] In fact, the
English never had the folly to call on the Acadians
to fight for them; and the greater part of this peace-
loving people were true to their promise not to take
arms against the English, though a considerable
number of them did so, especially at the beginning

---

[1] *Certificat de Charles de la Gaudalie, prêtre, curé missionnaire de la
paroisse des Mines, et Noël-Alexandre Noiville, . . . curé de l'Assomp-
tion et de la Sainte Famille de Pigiguit*; printed in Rameau, *Une
Colonie Féodale en Amérique* (ed. 1889), ii. 53.

of the Seven Years' War. It was to this promise, whether kept or broken, that they owed their name of Neutral French.

From first to last, the Acadians remained in a child-like dependence on their spiritual and temporal guides. Not one of their number stands out prominently from among the rest. They seem to have been totally devoid of natural leaders, and, unhappily for themselves, left their fate in the hands of others. Yet they were fully aware of their numerical strength, and had repeatedly declared, in a manner that the English officers called insolent, that they would neither leave the country nor swear allegiance to King George. The truth probably is that those who governed them had become convinced that this simple population, which increased rapidly, and could always be kept French at heart, might be made more useful to France in Acadia than out of it, and that it was needless further to oppose the taking of an oath which would leave them in quiet possession of their farms without making any change in their feelings, and probably none in their actions. By force of natural increase Acadia would in time become the seat of a large population ardently French and ardently Catholic; and while officials in France sometimes complained of the reluctance of the Acadians to move to Isle Royale, those who directed them in their own country seem to have become willing that they should stay where they were, and place themselves in such relations with the English as should leave them free to increase and multiply undisturbed. Deceived by the long apathy of the British government, French officials did not foresee that a time would come when it would bestir itself to make Acadia English in fact as well as in name.[1]

---

[1] The preceding chapter is based largely on two collections of documents relating to Acadia, — the *Nova Scotia Archives*, or *Selections from the Public Documents of Nova Scotia*, printed in 1869 by the government of that province, and the mass of papers collected by Rev. H. R. Casgrain and printed in the documentary department of *Le Canada-Français*, a review published under direction of Laval University at Quebec. Abbé Casgrain, with passionate industry, has labored to gather everything in Europe or America that could tell in favor of the French and against the English. Mr. Akins, the editor of the *Nova Scotia Archives*, leans to the other side, so that the two collections supplement each other. Both are copious and valuable. Besides these, I have made use of various documents from the archives of Paris not to be found in either of the above-named collections.

CHAPTER X.

1713–1724.

SEBASTIEN RALE.

BEFORE the Treaty of Utrecht, the present Nova Scotia, New Brunswick, and a part of Maine were collectively called Acadia by the French; but after the treaty gave Acadia to England, they insisted that the name meant only Nova Scotia. The English on their part claimed that the cession of Acadia made them owners, not only of the Nova Scotian peninsula, but of all the country north of it to the St. Lawrence, or at least to the dividing ridge or height of land.

This and other disputed questions of boundary were to be settled by commissioners of the two powers; but their meeting was put off for forty years, and then their discussions ended in the Seven Years'

War.   The claims of the rival nations were in fact so discordant that any attempt to reconcile them must needs produce a fresh quarrel.   The treaty had left a choice of evils.   To discuss the boundary question meant to renew the war; to leave it unsettled was a source of constant irritation; and while delay staved off a great war, it quickly produced a small one.

The river Kennebec, which was generally admitted by the French to be the dividing line between their possessions and New England,[1] was regarded by them with the most watchful jealousy.   Its headwaters approached those of the Canadian river Chaudière, the mouth of which is near Quebec; and by ascending the former stream and crossing to the headwaters of the latter, through an intricacy of forests, hills, ponds, and marshes, it was possible for a small band of hardy men, unencumbered by cannon, to reach the Canadian capital, — as was done long after by the followers of Benedict Arnold.   Hence it was thought a matter of the last importance to close the Kennebec against such an attempt.   The Norridgewock band of the Abenakis, who lived on the banks of that river, were used to serve this purpose and to form a sort of advance-guard to the French colony, while other kindred bands on the Penobscot, the St. Croix, and the St. John were expected to aid in opposing a living barrier to Eng-

[1] In 1700, however, there was an agreement, under the treaty of Ryswick, which extended the English limits as far as the river St. George, a little west of the Penobscot.

lish intrusion. Missionaries were stationed among all these Indians to keep them true to Church and King. The most important station, that of the Norridgewocks, was in charge of Father Sebastien Rale, the most conspicuous and interesting figure among the later French-American Jesuits.

Since the middle of the seventeenth century a change had come over the Jesuit missions of New France. Nothing is more striking or more admirable than the self-devoted apostleship of the earlier period.[1] The movement in Western Europe known as the Renaissance was far more than a revival of arts and letters, — it was an awakening of intellectual, moral, and religious life; the offspring of causes long in action, and the parent of other movements in action to this day. The Protestant Reformation was a part of it. That revolt against Rome produced a counter Renaissance in the bosom of the ancient Church herself. In presence of that peril she woke from sloth and corruption, and girded herself to beat back the invading heresies, by force or by craft, by inquisitorial fires, by the arms of princely and imperial allies, and by the self-sacrificing enthusiasm of her saints and martyrs. That time of danger produced the exalted zeal of Xavier and the intense, thoughtful, organizing zeal of Loyola. After a century had passed, the flame still burned, and it never shone with a purer or brighter radiance than in the early missions of New France.

[1] See "Jesuits in North America in the Seventeenth Century."

Such ardors cannot be permanent; they must subside, from the law of their nature. If the great Western mission had been a success, the enthusiasm of its founders might have maintained itself for some time longer; but that mission was extinguished in blood. Its martyrs died in vain, and the burning faith that had created it was rudely tried. Canada ceased to be a mission. The civil and military powers grew strong, and the Church no longer ruled with undivided sway. The times changed, and the men changed with them. It is a characteristic of the Jesuit Order, and one of the sources of its strength, that it chooses the workman for his work, studies the qualities of its members, and gives to each the task for which he is fitted best. When its aim was to convert savage hordes and build up another Paraguay in the Northern wilderness, it sent a Jogues, a Brébeuf, a Charles Garnier, and a Gabriel Lalemant, like a forlorn hope, to storm the stronghold of heathendom. In later times it sent other men to meet other needs and accomplish other purposes.

Before the end of the seventeenth century the functions of the Canadian Jesuit had become as much political as religious; but if the fires of his apostolic zeal burned less high, his devotion to the Order in which he had merged his personality was as intense as before. While in constant friction with the civil and military powers, he tried to make himself necessary to them, and in good measure he suc-

ceeded. Nobody was so able to manage the Indian
tribes and keep them in the interest of France.
"Religion," says Charlevoix, "is the chief bond by
which the savages are attached to us;" and it was
the Jesuit above all others who was charged to keep
this bond firm.

The Christianity that was made to serve this useful end did not strike a deep root. While humanity
is in the savage state, it can only be Christianized
on the surface; and the convert of the Jesuits remained a savage still. They did not even try to
civilize him. They taught him to repeat a catechism
which he could not understand, and practise rites of
which the spiritual significance was incomprehensible
to him. He saw the symbols of his new faith in
much the same light as the superstitions that had
once enchained him. To his eyes the crucifix was
a fetich of surpassing power, and the mass a benefi-
cent "medicine," or occult influence, of supreme
efficacy. Yet he would not forget his old rooted
beliefs, and it needed the constant presence of the
missionary to prevent him from returning to them.

Since the Iroquois had ceased to be a danger to
Canada, the active alliance of the Western Indians
had become less important to the colony. Hence the
missions among them had received less attention, and
most of these tribes had relapsed into heathenism.
The chief danger had shifted eastward, and was, or
was supposed to be, in the direction of New England.
Therefore the Eastern missions were cultivated with

diligence, — whether those within or adjoining the
settled limits of Canada, like the Iroquois mission of
Caughnawaga, the Abenaki missions of St. Francis
and Becancour, and the Huron mission of Lorette,
or those that served as outposts and advance-guards
of the colony, like the Norridgewock Abenakis of
the Kennebec, or the Penobscot Abenakis of the
Penobscot. The priests at all these stations were in
close correspondence with the government, to which
their influence over their converts was invaluable.
In the wilderness dens of the Hurons or the Iroquois,
the early Jesuit was a marvel of self-sacrificing zeal;
his successor, half missionary and half agent of the
King, had thought for this world as well as the
next.

Sebastien Rale,[1] born in Franche-Comté in 1657,
was sent to the American missions in 1689 at the age
of thirty-two. After spending two years among the
Abenakis of Canada, then settled near the mouth of
the Chaudière, he was sent for two years more to the
Illinois, and thence to the Abenakis of the Kennebec,
where he was to end his days.

Near where the town of Norridgewock now stands,
the Kennebec curved round a broad tongue of meadow
land, in the midst of a picturesque wilderness of hills
and forests. On this tongue of land, on ground a
few feet above the general level, stood the village of

---

[1] So written by himself in an autograph letter of 18 November,
1712. It is also spelled Rasle, Rasles, Ralle, and, very incorrectly,
Rallé, or Rallee.

the Norridgewocks, fenced with a stockade of round logs nine feet high. The enclosure was square; each of its four sides measured one hundred and sixty feet, and each had its gate. From the four gates ran two streets, or lanes, which crossed each other in the middle of the village. There were twenty-six Indian houses, or cabins, within the stockade, described as "built much after the English manner," though probably of logs. The church was outside the enclosure, about twenty paces from the east gate.[1]

Such was the mission village of Norridgewock in 1716. It had risen from its ashes since Colonel Hilton destroyed it in 1705, and the church had been rebuilt by New England workmen hired for the purpose.[2] A small bell, which is still preserved at Brunswick, rang for mass at early morning, and for vespers at sunset. Rale's leisure hours were few. He preached, exhorted, catechised the young converts, counselled their seniors for this world and the next, nursed them in sickness, composed their quar-

[1] The above particulars are taken from an inscription on a manuscript map in the library of the Maine Historical Society, made in 1716 by Joseph Heath, one of the principal English settlers on the Kennebec, and for a time commandant of the fort at Brunswick.

[2] When Colonel Westbrook and his men came to Norridgewock in 1722, they found a paper pinned to the church door, containing, among others, the following words, in the handwriting of Rale, meant as a fling at the English invaders: "It [the church] is ill built, because the English don't work well. It is not finished, although five or six Englishmen have wrought here during four years, and the Undertaker [contractor], who is a great Cheat, hath been paid in advance for to finish it." The money came from the Canadian government.

rels, tilled his own garden, cut his own firewood,
cooked his own food, which was of Indian corn, or,
at a pinch, of roots and acorns, worked at his Abenaki
vocabulary, and, being expert at handicraft, made
ornaments for the church, or moulded candles from
the fruit of the bayberry, or wax-myrtle.[1] Twice a
year, summer and winter, he followed his flock to
the sea-shore and the islands, where they lived at
their ease on fish and seals, clams, oysters, and
seafowl.

This Kennebec mission had been begun more than
half a century before; yet the conjurers, or "medicine
men," — natural enemies of the missionary, — still
remained obdurate and looked on the father askance,
though the body of the tribe were constant at mass
and confession, and regarded him with loving rever-
ence. He always attended their councils, and, as he
tells us, his advice always prevailed; but he was less
fortunate when he told them to practise no needless
cruelty in their wars, on which point they were often
disobedient children.[2]

Rale was of a strong, enduring frame, and a keen,
vehement, caustic spirit. He had the gift of tongues,
and was as familiar with the Abenaki and several

---

[1] *Myrica cerifera.*

[2] The site of the Indian village is still called Indian Old Point.
Norridgewock is the Naurantsouak, or Narantsouak, of the French.
For Rale's mission life, see two letters of his, 15 October, 1722, and
12 October, 1722, and a letter of Père La Chasse, Superior of the
Missions, 29 October, 1724. These are printed in the *Lettres Édifi-
antes,* xvii. xxiii.

other Indian languages as he was with Latin.[1] Of
the genuineness of his zeal there is no doubt, nor of
his earnest and lively interest in the fortunes of the
wilderness flock of which he was the shepherd for
half his life. The situation was critical for them
and for him. The English settlements were but a
short distance below, while those of the French
could be reached only by a hard journey of twelve
or fourteen days.

With two intervals of uneasy peace, the borders of
Maine had been harried by war-parties for thirty-
eight years; and since 1689 these raids had been
prompted and aided by the French. Thus it happened that extensive tracts, which before Philip's
War were dotted with farmhouses and fishing hamlets, had been abandoned, and cultivated fields were
turning again to forests. The village of Wells had
become the eastern frontier. But now the Treaty of
Utrecht gave promise of lasting tranquillity. The
Abenakis, hearing that they were to be backed no
longer by the French, became alarmed, sent messengers to Casco, and asked for peace. In July there
was a convention at Portsmouth, when delegates of
the Norridgewocks, Penobscots, Malicites, and other
Abenaki bands met Governor Dudley and the coun-

[1] Père La Chasse, in his eulogy of Rale, says that there was not
a language on the continent with which he had not some acquaintance. This is of course absurd. Besides a full knowledge of the
Norridgewock Abenaki, he had more or less acquaintance with two
other Algonquin languages, — the Ottawa and the Illinois, — and
also with the Huron ; which is enough for one man.

cillors of Massachusetts and New Hampshire. A
paper was read to them by sworn interpreters, in
which they confessed that they had broken former
treaties, begged pardon for "past rebellions, hostilities, and violations of promises," declared themselves
subjects of Queen Anne, pledged firm friendship
with the English, and promised them that they might
re-enter without molestation on all their former possessions. Eight of the principal Abenaki chiefs
signed this document with their totemic marks, and
the rest did so, after similar interpretation, at another
convention in the next year.[1] Indians when in trouble
can waive their pride, and lavish professions and
promises; but when they called themselves subjects
of Queen Anne, it is safe to say that they did not
know what the words meant.

Peace with the Indians was no sooner concluded
than a stream of settlers began to move eastward to
reoccupy the lands that they owned or claimed in the
region of the lower Kennebec. Much of this country
was held in extensive tracts, under old grants of the
last century, and the proprietors offered great induce-
ments to attract emigrants. The government of

---

[1] This treaty is given in full by Penhallow. It is also printed
from the original draft by Mr. Frederic Kidder, in his *Abenaki
Indians: their Treaties of* 1713 *and* 1717. The two impressions are
substantially the same, but with verbal variations. The version of
Kidder is the more complete, in giving not only the Indian totemic
marks, but also the autographs in facsimile of all the English
officials. Rale gives a dramatic account of the treaty, which he
may have got from the Indians, and which omits their submission
and their promises.

Massachusetts, though impoverished by three wars, of which it had borne the chief burden, added what encouragements it could. The hamlets of Saco, Scarborough, Falmouth, and Georgetown rose from their ashes; mills were built on the streams, old farms were retilled, and new ones cleared. A certain Dr. Noyes, who had established a sturgeon fishery on the Kennebec, built at his own charge a stone fort at Cushnoc, or Augusta; and it is said that as early as 1714 a blockhouse was built many miles above, near the mouth of the Sebasticook.[1] In the next year Fort George was built at the lower falls of the Androscoggin, and some years later Fort Richmond, on the Kennebec, at the site of the present town of Richmond.[2]

Some of the claims to these Kennebec lands were based on old Crown patents, some on mere prescription, some on Indian titles, good or bad. Rale says that an Englishman would give an Indian a bottle of rum, and get from him in return a large tract of land.[3] Something like this may have happened; though in other cases the titles were as good as Indian titles usually are, the deeds being in regular form and signed by the principal chiefs for a con-

---

[1] It was standing in 1852, and a sketch of it is given by Winsor, *Narrative and Critical History*, v. 185. I have some doubts as to the date of erection.

[2] Williamson, *History of Maine*, ii. 88, 97. Compare Penhallow.

[3] *Remarks out of the Fryar Sebastian Rale's Letter from Norridgewock, 7 February*, 1720, in the *Common Place Book* of Rev. Henry Flynt.

sideration which they thought sufficient. The lands of Indians, however, are owned, so far as owned at all, by the whole community; and in the case of the Algonquin tribes the chiefs had no real authority to alienate them without the consent of the tribesmen. Even supposing this consent to have been given, the Norridgewocks would not have been satisfied; for Rale taught them that they could not part with their lands, because they held them in trust for their children, to whom their country belonged as much as to themselves.

Long years of war and mutual wrong had embittered the Norridgewocks against their English neighbors, with whom, nevertheless, they wished to be at peace, because they feared them, and because their trade was necessary to them.

The English borderers, on their part, regarded the Indians less as men than as vicious and dangerous wild animals. In fact, the benevolent and philanthropic view of the American savage is for those who are beyond his reach: it has never yet been held by any whose wives and children have lived in danger of his scalping-knife. In Boston and other of the older and safer settlements, the Indians had found devoted friends before Philip's War; and even now they had apologists and defenders, prominent among whom was that relic of antique Puritanism, old Samuel Sewall, who was as conscientious and humane as he was prosy, narrow, and sometimes absurd, and whose benevolence towards the former owners of the soil was trebly reinforced by his notion that they were descendants of the ten lost tribes of Israel.[1]

The intrusion of settlers, and the building of forts and blockhouses on lands which they still called their own, irritated and alarmed the Norridgewocks, and their growing resentment was fomented by Rale, both because he shared it himself, and because he was prompted by Vaudreuil. Yet, dreading another war with the English, the Indians kept quiet for a year or two, till at length the more reckless among them began to threaten and pilfer the settlers.

In 1716 Colonel Samuel Shute came out to succeed Dudley as governor; and in the next summer he called the Indians to a council at Georgetown, a settlement on Arrowsick Island, at the mouth of the Kennebec. Thither he went in the frigate "Squirrel," with the councillors of Massachusetts and New Hampshire; while the deputies of the Norridgewocks, Penobscots, Pequawkets, or Abenakis of the Saco, and Assagunticooks, or Abenakis of the Androscoggin, came in canoes to meet him, and set up their wigwams on a neighboring island. The council opened on the ninth of August, under a large tent, over which waved the British flag. The oath was administered to the interpreters by the aged Judge Sewall, and Shute then made the Indians a speech in which he told them that the English and they were subjects of the great, good, and wise King George; that as

---

[1] Sewall's *Memorial relating to the Kennebec Indians* is an argument against war with them.

both peoples were under the same King, he would gladly see them also of the same religion, since it was the only true one; and to this end he gave them a Bible and a minister to teach them, — pointing to Rev. Joseph Baxter, who stood near by. And he further assured them that if any wrong should be done them, he would set it right. He then condescended to give his hand to the chiefs, telling them, through the interpreter, that it was to show his affection.

The Indians, after their usual custom, deferred their answer to the next day, when the council again met, and the Norridgewock chief, Wiwurna, addressed the governor as spokesman for his people. In defiance of every Indian idea of propriety, Shute soon began to interrupt him with questions and remarks. Wiwurna remonstrated civilly; but Shute continued his interruptions, and the speech turned to a dialogue, which may be abridged thus, Shute always addressing himself, not to the Indian orator, but to the interpreter.

The orator expressed satisfaction at the arrival of the governor, and hoped that peace and friendship would now prevail.

GOVERNOR (*to the interpreter*).   Tell them that if they behave themselves, I shall use them kindly.

ORATOR (*as rendered by the interpreter*).   Your Excellency was pleased to say that we must obey King George. We will if we like his way of treating us.

GOVERNOR.   They must obey him.

ORATOR.   We will if we are not disturbed on our lands.

GOVERNOR.   Nor must they disturb the English on theirs.

ORATOR.   We are pleased that your Excellency is ready to hear our complaints when wrong is done us.

GOVERNOR.   They must not pretend to lands that belong to the English.

ORATOR.   We beg leave to go on in order with our answer.

GOVERNOR.   Tell him to go on.

ORATOR.   If there should be any quarrel and bloodshed, we will not avenge ourselves, but apply to your Excellency.   We will embrace in our bosoms the English that have come to settle on our land.

GOVERNOR.   They must not call it their land, for the English have bought it of them and their ancestors.

ORATOR.   We pray leave to proceed with our answer, and talk about the land afterwards.

Wiwurna, then, with much civility, begged to be excused from receiving the Bible and the minister, and ended by wishing the governor good wind and weather for his homeward voyage.

There was another meeting in the afternoon, in which the orator declared that his people were willing that the English should settle on the west side of the Kennebec as far up the river as a certain mill; on which the governor said to the interpreter: "Tell them we want nothing but our own, and that that we will have;" and he ordered an old deed of sale, signed by six of their chiefs, to be shown and explained to them. Wiwurna returned that though his tribe were uneasy about their lands, they were willing that the English should keep what they had got, excepting the forts. On this point there was a sharp dialogue, and Shute said bluntly that if he saw fit, he should build a fort at every new settlement. At this all the Indians rose abruptly and went back to their camp, leaving behind an English flag that had been given them.

Rale was at the Indian camp, and some of them came back in the evening with a letter from him, in which he told Shute that the governor of Canada had asked the King of France whether he had ever given the Indians' land to the English, to which the King replied that he had not, and would help the Indians to repel any encroachment upon them. This cool assumption on the part of France of paramount right to the Abenaki country incensed Shute, who rejected the letter with contempt.

As between the governor and the Indian orator, the savage had shown himself by far the more mannerly; yet so unwilling were the Indians to break with the English that on the next morning, seeing Shute about to re-embark, they sent messengers to him to apologize for what they called their rudeness, beg that the English flag might be returned to them, and ask for another interview, saying that they

would appoint another spokesman instead of Wiwurna,
who had given so much offence. Shute consented,
and the meeting was held. The new orator presented a wampum belt, expressed a wish for peace,
and said that his people wished the English to extend
their settlements as far as they had formerly done.
Shute, on his part, promised that trading-houses
should be established for supplying their needs, and
that they should have a smith to mend their guns,
and an interpreter of their own choice. Twenty
chiefs and elders then affixed their totemic marks to
a paper, renewing the pledges made four years before
at Portsmouth, and the meeting closed with a dance
in honor of the governor.[1]

The Indians, as we have seen, had shown no
eagerness to accept the ministrations of Rev. Joseph
Baxter. The Massachusetts Assembly had absurdly
tried to counteract the influence of Rale by offering
£150 a year in their depreciated currency to any
one of their ministers who would teach Calvinism to
the Indians. Baxter, whom Rale, with characteristic
exaggeration, calls the ablest of the Boston ministers,
but who was far from being so, as he was the pastor of the small country village of Medfield, took up
the task, and, with no experience of Indian life or
knowledge of any Indian language, entered the lists

[1] A full report of this conference was printed at the time in
Boston. It is reprinted in *N. H. Historical Collections*, ii. 242, and
N. H. Provincial Papers, iii. 693. Penhallow was present at the
meeting, but his account of it is short. The accounts of Williamson
and Hutchinson are drawn from the above-mentioned report.

against an adversary who had spent half his days among savages, had gained the love and admiration of the Norridgewocks, and spoke their language fluently. Baxter, with the confidence of a novice, got an interpreter and began to preach, exhort, and launch sarcasms against the doctrines and practices of the Roman Church. Rale excommunicated such of his flock as listened to him;[1] yet some persisted in doing so, and three of these petitioned the English governor to order "a small praying-house" to be built for their use.[2]

Rale, greatly exasperated, opened a correspondence with Baxter, and wrote a treatise for his benefit, in which, through a hundred pages of polemical Latin, he proved that the Church of Rome was founded on a rock. This he sent to Baxter, and challenged him to overthrow his reasons. Baxter sent an answer for which Rale expresses great scorn as to both manner and matter. He made a rejoinder, directed not only against his opponent's arguments, but against his Latin, in which he picked flaws with great apparent satisfaction. He says that he heard no more from Baxter for a long time, but at last got another letter, in which there was nothing to the purpose, the minister merely charging him with an irascible and censorious spirit. This letter is still preserved, and

---

[1] *Shute to Rale*, 21 *February*, 1718.

[2] This petition is still in the Massachusetts Archives, and is printed by Dr. Francis in *Sparks's American Biography*, New Series, xvii. 259.

it does not answer to Rale's account of it. Baxter replies to his correspondent vigorously, defends his own Latin, attacks that of Rale, and charges him with losing temper.[1]

Rale's correspondence with the New England ministers seems not to have been confined to Baxter. A paper is preserved, translated apparently from a Latin original, and entitled, "Remarks out of the Fryar Sebastian Rale's Letter from Norridgewock, February 7, 1720." This letter appears to have been addressed to some Boston minister, and is of a scornful and defiant character, using language ill fitted to conciliate, as thus: "You must know that a missionary is not a cipher, like a minister;" or thus: "A Jesuit is not a Baxter or a Boston minister." The tone is one of exasperation dashed with contempt, and the chief theme is English encroachment and the inalienability of Indian lands.[2] Rale says that Baxter gave up his mission after receiving the treatise on the infallible supremacy of the true Church; but this is a mistake, as the minister made three successive visits to the Eastern country before he tired of his hopeless mission.

---

[1] This letter was given by Mr. Adams, of Medfield, a connection of the Baxter family, to the Massachusetts Historical Society, in whose possession it now is, in a worn condition. It was either captured with the rest of Rale's papers and returned to the writer, or else is a duplicate kept by Baxter.

[2] This curious paper is in the *Common Place Book* of Rev. Henry Flynt, of which the original is in the library of the Massachusetts Historical Society.

In the letter just quoted, Rale seems to have done
his best to rasp the temper of his New England correspondent.   He boasts of his power over the Indians,
who, as he declares, always do as he advises them.
"Any treaty with the governor," he goes on to say,
"and especially that of Arrowsick, is null and void if
I do not approve it, for I give them so many reasons
against it that they absolutely condemn what they
have done."   He says further that if they do not
drive the English from the Kennebec, he will leave
them, and that they will then lose both their lands
and their souls; and he adds that, if necessary, he
will tell them that they may make war.[1]   Rale wrote
also to Shute; and though the letter is lost, the
governor's answer shows that it was sufficiently
aggressive.

The wild Indian is unstable as water.   At Arrowsick, the Norridgewocks were all for peace; but
when they returned to their village their mood
changed, and, on the representations of Rale, they
began to kill the cattle of the English settlers on the
river below, burn their haystacks, and otherwise
annoy them.[2]   The English suspected that the

---

[1] See Francis, *Life of Rale*, where the entire passage is given.

[2] Rale wrote to the governor of Canada that it was "sur Les
Représentations qu'Il Avoit fait aux Sauvages de Sa Mission" that
they had killed "un grand nombre de Bestiaux apartenant aux
Anglois," and threatened them with attack if they did not retire.
(*Réponse fait par MM. Vaudreuil et Bégon au Mémoire du Roy du* 8
Juin, 1721.)   Rale told the governor of Massachusetts, on another
occasion, that his character as a priest permitted him to give the
Indians nothing but counsels of peace.   Yet as early as 1703 he

Jesuit was the source of their trouble; and as
they had always regarded the lands in question as
theirs, by virtue of the charter of the Plymouth
Company in 1620, and the various grants under it,
as well as by purchase from the Indians, their ire
against him burned high.   Yet afraid as the Indians were of another war, even Rale could scarcely
have stirred them to violence but for the indig-
nities put upon them by Indian-hating ruffians of
the border, vicious rum-selling traders, and hungry
land-thieves.   They had still another cause of
complaint. Shute had promised to build trading-
houses where their wants should be supplied without
fraud and extortion; but he had not kept his word,
and could not keep it, for reasons that will soon
appear.

In spite of such provocations, Norridgewock was
divided in opinion. Not only were the Indians in
great dread of war, but they had received English
presents to a considerable amount, chiefly from private persons interested in keeping them quiet.
Hence, to Rale's great chagrin, there was an English
party in the village so strong that when the English
authorities demanded reparation for the mischief
done to the settlers, the Norridgewocks promised
two hundred beaver-skins as damages, and gave four
hostages as security that they would pay for mis-

wrote to Vaudreuil that the Abenakis were ready, at a word from
him, to lift the hatchet against the English. *Beauharnois et Vaudreuil au Ministre*, 15 *Novembre*, 1703.

deeds in the past, and commit no more in the future.[1]

Rale now feared that his Indians would all go over to the English and tamely do their bidding; for though most of them, when he was present, would denounce the heretics and boast of the brave deeds they would do against them, yet after a meeting with English officials, they would change their minds and accuse their spiritual father of lying. It was clear that something must be done to end these waverings, lest the lands in dispute should be lost to France forever.

The Norridgewocks had been invited to another interview with the English at Georgetown; and Rale resolved, in modern American phrase, to "capture the meeting." Vaudreuil and the Jesuit La Chasse, superior of the mission, lent their aid. Messengers were sent to the converted Indians of Canada, whose attachment to France and the Church was past all doubt, and who had been taught to abhor the English as children of the Devil. The object of the message was to induce them to go to the meeting at Georgetown armed and equipped for any contingency.

They went accordingly, — Abenakis from Becancour

---

[1] *Joseph Heath and John Minot to Shute*, 1 *May*, 1719. Rale says that these hostages were seized by surprise and violence; but Vaudreuil complains bitterly of the faintness of heart which caused the Indians to give them (*Vaudreuil à Rale*, 15 *Juin*, 1721), and both he and the intendant lay the blame on the English party at Norridgewock, who, "with the consent of all the Indians of that mission, had the weakness to give four hostages." *Réponse de Vaudreuil et Bégon au Mémoire du Roy du* 8 *Juin*, 1721.

and St. Francis, Hurons from Lorette, and Iroquois from Caughnawaga, besides others, all stanch foes of heresy and England. Rale and La Chasse directed their movements and led them first to Norridgewock, where their arrival made a revolution. The peace party changed color like a chameleon, and was all for war. The united bands, two hundred and fifty warriors in all, paddled down the Kennebec along with the two Jesuits and two French officers, Saint-Castin and Croisil. In a few days the English at Georgetown saw them parading before the fort, well armed, displaying French flags, — feathers dangling from their scalp-locks, and faces fantastically patterned in vermilion, ochre, white clay, soot, and such other pigments as they could find or buy.

They were met by Captain Penhallow and other militia officers of the fort, to whom they gave the promised two hundred beaver-skins, and demanded the four hostages in return; but the hostages had been given as security, not only for the beaver-skins, but also for the future good behavior of the Indians, and Penhallow replied that he had no authority to surrender them. On this they gave him a letter to the governor, written for them by Père de la Chasse, and signed by their totems. It summoned the English to leave the country at once, and threatened to rob and burn their houses in case of refusal.[1] The

---

[1] *Eastern Indians' Letter to the Governour*, 27 *July*, 1721, in *Mass., Hist. Coll., Second Series*, viii. 259. This is the original French. It is signed with totems of all the Abenaki bands, and also of the

threat was not executed, and they presently disappeared, but returned in September in increased numbers, burned twenty-six houses and attacked the fort,
in which the inhabitants had sought refuge. The
garrison consisted of forty men, who, being reinforced
by the timely arrival of several whale-boats bringing
thirty more, made a sortie. A skirmish followed;
but being outnumbered and outflanked, the English
fell back behind their defences.[1]

The French authorities were in a difficult position.
They thought it necessary to stop the progress of
English settlement along the Kennebec; and yet, as
there was peace between the two Crowns, they could
not use open force. There was nothing for it but to
set on the Abenakis to fight for them. "I am well
pleased," wrote Vaudreuil to Rale, "that you and

Caughnawagas, Iroquois of the Mountain, Hurons, Micmacs, Mon-
tagnais, and several other tribes. On this interview, Penhallow;
Belknap, ii. 51; *Shute to Vaudreuil*, 21 July, 1721 (O. S.); *Ibid.*, 23
April, 1722; Rale in *Lettres Édifiantes*, xvii. 285. Rale blames Shute
for not being present at the meeting, but a letter of the governor
shows that he had never undertaken to be there. He could not
have come in any case, from the effects of a fall, which disabled
him for some months even from going to Portsmouth to meet the
Legislature. *Provincial Papers of New Hampshire*, iii. 822.

[1] Williamson, *Hist. of Maine*, ii. 119; Penhallow. Rale's account
of the affair, found among his papers at Norridgewock, is curiously
exaggerated. He says that he himself was with the Indians, and
"to pleasure the English" showed himself to them several times, —
a point which the English writers do not mention, though it is one
which they would be most likely to seize upon. He says that fifty
houses were burned, and that there were five forts, two of which
were of stone, and that in one of these six hundred armed men,
besides women and children, had sought refuge, though there was
not such a number of men in the whole region of the Kennebec.

Père de la Chasse have prompted the Indians to treat the English as they have done. My orders are to let them want for nothing, and I send them plenty of ammunition." Rale says that the King allowed him a pension of six thousand livres a year, and that he spent it all "in good works." As his statements are not remarkable for precision, this may mean that he was charged with distributing the six thousand livres which the King gave every year in equal shares to the three Abenaki missions of Medoctec, Norridgewock, and Panawamské, or Penobscot, and which generally took the form of presents of arms, gunpowder, bullets, and other munitions of war, or of food and clothing to support the squaws and children while the warriors were making raids on the English.[1]

Vaudreuil had long felt the delicacy of his position, and even before the crisis seemed near he tried to provide against it, and wrote to the minister that he had never called the Abenakis subjects of France, but only allies, in order to avoid responsibility for anything they might do.[2] "The English," he says elsewhere, "must be prevented from settling on Abenaki lands; and to this end we must let the Indians act for us (*laisser agir les sauvages*)."[3]

Yet while urging the need of precaution, he was too zealous to be always prudent; and once, at least,

---

[1] Vaudreuil, *Mémoire adressé au Roy, 5 Juin,* 1723.

[2] *Vaudreuil au Ministre,* 6 *Septembre,* 1716.

[3] *Extrait d'une Liasse de Papiers concernant le Canada,* 1720 (Archives du Ministère des Affaires Étrangères.)

he went so far as to suggest that French soldiers should be sent to help the Abenakis, — which, he thought, would frighten the English into retreating from their settlements; whereas if such help were refused, the Indians would go over to the enemy.[1] The court was too anxious to avoid a rupture to permit the use of open force, and would only promise plenty of ammunition to Indians who would fight the English, directing at the same time that neither favors nor attentions should be given to those who would not.[2]

The half-breed officer, Saint-Castin, son of Baron Vincent de Saint-Castin by his wife, a Penobscot squaw, bore the double character of a French lieutenant and an Abenaki chief, and had joined with the Indians in their hostile demonstration at Arrowsick Island. Therefore, as chief of a tribe styled subjects of King George, the English seized him, charged him with rebellion, and brought him to Boston, where he was examined by a legislative committee. He showed both tact and temper, parried the charges against him, and was at last set at liberty. His arrest, however, exasperated his tribesmen, who soon began to burn houses, kill settlers, and commit various acts of violence, for all of which Rale was believed to be mainly answerable. There was great indignation against him. He himself says that a reward of a thousand pounds sterling was

[1] *Réponse de Vaudreuil et Bégon au Mémoire du Roy*, 8 *Juin*, 1721.
[2] *Bégon à Rale*, 14 *Juin*, 1721.

offered for his head, but that the English should not
get it for all their sterling money.   It does not appear
that such a reward was offered, though it is true
that the Massachusetts House of Representatives once
voted five hundred pounds in their currency — then
equal to about a hundred and eighty pounds sterling
— for the same purpose; but as the governor and
Council refused their concurrence, the Act was of no
effect.

All the branches of the government, however,
presently joined in sending three hundred men to
Norridgewock, with a demand that the Indians
should give up Rale "and the other heads and
fomenters of their rebellion." In case of refusal
they were to seize the Jesuit and the principal chiefs
and bring them prisoners to Boston.   Colonel Westbrook was put in command of the party.   Rale, being
warned of their approach by some of his Indians,
swallowed the consecrated wafers, hid the sacred
vessels, and made for the woods, where, as he thinks,
he was saved from discovery by a special intervention of Providence.   His papers fell into the hands
of Westbrook, including letters that proved beyond
all doubt that he had acted as agent of the Canadian
authorities in exciting his flock against the English.[1]

---

[1] Some of the papers found in Rale's " strong box " are still preserved in the Archives of Massachusetts, including a letter to him
from Vaudreuil, dated at Quebec, 25 September, 1721, in which the
French governor expresses great satisfaction at the missionary's
success in uniting the Indians against the English, and promises
military aid, if necessary.

Incensed by Westbrook's invasion, the Indians came down the Kennebec in large numbers, burned the village of Brunswick, and captured nine families at Merry-meeting Bay; though they soon set them free, except five men whom they kept to exchange for the four hostages still detained at Boston.[1] At the same time they seized several small vessels in the harbors along the coast. On this the governor and Council declared war against the Eastern Indians, meaning the Abenakis and their allies, whom they styled traitors and robbers.

In Massachusetts many persons thought that war could not be justified, and were little disposed to push it with vigor. The direction of it belonged to the governor in his capacity of Captain-General of the Province. Shute was an old soldier who had served with credit as lieutenant-colonel under Marlborough; but he was hampered by one of those disputes which in times of crisis were sure to occur in every British province whose governor was appointed by the Crown. The Assembly, jealous of the representative of royalty, and looking back mournfully to their virtual independence under the lamented old charter, had from the first let slip no opportunity to increase its own powers and abridge those of the governor, refused him the means of establishing the promised trading-houses in the Indian country, and would grant no money for presents to conciliate the Norridgewocks. The House now wanted, not only

[1] Wheeler, *History of Brunswick, Topsham, and Harpswell,* 54.

to control supplies for the war, but to direct the war itself and conduct operations by committees of its own. Shute made his plans of campaign, and proceeded to appoint officers from among the frontier inhabitants, who had at least the qualification of being accustomed to the woods.   One of them, Colonel Walton, was obnoxious to some of the representatives, who brought charges against him, and the House demanded that he should be recalled from the field to answer to them for his conduct.   The governor objected to this as an encroachment on his province as commander-in-chief.   Walton was now accused of obeying orders of the governor in contravention of those of the representatives, who thereupon passed a vote requiring him to lay his journal before them.   This was more than Shute could bear. He had the character of a good-natured man; but the difficulties and mortifications of his position had long galled him, and he had got leave to return to England and lay his case before the King and Council.   The crisis had now come.   The Assembly were for usurping all authority, civil and military. Accordingly, on the first of January, 1723, the governor sailed in a merchant ship, for London, without giving notice of his intention to anybody except two or three servants.[1]

The burden of his difficult and vexatious office fell upon the lieutenant-governor, William Dummer.

---

[1] Hutchinson, ii. 261. On these dissensions compare Palfrey, *Hist. of New England*, **iv**. 406–428.

GOV. WILLIAM DUMMER.

When he first met the Council in his new capacity, a whimsical scene took place. Here, among the rest, was the aged, matronly countenance of the worthy Samuel Sewall, deeply impressed with the dignity and importance of his position as senior member of the Board. At his best he never had the faintest sense of humor or perception of the ludicrous, and being now perhaps touched with dotage, he thought it incumbent upon him to address a few words of exhortation and encouragement to the incoming chief magistrate. He rose from his seat with long locks, limp and white, drooping from under his black skull-cap, — for he abhorred a wig as a sign of backsliding, — and in a voice of quavering solemnity spoke thus: —

"If your Honour and this Honourable Board please to give me leave, I would speak a Word or two upon this solemn Occasion. Altho the unerring Providence of God has brought you to the Chair of Government in a cloudy and tempestuous season, yet you have this for your Encouragement, that the people you Have to do with are a part of the Israel of God, and you may expect to have of the Prudence and Patience of Moses communicated to you for your Conduct. It is evident that our Almighty Saviour counselled the first planters to remove hither and Settle here, and they dutifully followed his Advice, and therefore He will never leave nor forsake them nor Theirs; so that your Honour must needs be happy in sincerely seeking their Interest and Welfare, which your Birth and Education will incline you to do. *Difficilia quæ pulchra.*

I promise myself that they who sit at this Board will
yield their Faithful Advice to your Honour according to
the Duty of their Place."

Having thus delivered himself to an audience not
much more susceptible of the ludicrous than he was,
the old man went home well pleased, and recorded
in his diary that the lieutenant-governor and councillors rose and remained standing while he was speaking, "and they expressed a handsom Acceptance of
what I had said; *Laus Deo.*" [1]

Dummer was born in New England, and might,
therefore, expect to find more favor than had fallen
to his predecessor; but he was the representative of
royalty, and could not escape the consequences of
being so. In earnest of what was in store for him,
the Assembly would not pay his salary, because he
had sided with the governor in the late quarrel.
The House voted to dismiss Colonel Walton and
Major Moody, the chief officers appointed by Shute;
and when Dummer reminded it that this was a
matter belonging to him as commander-in-chief, it
withheld the pay of the obnoxious officers and refused
all supplies for the war till they should be removed.
Dummer was forced to yield. [2] The House would
probably have pushed him still farther, if the members had not dreaded the effect of Shute's representations at court, and feared lest persistent encroachment
on the functions of the governor might cost them

---

[1] *Sewall Papers*, iii. 317, 318.   [2] Palfrey, iv. 432, 433.

their charter, to which, insufficient as they thought it, and far inferior to the one they had lost, they clung tenaciously as the palladium of their liberties. Yet Dummer needed the patience of Job; for his Assembly seemed more bent on victories over him than over the Indians.

There was another election, which did not improve the situation. The new House was worse than the old, being made up largely of narrow-minded rustics, who tried to relieve the governor of all conduct of the war by assigning it to a committee chosen from among themselves; but the Council would not concur with them.

Meanwhile the usual ravages went on. Farmhouses were burned, and the inmates waylaid and killed, while the Indians generally avoided encounters with armed bodies of whites. Near the village of Oxford four of them climbed upon the roof of a house, cut a hole in it with their hatchets, and tried to enter. A woman who was alone in the building, and who had two loaded guns and two pistols, seeing the first savage struggling to shove himself through the hole, ran to him in desperation and shot him; on which the others dragged the body back and disappeared.[1]

There were several attempts of a more serious kind. The small wooden fort at the river St. George, the most easterly English outpost, was attacked, but the assailants were driven off. A few weeks later it

---

[1] Penhallow. Hutchinson, ii. 279.

was attacked again by the Penobscots under their missionary, Father Lauverjat. Other means failing, they tried to undermine the stockade; but their sap caved in from the effect of rains, and they retreated, with severe loss. The warlike contagion spread to the Indians of Nova Scotia. In July the Micmacs seized sixteen or seventeen fishing smacks at Canseau; on which John Eliot, of Boston, and John Robinson, of Cape Ann, chased the marauders in two sloops, retook most of the vessels, and killed a good number of the Indians. In the autumn a war-party, under the noted chief Grey Lock, prowled about the village of Rutland, met the minister, Joseph Willard, and attacked him. He killed one savage and wounded another, but was at last shot and scalped.[1]

The representatives had long been bent on destroying the mission village of the Penobscots on the river of that name; and one cause of their grudge against Colonel Walton was that, by order of the governor, he had deferred a projected attack upon it. His successor, Colonel Westbrook, now took the work in hand, went up the Penobscot in February with two hundred and thirty men in sloops and whale-boats, left these at the head of navigation, and pushed through the forest to the Indian town called Panawamské by the French. It stood apparently above Bangor, at or near Passadumkeag. Here the party found a stockade enclosure fourteen feet high, seventy yards long, and fifty yards wide, containing

[1] Penhallow. Temple and Sheldon, *History of Northfield*, 195.

twenty-three houses, which Westbrook, a better woodsman than grammarian, reports to have been "built regular." Outside the stockade stood the chapel, "well and handsomely furnished within and without, and on the south side of that the Fryer's dwelling-house." [1] This "Fryer" was Father Lauverjat, who had led his flock to the attack of the fort at the St. George. Both Indians and missionary were gone. Westbrook's men burned the village and chapel, and sailed back to the St. George. In the next year, 1724, there was a more noteworthy stroke; for Dummer, more pliant than Shute, had so far soothed his Assembly that it no longer refused money for the war. It was resolved to strike at the root of the evil, seize Rale, and destroy Norridgewock. Two hundred and eight men in four companies, under Captains Harmon, Moulton, and Brown, and Lieutenant Bean, set out from Fort Richmond in seventeen whaleboats on the eighth of August. They left the boats at Taconic Falls in charge of a lieutenant and forty men, and on the morning of the tenth the main body, accompanied by three Mohawk Indians, marched through the forest for Norridgewock. Towards evening they saw two squaws, one of whom they brutally shot, and captured the other, who proved to be the wife of the noted chief Bomazeen. She gave them a full account of the state of the village, which they approached early in the afternoon

---

[1] *Westbrook to Dummer*, 23 *March*, 1723, in *Collections Mass. Hist. Soc., Second Series.* viii. 264.

of the twelfth.   In the belief that some of the Indians would be in their cornfields on the river above, Harmon, who was in command, divided the force, and moved up the river with about eighty men, while Moulton, with as many more, made for the village, advancing through the forest with all possible silence. About three o'clock he and his men emerged from a tangle of trees and bushes, and saw the Norridgewock cabins before them, no longer enclosed with a stockade, but open and unprotected.   Not an Indian was stirring, till at length a warrior came out from one of the huts, saw the English, gave a startled war-whoop, and ran back for his gun.   Then all was dismay and confusion.   Squaws and children ran screaming for the river, while the warriors, fifty or sixty in number, came to meet the enemy.   Moulton ordered his men to reserve their fire till the Indians had emptied their guns.   As he had foreseen, the excited savages fired wildly, and did little or no harm.   The English, still keeping their ranks, returned a volley with deadly effect.   The Indians gave one more fire, and then ran for the river.   Some tried to wade to the farther side, the water being low; others swam across, while many jumped into their canoes, but could not use them, having left the paddles in their houses.   Moulton's men followed close, shooting the fugitives in the water or as they climbed the farther bank.

When they returned to the village they found Rale in one of the houses, firing upon some of their comrades who had not joined in the pursuit. He presently wounded one of them, on which a lieutenant named Benjamin Jaques burst open the door of the house, and, as he declared, found the priest loading his gun for another shot. The lieutenant said further that he called on him to surrender, and that Rale replied that he would neither give quarter nor take it; on which Jaques shot him through the head.[1] Moulton, who had given orders that Rale should not be killed, doubted this report of his subordinate so far as concerned the language used by Rale, though believing that he had exasperated the lieutenant by provoking expressions of some kind. The old chief Mogg had shut himself up in another house, from which he fired and killed one of Moulton's three Mohawks, whose brother then beat in the door and shot the chief dead. Several of the English followed, and brutally murdered Mogg's squaw and his two children. Such plunder as the village afforded, consisting of three barrels of gunpowder, with a few guns, blankets, and kettles, was then seized; and the Puritan militia thought it a meritorious act to break what they called the "idols" in the church, and carry off the sacred vessels.

Harmon and his party returned towards night from their useless excursion to the cornfields, where they found nobody. In the morning a search was

---

[1] Hutchinson, ii. 283 (ed. 1795). Hutchinson had the story from Moulton. Compare the tradition in the family of Jaques, as told by his great-grandson, in *Historical Magazine*, viii. 177.

made for the dead, and twenty-six Indians were
found and scalped, including the principal chiefs and
warriors of the place.   Then, being anxious for the
safety of their boats, the party marched for Taconic
Falls.   They had scarcely left the village when one
of the two surviving Mohawks, named Christian,
secretly turned back, set fire to the church and the
houses, and then rejoined the party.   The boats
were found safe, and embarking, they rowed down
to Richmond with their trophies.[1]

The news of the fate of the Jesuit and his mission
spread joy among the border settlers, who saw in it
the end of their troubles.   In their eyes Rale was
an incendiary, setting on a horde of bloody savages
to pillage and murder.   While they thought him a
devil, he passed in Canada for a martyred saint.
He was neither the one nor the other, but a man
with the qualities and faults of a man, — fearless,

---

[1] The above rests on the account of Hutchinson, which was
taken from the official Journal of Harmon, the commander of the
expedition, and from the oral statements of Moulton, whom Hutchinson examined on the subject.   Charlevoix, following a letter of
La Chasse in the Jesuit *Lettres Édifiantes,* gives a widely different
story.   According to him, Norridgewock was surprised by eleven
hundred men, who first announced their presence by a general volley, riddling all the houses with bullets.   Rale, says La Chasse,
ran out to save his flock by drawing the rage of the enemy on himself; on which they raised a great shout and shot him dead at the
foot of the cross in the middle of the village.   La Chasse does not
tell us where he got the story; but as there were no French wit-
nesses, the story must have come from the Indians, who are notorious liars where their interest and self-love are concerned.   Nobody
competent to judge of evidence can doubt which of the two statements is the more trustworthy.

resolute, enduring; boastful, sarcastic, often bitter
and irritating; a vehement partisan; apt to see things,
not as they were, but as he wished them to be; given
to inaccuracy and exaggeration, yet no doubt sincere
in opinions and genuine in zeal; hating the English
more than he loved the Indians; calling himself their
friend, yet using them as instruments of worldly
policy, to their danger and final ruin. In considering the ascription of martyrdom, it is to be remembered that he did not die because he was an apostle
of the faith, but because he was the active agent of
the Canadian government.

There is reason to believe that he sometimes exer-
cised a humanizing influence over his flock. The
war which he helped to kindle was marked by fewer
barbarities — fewer tortures, mutilations of the dead,
and butcheries of women and infants — than either
of the preceding wars. It is fair to assume that this
was due in part to him, though it was chiefly the
result of an order given, at the outset, by Shute that
non-combatants in exposed positions should be sent
to places of safety in the older settlements.[1]

[1] It is also said that Rale taught some of his Indians to read and
write, — which was unusual in the Jesuit missions. On his character, compare the judicial and candid *Life of Rale,* by Dr. Convers
Francis, in Sparks's *American Biography, New Series,* **vii.**

CHAPTER XI.

1724, 1725.

LOVEWELL'S FIGHT.

VAUDREUIL AND DUMMER. — EMBASSY TO CANADA. — INDIANS IN-
TRACTABLE. — TREATY OF PEACE. — THE PEQUAWKETS. — JOHN
LOVEWELL. — A HUNTING PARTY. — ANOTHER EXPEDITION. —
THE AMBUSCADE. — THE FIGHT. — CHAPLAIN FRYE: HIS FATE.
— THE SURVIVORS. — SUSANNA ROGERS.

THE death of Rale and the destruction of Norridgewock did not at once end the war. Vaudreuil turned
all the savages of the Canadian missions against the
borders, not only of Maine, but of western Massachusetts, whose peaceful settlers had given no offence.
Soon after the Norridgewock expedition, Dummer
wrote to the French governor, who had lately proclaimed the Abenakis his allies: "As they are subjects of his Britannic Majesty, they cannot be your
allies, except through me, his representative. You
have instigated them to fall on our people in the most
outrageous manner. I have seen your commission
to Sebastien Rale. But for your protection and in-
citements they would have made peace long ago."[1]

In reply, Vaudreuil admitted that he had given a
safe-conduct and a commission to Rale, which he

[1] *Dummer to Vaudreuil*, 15 *September*, 1724.

could not deny, as the Jesuit's papers were in the hands of the English governor. "You will have to answer to your king for his murder," he tells Dummer. "It would have been strange if I had abandoned our Indians to please you. I cannot help taking the part of our allies. You have brought your troubles upon yourself. I advise you to pull down all the forts you have built on the Abenaki lands since the Peace of Utrecht. If you do so, I will be your mediator with the Norridgewocks. As to the murder of Rale, I leave that to be settled between the two Crowns."[1]

Apparently the French court thought it wise to let the question rest, and make no complaint. Dummer, however, gave his views on the subject to Vaudreuil. "Instead of preaching peace, love, and friendship, agreeably to the Christian religion, Rale was an incendiary, as appears by many letters I have by me. He has once and again appeared at the head of a great many Indians, threatening and insulting us. If such a disturber of the peace has been killed in the heat of action, nobody is to blame but himself. I have much more cause to complain that Mr. Willard, minister of Rutland, who is innocent of all that is charged against Rale, and always confined himself to preaching the Gospel, was slain and scalped by your Indians, and his scalp carried in triumph to Quebec."

Dummer then denies that France has any claim to

---

[1] *Vaudreuil à Dummer, 29 Octobre,* 1724.

the Abenakis, and declares that the war between them and the English is due to the instigations of Rale and the encouragements given them by Vaudreuil. But he adds that in his wish to promote peace he sends two prominent gentlemen, Colonel Samuel Thaxter and Colonel William Dudley, as bearers of his letter.[1]

Mr. Atkinson, envoy on the part of New Hampshire, joined Thaxter and Dudley, and the three set out for Montreal, over the ice of Lake Champlain. Vaudreuil received them with courtesy. As required by their instructions, they demanded the release of the English prisoners in Canada, and protested against the action of the French governor in setting on the Indians to attack English settlements when there was peace between the two Crowns. Vaudreuil denied that he had done so, till they showed him his own letters to Rale, captured at Norridgewock. These were unanswerable; but Vaudreuil insisted that the supplies sent to the Indians were only the presents which they received every year from the King. As to the English prisoners, he said that those in the hands of the Indians were beyond his power; but that the envoys could have those whom the French had bought from their captors, on paying back the price they had cost. The demands were exorbitant, but sixteen prisoners were ransomed, and bargains were made for ten more. Vaudreuil proposed

---

[1] *Dummer to Vaudreuil*, 19 *January*, 1725. This, with many other papers relating to these matters, is in the Massachusetts Archives.

to Thaxter and his colleagues to have an interview with the Indians, which they at first declined, saying that they had no powers to treat with them, though, if the Indians wished to ask for peace, they were ready to hear them. At length a meeting was arranged. The French governor writes: "Being satisfied that nothing was more opposed to our interests than a peace between the Abenakis and the English, I thought that I would sound the chiefs before they spoke to the English envoys, and insinuate to them everything that I had to say."[1] This he did with such success that, instead of asking for peace, the Indians demanded the demolition of the English forts, and heavy damages for burning their church and killing their missionary. In short, to Vaudreuil's great satisfaction, they talked nothing but war. The French despatch reporting this interview has the following marginal note: "Nothing better can be done than to foment this war, which at least retards the settlements of the English;" and against this is written, in the hand of the colonial minister, the word "*Approved*."[2] This was, in fact, the policy pursued from the first, and Rale had been an instrument of it. The Jesuit La Chasse, who

---

[1] *Dépêche de Vaudreuil*, 7 *Août*, 1725. "Comme j'ai toujours été persuadé que rien n'est plus opposé à nos intérêts que la paix des Abenakis avec les Anglais (la sureté de cette colonie du côté de l'est ayant été l'unique objet de cette guerre), je songeai à pressentir ces sauvages avant qu'ils parlassant aux Anglais et à leur insinuer tout ce que j'avais à leur dire." — *Vaudreuil au Ministre*, 22 *Mai*, 1725.

[2] *N. Y Col. Docs.*, ix. 949.

spoke both English and Abenaki, had acted as interpreter, and so had had the meeting in his power, as he could make both parties say what he pleased. The envoys thought him more anti-English than Vaudreuil himself, and ascribed the intractable mood of the Indians to his devices. Under the circumstances, they made a mistake in consenting to the interview at all. The governor, who had treated them with civility throughout, gave them an escort of soldiers for the homeward journey, and they and the redeemed prisoners returned safely to Albany.

The war went on as before, but the Indians were fast growing tired of it. The Penobscots had made themselves obnoxious by their attacks on Fort St. George, and Captain Heath marched across country from the Kennebec to punish them. He found their village empty. It was built, since Westbrook's attack, at or near the site of Bangor, a little below Indian Old Town, — the present abode of the tribe, — and consisted of fifty wigwams, which Heath's men burned to the ground.

One of the four hostages still detained at Boston, together with another Indian captured in the war, was allowed to visit his people, under a promise to return. Strange to say, the promise was kept. They came back bringing a request for peace from their tribesmen. On this, commissioners were sent to the St. George, where a conference was held with some of the Penobscot chiefs, and it was arranged that deputies of that people should be sent to Boston to

conclude a solid peace.   After long delay, four
chiefs appeared, fully empowered, as they said, to
make peace, not for the Penobscots only, but for the
other Abenaki tribes, their allies.   The speeches and
ceremonies being at last ended, the four deputies
affixed their marks to a paper in which, for themselves and those they represented, they made submission "unto his most excellent Majesty George, by
the grace of God king of Great Britain, France, and
Ireland, defender of the Faith," etc., promising to
"cease and forbear all acts of hostility, injuries, and
discord towards all his subjects, and never confederate
or combine with any other nation to their prejudice."
Here was a curious anomaly.   The English claimed
the Abenakis as subjects of the British Crown, and
at the same time treated with them as a foreign
power.   Each of the four deputies signed the above-
mentioned paper, one with the likeness of a turtle,
the next with that of a bird, the third with the untutored portrait of a beaver, and the fourth with an
extraordinary scrawl, meant, it seems, for a lobster,
— such being their respective totems.   To these the
lieutenant-governor added the seal of the province
of Massachusetts, coupled with his own autograph.

In the next summer, and again a year later, other
meetings were held at Casco Bay with the chiefs of
the various Abenaki tribes, in which, after prodigious
circumlocution, the Boston treaty was ratified, and
the war ended.[1]   This time the Massachusetts

[1] Penhallow gives the Boston treaty.   For the ratifications, see
Collections of the Maine Hist. Soc., iii. 377, 407.

Assembly, taught wisdom by experience, furnished a guarantee of peace by providing for government trading-houses in the Indian country, where goods were supplied, through responsible hands, at honest prices.

The Norridgewocks, with whom the quarrel began, were completely broken. Some of the survivors joined their kindred in Canada, and others were merged in the Abenaki bands of the Penobscot, Saco, or Androscoggin. Peace reigned at last along the borders of New England; but it had cost her dear. In the year after the death of Rale, there was an incident of the conflict too noted in its day, and too strongly rooted in popular tradition, to be passed unnoticed.

Out of the heart of the White Mountains springs the river Saco, fed by the bright cascades that leap from the crags of Mount Webster, brawling among rocks and bowlders down the great defile of the Crawford Notch, winding through the forests and intervales of Conway, then circling northward by the village of Fryeburg in devious wanderings by meadows, woods, and mountains, and at last turning eastward and southward to join the sea.

On the banks of this erratic stream lived an Abenaki tribe called the Sokokis. When the first white man visited the country, these Indians lived at the Falls, a few miles from the mouth of the river. They retired before the English settlers, and either joined their kindred in Maine, or migrated to St. Francis

and other Abenaki settlements in Canada; but a
Sokoki band called Pigwackets, or Pequawkets, still
kept its place far in the interior, on the upper waters
of the Saco, near Pine Hill, in the present town of
Fryeburg.   Except a small band of their near kindred
on Lake Ossipee, they were the only human tenants
of a wilderness many thousand square miles in extent.   In their wild and remote abode they were difficult of access, and the forest and the river were well
stocked with moose, deer, bear, beaver, otter, lynx,
fisher, mink, and marten.   In this, their happy
hunting-ground, the Pequawkets thought themselves
safe; and they would have been so for some time
longer if they had not taken up the quarrel of the
Norridgewocks and made bloody raids against the
English border, under their war-chief, Paugus.

Not far from where their wigwams stood clustered
in a bend of the Saco was the small lake now called
Lovewell's Pond, named for John Lovewell of
Dunstable, a Massachusetts town on the New Hampshire line.   Lovewell's father, a person of consideration in the village, where he owned a "garrison
house," had served in Philip's War, and taken part
in the famous Narragansett Swamp Fight.   The
younger Lovewell, now about thirty-three years of
age, lived with his wife, Hannah, and two or three
children on a farm of two hundred acres.   The
inventory of his effects, made after his death, includes
five or six cattle, one mare, two steel traps with
chains, a gun, two or three books, a feather-bed, and

"under-bed," or mattress, along with sundry tools, pots, barrels, chests, tubs, and the like, — the equipment, in short, of a decent frontier yeoman of the time.[1] But being, like the tough veteran, his father, of a bold and adventurous disposition, he seems to have been less given to farming than to hunting and bush-fighting.

Dunstable was attacked by Indians in the autumn of 1724, and two men were carried off. Ten others went in pursuit, but fell into an ambush, and nearly all were killed, Josiah Farwell, Lovewell's brother-in-law, being, by some accounts, the only one who escaped.[2] Soon after this, a petition, styled a "Humble Memorial," was laid before the House of Representatives at Boston. It declares that in order "to kill and destroy their enemy Indians," the petitioners and forty or fifty others are ready to spend one whole year in hunting them, "provided they can meet with Encouragement suitable." The petition is signed by John Lovewell, Josiah Farwell, and Jonathan Robbins, all of Dunstable, Lovewell's name being well written, and the others after a cramped and unaccustomed fashion. The representatives accepted the proposal and voted to give each adventurer two shillings and sixpence a day, — then equal in

[1] See the inventory, in Kidder, *The Expeditions of Captain John Lovewell*, 93, 94.

[2] Other accounts say that eight of the ten were killed. The head-stone of one of the number, Thomas Lund, has these words : "This man, with seven more that lies in this grave, was slew All in A day by the Indiens."

Massachusetts currency to about one English shilling, — out of which he was to maintain himself. The men were, in addition, promised large rewards for the scalps of male Indians old enough to fight.

A company of thirty was soon raised. Lovewell was chosen captain, Farwell, lieutenant, and Robbins, ensign. They set out towards the end of November, and reappeared at Dunstable early in January, bringing one prisoner and one scalp. Towards the end of the month Lovewell set out again, this time with eighty-seven men, gathered from the villages of Dunstable, Groton, Lancaster, Haverhill, and Billerica. They ascended the frozen Merrimac, passed Lake Winnepesaukee, pushed nearly to the White Mountains, and encamped on a branch of the upper Saco. Here they killed a moose, — a timely piece of luck, for they were in danger of starvation, and Lovewell had been compelled by want of food to send back a good number of his men. The rest held their way, filing on snow-shoes through the deathlike solitude that gave no sign of life except the light track of some squirrel on the snow, and the brisk note of the hardy little chickadee, or black-capped titmouse, so familiar to the winter woods. Thus far the scouts had seen no human footprint; but on the twentieth of February they found a lately abandoned wigwam, and, following the snow-shoe tracks that led from it, at length saw smoke rising at a distance out of the gray forest. The party lay close till two o'clock in the morning; then cautiously approached, found one

received from Indians some time before, that he could not keep on with the rest, and Lovewell sent him back in charge of a kinsman, thus reducing their number to forty-four.   When they reached the west shore of Lake Ossipee, Benjamin Kidder, of Nutfield, fell seriously ill.   To leave him defenceless in a place so dangerous was not to be thought of; and his comrades built a small fort, or palisaded log-cabin, near the water, where they left the sick man in charge of the surgeon, together with Sergeant Woods and a guard of seven men.   The rest, now reduced to thirty-four, continued their march through the forest northeastward towards Pequawket, while the savage heights of the White Mountains, still covered with snow, rose above the dismal, bare forests on their left.   They seem to have crossed the Saco just below the site of Fryeburg, and in the night of May 7, as they lay in the woods near the northeast end of Lovewell's Pond, the men on guard heard sounds like Indians prowling about them.   At daybreak the next morning, as they stood bareheaded, listening to a prayer from the young chaplain, they heard the report of a gun, and soon after discovered an Indian on the shore of the pond at a considerable distance. Apparently he was shooting ducks; but Lovewell, suspecting a device to lure them into an ambuscade, asked the men whether they were for pushing forward or falling back, and with one voice they called upon him to lead them on.   They were then in a piece of open pine woods traversed by a small brook.

He ordered them to lay down their packs and advance with extreme caution. They had moved forward for some time in this manner when they met an Indian coming towards them through the dense trees and bushes. He no sooner saw them than he fired at the leading men. His gun was charged with beaver-shot; but he was so near his mark that the effect was equal to that of a bullet, and he severely wounded Lovewell and one Whiting; on which Seth Wyman shot him dead, and the chaplain and another man scalped him. Lovewell, though believed to be mortally hurt, was still able to walk, and the party fell back to the place where they had left their packs. The packs had disappeared, and suddenly, with frightful yells, the whole body of the Pequawket warriors rushed from their hiding-places, firing as they came on. The survivors say that they were more than twice the number of the whites, — which is probably an exaggeration, though their conduct, so unusual with Indians, in rushing forward instead of firing from their ambush, shows a remarkable confidence in their numerical strength.[1] They no doubt expected to strike their enemies with a panic. Lovewell received another mortal wound; but he fired more than once on the Indians as he lay dying. His two lieutenants, Farwell and Robbins, were also badly hurt. Eight others fell; but the rest stood their

---

[1] Penhallow puts their number at seventy, Hutchinson at eighty, Williamson at sixty-three, and Belknap at forty-one. In such cases the smallest number is generally nearest the truth.

ground, and pushed the Indians so hard that they drove them back to cover with heavy loss. One man played the coward, Benjamin Hassell, of Dunstable, who ran off, escaped in the confusion, and made with his best speed for the fort at Lake Ossipee.

The situation of the party was desperate, and nothing saved them from destruction but the prompt action of their surviving officers, only one of whom, Ensign Wyman, had escaped unhurt. It was probably under his direction that the men fell back steadily to the shore of the pond, which was only a few rods distant. Here the water protected their rear, so that they could not be surrounded; and now followed one of the most obstinate and deadly bush-fights in the annals of New England. It was about ten o'clock when the fight began, and it lasted till night. The Indians had the greater agility and skill in hiding and sheltering themselves, and the whites the greater steadiness and coolness in using their guns. They fought in the shade; for the forest was dense, and all alike covered themselves as they best could behind trees, bushes, or fallen trunks, where each man crouched with eyes and mind intent, firing whenever he saw, or thought he saw, the head, limbs, or body of an enemy exposed to sight for an instant. The Indians howled like wolves, yelled like enraged cougars, and made the forest ring with their whoops; while the whites replied with shouts and cheers. At one time the Indians ceased firing and drew back among the trees and undergrowth, where, by the noise they made, they seemed to be holding a "pow-wow," or incantation to procure victory; but the keen and fearless Seth Wyman crept up among the bushes, shot the chief conjurer, and broke up the meeting. About the middle of the afternoon young Frye received a mortal wound. Unable to fight longer, he lay in his blood, praying from time to time for his comrades in a faint but audible voice.

Solomon Keyes, of Billerica, received two wounds, but fought on till a third shot struck him. He then crawled up to Wyman in the heat of the fight, and told him that he, Keyes, was a dead man, but that the Indians should not get his scalp if he could help it. Creeping along the sandy edge of the pond, he chanced to find a stranded canoe, pushed it afloat, rolled himself into it, and drifted away before the wind.

Soon after sunset the Indians drew off and left the field to their enemies, living and dead, not even stopping to scalp the fallen, — a remarkable proof of the completeness of their discomfiture. Exhausted with fatigue and hunger, — for, having lost their packs in the morning, they had no food, — the surviving white men explored the scene of the fight. Jacob Farrar lay gasping his last by the edge of the water. Robert Usher and Lieutenant Robbins were unable to move. Of the thirty-four men, nine had escaped without serious injury, eleven were badly wounded, and the rest were dead or dying, except the coward who had run off.

About midnight, an hour or more before the setting of the moon, such as had strength to walk left the ground.   Robbins, as he lay helpless, asked one of them to load his gun, saying, "The Indians will come in the morning to scalp me, and I 'll kill another of 'em if I can."   They loaded the gun and left him.

To make one's way even by daylight through the snares and pitfalls of a New England forest is often a difficult task; to do so in the darkness of night and overshadowing boughs, among the fallen trees and the snarl of underbrush, was wellnigh impossible. Any but the most skilful woodsmen would have lost their way.   The Indians, sick of fighting, did not molest the party.   After struggling on for a mile or more, Farwell, Frye, and two other wounded men, Josiah Jones and Eleazer Davis, could go no farther, and, with their consent, the others left them, with a promise to send them help as soon as they should reach the fort.   In the morning the men divided into several small bands, the better to elude pursuit. One of these parties was tracked for some time by the Indians, and Elias Barron, becoming separated from his companions, was never again heard of, though the case of his gun was afterwards found by the bank of the river Ossipee.

Eleven of the number at length reached the fort, and to their amazement found nobody there.   The runaway, Hassell, had arrived many hours before them, and to excuse his flight told so frightful a story of the fate of his comrades that his hearers were seized with a panic, shamefully abandoned their post, and set out for the settlements, leaving a writing on a piece of birch-bark to the effect that all the rest were killed. They had left a supply of bread and pork, and while the famished eleven rested and refreshed themselves they were joined by Solomon Keyes, the man who, after being thrice wounded, had floated away in a canoe from the place of the fight. After drifting for a considerable distance, the wind blew him ashore, when, spurred by necessity and feeling himself "wonderfully strengthened," he succeeded in gaining the fort.

Meanwhile Frye, Farwell, and their two wounded companions, Davis and Jones, after waiting vainly for the expected help, found strength to struggle forward again, till the chaplain stopped and lay down, begging the others to keep on their way, and saying to Davis, "Tell my father that I expect in a few hours to be in eternity, and am not afraid to die." They left him, and, says the old narrative, "he has not been heard of since." He had kept the journal of the expedition, which was lost with him.

Farwell died of exhaustion. The remaining two lost their way and became separated. After wandering eleven days, Davis reached the fort at Lake Ossipee, and, finding food there, came into Berwick on the twenty-seventh. Jones, after fourteen days in the woods, arrived, half dead, at the village of Biddeford.

Some of the eleven who had first made their way to the fort, together with Keyes, who joined them there, came into Dunstable during the night of the thirteenth, and the rest followed one or two days later. Ensign Wyman, who was now the only commissioned officer left alive, and who had borne himself throughout with the utmost intrepidity, decision, and good sense, reached the same place along with three other men on the fifteenth.

The runaway, Hassell, and the guard at the fort, whom he had infected with his terror, had lost no time in making their way back to Dunstable, which they seem to have reached on the evening of the eleventh.   Horsemen were sent in haste to carry the doleful news to Boston, on which the governor gave orders to Colonel Tyng of the militia, who was then at Dunstable, to gather men in the border towns, march with all speed to the place of the fight, succor the wounded if any were still alive, and attack the Indians, if he could find them.   Tyng called upon Hassell to go with him as a guide; but he was ill, or pretended to be so, on which one of the men who had been in the fight and had just returned offered to go in his place.

When the party reached the scene of the battle, they saw the trees plentifully scarred with bullets, and presently found and buried the bodies of Lovewell, Robbins, and ten others.   The Indians, after their usual custom, had carried off or hidden their own dead; but Tyng's men discovered three of them buried together, and one of these was recognized as the war-chief Paugus, killed by Wyman, or, according to a more than doubtful tradition, by John Chamberlain.[1] Not a living Indian was to be seen.

The Pequawkets were cowed by the rough handling they had met when they plainly expected a victory. Some of them joined their Abenaki kinsmen in Canada and remained there, while others returned after the peace to their old haunts by the Saco; but they never again raised the hatchet against the English.

Lovewell's Pond, with its sandy beach, its two green islands, and its environment of lonely forests, reverted for a while to its original owners, — the wolf, bear, lynx, and moose. In our day all is changed. Farms and dwellings possess those peaceful shores, and hard by, where, at the bend of the Saco, once stood, in picturesque squalor, the wigwams of the vanished Pequawkets, the village of Fryeburg preserves the name of the brave young

---

[1] The tradition is that Chamberlain and Paugus went down to the small brook, now called Fight Brook, to clean their guns, hot and foul with frequent firing; that they saw each other at the same instant, and that the Indian said to the white man, in his broken English, "Me kill you quick!" at the same time hastily loading his piece; to which Chamberlain coolly replied, "Maybe not." His firelock had a large touch-hole, so that the powder could be shaken out into the pan, and the gun made to prime itself. Thus he was ready for action an instant sooner than his enemy, whom he shot dead just as Paugus pulled trigger, and sent a bullet whistling over his head. The story has no good foundation, while the popular ballad, written at the time, and very faithful to the facts, says that, the other officers being killed, the English made Wyman their captain, —

"Who shot the old chief Paugus, which did the foe defeat,
Then set his men in order and brought off the retreat."

chaplain, whose memory is still cherished, in spite of his uncanonical turn for scalping.[1]   He had engaged himself to a young girl of a neighboring village, Susanna Rogers, daughter of John Rogers, minister of Boxford.   It has been said that Frye's parents thought her beneath him in education and position; but this is not likely, for her father belonged to what has been called the "Brahmin caste" of New England, and, like others of his family, had had, at Harvard, the best education that the country could supply.   The girl herself, though only fourteen years old, could make verses, such as they were; and she wrote an elegy on the death of her lover which, bating some grammatical lapses, deserves the modest praise of being no worse than many New England rhymes of that day.

The courage of Frye and his sturdy comrades contributed greatly to the pacification which in the next year relieved the borders from the scourge of Indian war.[2]

---

[1] The town, however, was not named for the chaplain, but for his father's cousin, General Joseph Frye, the original grantee of the land.

[2] Rev. Thomas Symmes, minister of Bradford, preached a sermon on the fate of Lovewell and his men immediately after the return of the survivors, and printed it, with a much more valuable introduction, giving a careful account of the affair, on the evidence of "the Valorous Captain Wyman and some others of good Credit that were in the Engagement." Wyman had just been made a captain, in recognition of his conduct. The narrative is followed by an attestation of its truth signed by him and two others of Lovewell's band.

A considerable number of letters relating to the expedition are preserved in the Massachusetts Archives, from Benjamin Hassell, Colonel Tyng, Governor Dummer of Massachusetts, and Governor Wentworth of New Hampshire. They give the various reports received from those in the fight, and show the action taken in consequence. The Archives also contain petitions from the survivors and the families of the slain; and the legislative Journals show that the petitioners received large grants of land. Lovewell's debts contracted in raising men for his expeditions were also paid.

The papers mentioned above, with other authentic records concerning the affair, have been printed by Kidder in his *Expeditions of Captain John Lovewell*, a monograph of thorough research. The names of all Lovewell's party, and biographical notices of some of them, are also given by Mr. Kidder. Compare Penhallow, Hutchinson, Fox, *History of Dunstable*, and Bouton, *Lovewell's Great Fight*. For various suggestions touching Lovewell's Expedition, I am indebted to Mr. C. W. Lewis, who has made it the subject of minute and careful study.

A ballad which was written when the event was fresh, and was long popular in New England, deserves mention, if only for its general fidelity to the facts. The following is a sample of its eighteen stanzas : —

> "'T was ten o'clock in the morning when first the fight begun,
> And fiercely did continue till the setting of the sun,
> Excepting that the Indians, some hours before 't was night,
> Drew off into the bushes, and ceased awhile to fight ;

> "But soon again returnèd in fierce and furious mood,
> Shouting as in the morning, but yet not half so loud ;
> For, as we are informèd, so thick and fast they fell,
> Scarce twenty of their number at night did get home well.

> .   .   .   .

> "Our worthy Captain Lovewell among them there did die;
> They killed Lieutenant Robbins, and wounded good young **Frye**,
> Who was our English chaplain ; he many Indians slew,
> And some of them he scalped when bullets round him flew."

Frye, as mentioned in the text, had engaged himself to Susanna Rogers, a young girl of the village of Boxford, who, after his death, wrote some untutored verses to commemorate his fate. They **are** entitled, *A Mournful Elegy on Mr. Jonathan Frye*, and begin thus ·

"Assist, ye muses, help my quill,
  Whilst floods of tears does down distil;
  Not from mine eyes alone, but all
  That hears the sad and doleful fall
  Of that young student, Mr. Frye,
  Who in his blooming youth did die.
  Fighting for his dear country's good,
  He lost his life and precious blood.
  His father's only son was he;
  His mother loved him tenderly;
  And all that knew him loved him well;
  For in bright parts he did excel
  Most of his age; for he was young, —
  Just entering on twenty-one;
  A comely youth, and pious too;
  This l affirm, for him I knew."

She then describes her lover's brave deeds, and sad but heroic
death, alone in a howling wilderness; condoles with the bereaved
parents, exhorts them to resignation, and touches modestly on her
own sorrow.

In more recent times the fate of Lovewell and his companions
has inspired several poetical attempts, which need not be dwelt
upon. Lovewell's Fight, as Dr. Palfrey observes, was long as
famous in New England as Chevy Chase on the Scottish Border.

CHAPTER XII.

1712.

THE OUTAGAMIES AT DETROIT.

THE WEST AND THE FUR-TRADE. — NEW YORK AND CANADA. — INDIAN POPULATION. — THE FIREBRANDS OF THE WEST. — DETROIT IN 1712. — DANGEROUS VISITORS. — SUSPENSE. — TIMELY SUCCORS. — THE OUTAGAMIES ATTACKED: THEIR DESPERATE POSITION. — OVERTURES. — WAVERING ALLIES. — CONDUCT OF DUBUISSON. — ESCAPE OF THE OUTAGAMIES. — PURSUIT AND ATTACK. — VICTORY AND CARNAGE.

WE have seen that the Peace of Utrecht was followed by a threefold conflict for ascendency in America, — the conflict for Acadia, the conflict for northern New England, and the conflict for the Great West; which last could not be said to take at once an international character, being essentially a competition for the fur-trade. Only one of the English colonies took an active part in it, — the province of New York. Alone among her sister communities she had a natural thoroughfare to the West, not comparable, however, with that of Canada, to whose people the St. Lawrence, the Great Lakes, and their tributary waters were a continual invitation to the vast interior.

Virginia and Pennsylvania were not yet serious rivals in the fur-trade; and New England, the most active of the British colonies, was barred out from it by the interposition of New York, which lay across her westward path, thus forcing her to turn her energies to the sea, where half a century later her achievements inspired the glowing panegyrics of Burke before the House of Commons.

New York, then, was for many years the only rival of Canada for the control of the West. It was a fatal error in the rulers of New France that they did not, in the seventeenth century, use more strenuous efforts to possess themselves, by purchase, exchange, or conquest, of this troublesome and dangerous neighbor. There was a time, under the reign of Charles II., when negotiation for the purchase of New York might have been successful; and if this failed, the conquest of the province, if attempted by forces equal to the importance of the object, would have been far from hopeless. With New York in French hands, the fate of the continent would probably have been changed. The British possessions would have been cut in two. New England, isolated and placed in constant jeopardy, would have vainly poured her unmanageable herds of raw militia against the disciplined veterans of Old France intrenched at the mouth of the Hudson. Canada would have gained complete control of her old enemies, the Iroquois, who would have been wholly dependent on her for the arms and ammunition without which they could do nothing.

The Iroquois, as the French had been accustomed to call them, were known to the English as the Five

Nations, — a name which during the eighteenth century the French also adopted. Soon after the Peace of Utrecht, a kindred tribe, the Tuscaroras, was joined to the original five members of the confederacy, which thenceforward was sometimes called the Six Nations, though the Tuscaroras were never very prominent in its history; and, to avoid confusion, we will keep the more familiar name of the Five Nations, which the French used to the last.

For more than two generations this league of tribes had held Canada in terror, and more than once threatened it with destruction. But now a change had come over the confederates. Count Frontenac had humbled their pride. They were crowded between the rival European nations, both of whom they distrusted. Their traditional hatred of the French would have given the English of New York a controlling influence over them if the advantage had been used with energy and tact. But a narrow and short-sighted conduct threw it away. A governor of New York, moreover, even were he as keen and far-seeing as Frontenac himself, would often have been helpless. When the Five Nations were attacked by the French, he had no troops to defend them, nor could he, like a Canadian governor, call out the forces of his province by a word, to meet the exigency. The small revenues of New York were not at his disposal. Without the votes of the frugal representatives of an impoverished people, his hands were tied. Hence the Five Nations, often left unaided when they most needed help, looked upon their Dutch and English neighbors as slothful and unwarlike.

Yet their friendship was of the greatest importance to the province, in peace as well as in war, and was indispensable in the conflict that New York was waging single-handed for the control of the western fur-trade. The Five Nations, as we have seen,[1] acted as middlemen between the New York merchants and the tribes of the far interior, and through them English goods and English influence penetrated all the lake country, and reached even to the Mississippi.

These vast western regions, now swarming with laborious millions, were then scantily peopled by savage hordes, whose increase was stopped by incessant mutual slaughter. This wild population had various centres or rallying-points, usually about the French forts, which protected them from enemies and supplied their wants. Thus the Pottawattamies, Ottawas, and Hurons were gathered about Detroit, and the Illinois about Fort St. Louis, on the river Illinois, where Henri de Tonty and his old comrade, La Forest, with fifteen or twenty Frenchmen, held a nominal monopoly of the neighboring fur-trade. Another focus of Indian population was near the Green Bay of Lake Michigan, and on Fox River, which enters it. Here were grouped the Sacs, Winnebagoes, and Menominies, with the Outagamies, or Foxes, a formidable tribe, the source of endless trouble to the French.

[1] See Chapter I.

The constant aim of the Canadian authorities was
to keep these western savages at peace among themselves, while preventing their establishing relations
of trade with the Five Nations, and carrying their
furs to them in exchange for English goods.   The
position was delicate, for while a close understanding
between the western tribes and the Five Nations
would be injurious to French interests, a quarrel
would be still more so, since the French would then
be forced to side with their western allies, and so be
drawn into hostilities with the Iroquois confederacy,
which of all things they most wished to avoid.   Peace
and friendship among the western tribes; peace without friendship between these tribes and the Five
Nations, — thus became maxims of French policy.
The Canadian governor called the western Indians
his "children," and a family quarrel among them
would have been unfortunate, since the loving father
must needs have become involved in it, to the detri-
ment of his trading interests.

Yet to prevent such quarrels was difficult, partly
because they had existed time out of mind, and partly
because it was the interest of the English to promote
them.   Dutch and English traders, it is true, took
their lives in their hands if they ventured among the
western Indians, who were encouraged by their
French father to plunder and kill them, and who on
occasion rarely hesitated to do so.   Hence English
communication with the West was largely carried
on through the Five Nations.   Iroquois messengers,

hired for the purpose, carried wampum belts "underground "— that is, secretly — to such of the interior tribes as were disposed to listen with favor to the words of Corlaer, as they called the governor of New York.

In spite of their shortcomings, the English had one powerful attraction for all the tribes alike. This was the abundance and excellence of their goods, which, with the exception of gunpowder, were better as well as cheaper than those offered by the French. The Indians, it is true, liked the taste of French brandy more than that of English rum; yet as their chief object in drinking was to get drunk, and as rum would supply as much intoxication as brandy at a lower price, it always found favor in their eyes. In the one case, to get thoroughly drunk often cost a beaver-skin; in the other, the same satisfaction could generally be had for a mink-skin.

Thus the French found that some of their western children were disposed to listen to English seductions, look askance at their father Onontio, and turn their canoes, not towards Montreal, but towards Albany. Nor was this the worst; for there were some of Onontio's wild and unruly western family too ready to lift their hatchets against their brethren and fill the wilderness with discord. Consequences followed most embarrassing to the French, and among them an incident prominent in the early annals of Detroit, that new establishment so obnoxious to the English, because it barred their way to the northern lakes, so that they were extremely anxious to rid themselves of it.

In the confused and tumultuous history of the savages of this continent one now and then sees some tribe or league of tribes possessed for a time with a spirit of conquest and havoc that made it the terror of its neighbors.   Of this the foremost example is that of the Five Nations of the Iroquois, who, towards the middle of the seventeenth century, swept all before them and made vast regions a solitude.   They were now comparatively quiet; but far in the North-west, another people, inferior in number, organiza-tion, and mental capacity, but not in ferocity or courage, had begun on a smaller scale, and with less conspicuous success, to play a similar part.   These were the Outagamies, or Foxes, with their allies, the Kickapoos and the Mascoutins, all living at the time within the limits of the present States of Wis-consin and Illinois, — the Outagamies near Fox River, and the others on Rock River.[1]   The Outagamies, in particular, seem to have been seized with an access of homicidal fury.   Their hand was against every man, and for twenty years and more they were the firebrands of the West, and a ceaseless peril to French interests in that region.   They were, however, on good terms with the Five Nations, by means of whom, as French writers say, the Dutch and English of Albany sent them gifts and messages to incite

[1] *Memoir on the Indians between Lake Erie and the Mississippi*, in *N. Y. Col. Docs.*, ix. 885.

them to kill French traders and destroy the French fort at Detroit. This is not unlikely, though the evidence on the point is far from conclusive.

Fort Ponchartrain, better known as Fort Detroit, was an enclosure of palisades, flanked by blockhouses at the corners, with an open space within to serve as a parade-ground, around which stood small wooden houses thatched with straw or meadow-grass. La Mothe-Cadillac, founder of the post, had been made governor of the new colony of Louisiana, and the Sieur Dubuisson now commanded at Detroit. There were about thirty French traders, *voyageurs*, and *coureurs de bois* in the place, but at this time no soldiers.

The village of the Pottawattamies was close to the French fort; that of the Hurons was not far distant, by the edge of the river. Their houses were those structures of bark, "very high, very long, and arched like garden arbors," which were common to all the tribes of Iroquois stock, and both villages were enclosed by strong double or triple stockades, such as Cartier had found at Hochelaga, and Champlain in the Onondaga country. Their neighbors, the Ottawas, who were on the east side of the river, had imitated, with imperfect success, their way of housing and fortifying themselves. These tribes raised considerable crops of peas, beans, and Indian corn; and except when engaged in their endless dances and games of ball, dressed, like the converts of the mission villages, in red or blue cloth.[1] The Hurons

---

[1] *Memoir on the Indians between Lake Erie and the Mississippi.*

were reputed the most intelligent as well as the bravest of all the western tribes, and, being incensed by various outrages, they bore against the Outagamies a deadly grudge, which was shared by the other tribes, their neighbors.

All these friendly Indians were still absent on their winter hunt, when, at the opening of spring, Dubuisson and his Frenchmen were startled by a portentous visitation. Two bands of Outagamies and Mascoutins, men, women, and children, counting in all above a thousand, of whom about three hundred were warriors, appeared on the meadows behind the fort, approached to within pistol-shot of the palisades, and encamped there. It is by no means certain that they came with deliberate hostile intent. Had this been the case, they would not have brought their women and children. A paper ascribed to the engineer Léry says, moreover, that their visit was in consequence of an invitation from the late commandant, La Mothe-Cadillac, whose interest it was to attract to Detroit as many Indians as possible, in order to trade for their furs.[1] Dubuisson, however, was satisfied that they meant mischief, especially when, in spite of all his efforts to prevent them, they fortified themselves by cutting down young trees and surrounding their wigwams with a rough fence of palisades. They were rude and insolent, declared that all that country was theirs, and killed fowls and pigeons

[1] This paper is printed, not very accurately, in the *Collection de Documents relatifs à la Nouvelle France*, i. 623 (Québec, 1883).

belonging to the French, who, in the absence of their friends, the Hurons and Ottawas, dared not even remonstrate. Dubuisson himself was forced to submit to their insults in silence, till a party of them came one day into the fort bent on killing two of the French, a man and a girl, against whom they had taken some offence. The commandant then ordered his men to drive them out; which was done, and henceforward he was convinced that the Outagamies and Mascoutins were only watching their opportunity to burn the fort and butcher its inmates. Soon after, their excitement redoubled. News came that a band of Mascoutins, who had wintered on the river St. Joseph, had been cut off by the Ottawas and Pottawattamies, led by an Ottawa chief named Saguina; on which the behavior of the dangerous visitors became so threatening that Dubuisson hastily sent a canoe to recall the Hurons and Ottawas from their hunting-grounds, and a second to invite the friendly Ojibwas and Mississagas to come to his aid. No doubt there was good cause for alarm; yet if the dangerous strangers had resolved to strike, they would have been apt to strike at once, instead of waiting week after week, when they knew that the friends and allies of the French might arrive at any time. Dubuisson, however, felt that the situation was extremely critical, and he was confirmed in his anxiety by a friendly Outagamie, who, after the news of the massacre on the St. Joseph, told him that his tribesmen meant to burn the fort.

The church was outside the palisade, as were also several houses, one of which was stored with wheat. This the Outagamies tried to seize. The French fired on them, drove them back, and brought most of the wheat into the fort; then they demolished the church and several of the houses, which would have given cover to the assailants and enabled them to set fire to the palisade, close to which the buildings stood. The French worked at their task in the excitement of desperation, for they thought that all was lost.

The irritation of their savage neighbors so increased that an outbreak seemed imminent, when, on the thirteenth of May, the Sieur de Vincennes arrived, with seven or eight Frenchmen, from the Miami country. The reinforcement was so small that instead of proving a help it might have provoked a crisis. Vincennes brought no news of the Indian allies, who were now Dubuisson's only hope. "I did not know on what saint to call," he writes, almost in despair, when suddenly a Huron Indian came panting into the fort with the joyful news that both his people and the Ottawas were close at hand. Nor was this all. The Huron messenger announced that Makisabie, war-chief of the Pottawattamies, was then at the Huron fort, and that six hundred warriors of various tribes, deadly enemies of the Outagamies and Mascoutins, would soon arrive and destroy them all.

Here was an unlooked-for deliverance. Yet the danger was not over; for there was fear lest the Outagamies and their allies, hearing of the approaching succor, might make a desperate onslaught, burn the French fort, and kill its inmates before their friends could reach them.   An interval of suspense followed, relieved at last by a French sentinel, who called to Dubuisson that a crowd of Indians was in sight.   The commandant mounted to the top of a blockhouse, and, looking across the meadows behind the fort, saw a throng of savages coming out of the woods, — Pottawattamies, Sacs, Menominies, Illinois, Missouris, and other tribes yet more remote, each band distinguished by a kind of ensign.   These were the six hundred warriors promised by the Huron messenger, and with them, as it proved, came the Ottawa war-chief Saguina.   Having heard during the winter that the Outagamies and Mascoutins would go to Detroit in the spring, these various tribes had combined to attack the common enemy; and they now marched with great ostentation and some show of order, not to the French fort, but to the fortified village of the Hurons, who with their neighbors, the Ottawas, had arrived just before them.

The Hurons were reputed leaders among the western tribes, and they hated the Outagamies, not only by reason of bitter wrongs, but also through jealousy of the growing importance which these fierce upstarts had won by their sanguinary prowess.   The Huron chiefs came to meet the motley crew of warriors, and urged them to instant action.   "You must not stop to encamp," said the Huron spokesman; "we must all go this moment to the fort of our fathers, the French, and fight for them." Then, turning to the Ottawa war-chief: "Do you see that smoke, Saguina, rising from the camp of our enemies? They are burning three women of your village, and your wife is one of them." The Outagamies had, in fact, three Ottawa squaws in their clutches; but the burning was an invention of the crafty Huron. It answered its purpose, and wrought the hearers to fury. They ran with yells and whoops towards the French fort, the Hurons and Ottawas leading the way. A burst of answering yells rose from the camp of the enemy, and about forty of their warriors ran out in bravado, stripped naked and brandishing their weapons; but they soon fell back within their defences before the approaching multitude.

Just before the arrival of the six hundred allies, Dubuisson, whose orders were to keep the peace, if he could, among the western tribes, had sent Vincennes to the Huron village with a proposal that they should spare the lives of the Outagamies and Mascoutins, and rest content with driving them away; to which the Hurons returned a fierce and haughty refusal. There was danger that, if vexed or thwarted, the rabble of excited savages now gathered before the fort might turn from friends into enemies, and in some burst of wild caprice lift parricidal tomahawks against their French fathers. Dubuisson saw no choice but to humor them, put himself at their head, aid them in their vengeance, and even set them on. Therefore, when they called out for admittance, he did not venture to refuse it, but threw open the gate.

The savage crew poured in till the fort was full. The chiefs gathered for council on the parade, and the warriors crowded around, a living wall of dusky forms, befeathered heads, savage faces, lank snaky locks, and deep-set eyes that glittered with a devilish light. Their orator spoke briefly, but to the purpose. He declared that all present were ready to die for their French father, who had stood their friend against the bloody and perfidious Outagamies. Then he begged for food, tobacco, gunpowder, and bullets. Dubuisson replied with equal conciseness, thanked them for their willingness to die for him, said that he would do his best to supply their wants, and promised an immediate distribution of powder and bullets; to which the whole assembly answered with yells of joy.

Then the council dissolved, and the elder warriors stalked about the fort, haranguing their followers, exhorting them to fight like men and obey the orders of their father. The powder and bullets were served out, after which the whole body, white men and red, yelled the war-whoop together, — "a horrible cry, that made the earth tremble," writes Dubuisson.[1] An answering howl, furious and defiant, rose close at hand from the palisaded camp of the enemy, the firing began on both sides, and bullets and arrows filled the air.

[1] "Cri horrible, dont la terre trembla." — *Dubuisson à Vaudreuil*, 15 *Juin*, 1712. This is the official report of the affair.

The French and their allies outnumbered their enemies fourfold, while the Outagamie and Mascoutin warriors were encumbered with more than seven hundred women and children. Their frail defences might have been carried by assault; but the loss to the assailants must needs have been great against so brave and desperate a foe, and such a mode of attack is repugnant to the Indian genius. Instead, therefore, of storming the palisaded camp, the allies beleaguered it with vindictive patience, and wore out its defenders by a fire that ceased neither day nor night. The French raised two tall scaffolds, from which they overlooked the palisade, and sent their shot into the midst of those within, who were forced, for shelter, to dig holes in the ground four or five feet deep, and ensconce themselves there. The situation was almost hopeless, but their courage did not fail. They raised twelve red English blankets on poles as battle-flags, to show that they would fight to the death, and hung others over their palisades, calling out that they wished to see the whole earth red, like them, with blood; that they had no fathers but the English, and that the other tribes had better do as they did, and turn their backs to Onontio.

The great war-chief of the Pottawattamies now mounted to the top of one of the French scaffolds, and harangued the enemy to this effect: "Do you think, you wretches, that you can frighten us by hanging out those red blankets? If the earth is red with blood, it will be your own. You talk about the

English. Their bad advice will be your ruin. They are enemies of religion, and that is why the Master of Life punishes both them and you. They are cowards, and can only defend themselves by poisoning people with their firewater, which kills a man the instant he drinks it. We shall soon see what you will get for listening to them."

This Homeric dialogue between the chief combatants was stopped by Dubuisson, who saw that it distracted the attention of the warriors, and so enabled the besieged to run to the adjacent river for water. The firing was resumed more fiercely than ever. Before night twelve of the Indian allies were killed in the French fort, though the enemy suffered a much greater loss. One house had been left standing outside the French palisades, and the Outagamies raised a scaffold behind its bullet-proof gable, under cover of which they fired with great effect. The French at length brought two swivels to bear upon the gable, pierced it, knocked down the scaffold, killed some of the marksmen, and scattered the rest in consternation.

Famine and thirst were worse for the besieged than the bullets and arrows of the allies. Parched, starved, and fainting, they could no longer find heart for bravado, and they called out one evening from behind their defences to ask Dubuisson if they might come to speak with him. He called together the allied chiefs, and all agreed that here was an opportunity to get out of the hands of the Outagamies the three

Ottawa women whom they held prisoners.   The commandant, therefore, told them that if they had anything to say to their father before dying, they might come and say it in safety.

In the morning all the red blankets had disappeared, and a white flag was waving over the hostile camp. The great Outagamie chief, Pemoussa, presently came out, carrying a smaller white flag and followed by two Indian slaves.· Dubuisson sent his interpreter to protect him from insult and conduct him to the parade, where all the allied chiefs presently met to hear him.

"My father," he began, "I am a dead man.   The sky is bright for you, and dark as night for me." Then he held out a belt of wampum, and continued: "By this belt I ask you, my father, to take pity on your children, and grant us two days in which our old men may counsel together to find means of appeasing your wrath."   Then, offering another belt to the assembled chiefs, "This belt is to pray you to remember that you are of our kin.   If you spill our blood, do not forget that it is also your own.   Try to soften the heart of our father, whom we have offended so often.   These two slaves are to replace some of the blood you have lost.   Grant us the two days we ask, for I cannot say more till our old men have held counsel."

To which Dubuisson answered in the name of all: "If your hearts were really changed, and you honestly accepted Onontio as your father, you would have

brought back the three women who are prisoners in
your hands. As you have not done so, I think that
your hearts are still bad. First bring them to me,
if you expect me to hear you. I have no more to
say."

"I am but a child," replied the envoy. "I will go
back to my village, and tell our old men what you
have said."

The council then broke up, and several Frenchmen
conducted the chief back to his followers.

Three other chiefs soon after appeared, bearing a
flag and bringing the Ottawa squaws, one of whom
was the wife of the war-chief, Saguina. Again the
elders met in council on the parade, and the orator
of the deputation spoke thus: "My father, here are
the three pieces of flesh that you ask of us. We
would not eat them, lest you should be angry. Do
with them what you please, for you are the master.
Now we ask that you will send away the nations that
are with you, so that we may seek food for our
women and children, who die of hunger every day.
If you are as good a father as your other children say
you are, you will not refuse us this favor."

But Dubuisson, having gained his point and recovered the squaws, spoke to them sternly, and referred
them to his Indian allies for their answer. Whereupon the head chief of the Illinois, being called upon
by the rest to speak in their behalf, addressed the
envoys to this effect: "Listen to me, you who have
troubled all the earth. We see plainly that you

mean only to deceive our father. If we should leave him, as you wish, you would fall upon him and kill him. You are dogs who have always bitten him. You thought that we did not know all the messages you have had from the English, telling you to cut our father's throat, and then bring them into this our country. We will not leave him alone with you. We shall see who will be the master. Go back to your fort. We are going to fire at you again."

The envoys went back with a French escort to prevent their being murdered on the way, and then the firing began again. The Outagamies and Mascoutins gathered strength from desperation, and sent flights of fire-arrows into the fort to burn the straw-thatched houses. The flames caught in many places; but with the help of the Indians they were extinguished, though several Frenchmen were wounded, and there was great fright for a time. But the thatch was soon stripped off and the roofs covered with deer and bear skins, while mops fastened to long poles, and two large wooden canoes filled with water, were made ready for future need.

A few days after, a greater peril threatened the French. If the wild Indian has the passions of a devil, he has also the instability of a child; and this is especially true when a number of incoherent tribes or bands are joined in a common enterprise. Dubuisson's Indians became discouraged, partly at the stubborn resistance of the enemy, and partly at the scarcity of food. Some of them declared openly that they could never conquer those people; that they knew them well, and that they were braver than anybody else. In short, the French saw themselves on the point of being abandoned by their allies to a fate the most ghastly and appalling; and they urged upon the commandant the necessity of escaping to Michilimackinac before it was too late. Dubuisson appears to have met the crisis with equal resolution and address. He braced the shaken nerves of his white followers by appeals to their sense of shame, threats of the governor's wrath, and assurances that all would yet be well; then set himself to the more difficult task of holding the Indian allies to their work. He says that he scarcely ate or slept for four days and nights, during which time he was busied without ceasing in private and separate interviews with all the young war-chiefs, persuading them, flattering them, and stripping himself of all he had to make them presents. When at last he had gained them over, he called the tribes to a general council.

"What, children!" thus he addressed them, "when you are on the very point of destroying these wicked people, do you think of shamefully running away? How could you ever hold up your heads again? All the other nations would say: 'Are these the brave warriors who deserted the French and ran like cowards?'" And he reminded them that their enemies were already half dead with famine, and that they could easily make an end of them, thereby gaining great honor among the nations, besides the thanks and favors of Onontio, the father of all.

At this the young war-chiefs whom he had gained over interrupted him and cried out, "My father, somebody has been lying to you. We are not cowards. We love you too much to abandon you, and we will stand by you till the last of your enemies is dead." The elder men caught the contagion, and cried, "Come on, let us show our father that those who have spoken ill of us are liars." Then they all raised the war-whoop, sang the war-song, danced the war-dance, and began to fire again.

Among the enemy were some Sakis, or Sacs, fighting for the Outagamies, while others of their tribe were among the allies of the French. Seeing the desperate turn of affairs, they escaped from time to time and came over to the winning side, bringing reports of the state of the beleaguered camp. They declared that sixty or eighty women and children were already dead from hunger and thirst, besides those killed by bullets and arrows; that the fire of the besiegers was so hot that the bodies could not be buried, and that the camp of the Outagamies and Mascoutins was a den of infection.

The end was near. The besieged savages called from their palisades to ask if they might send another deputation, and were told that they were free to do so. The chief, Pemoussa, soon appeared at the gate of the fort, naked, painted from head to foot with green earth, wearing belts of wampum about his waist, and others hanging from his shoulders, besides a kind of crown of wampum beads on his head. With him came seven women, meant as a peace-offering, all painted and adorned with wampum. Three other principal chiefs followed, each with a gourd rattle in his hand, to the cadence of which the whole party sang and shouted at the full stretch of their lungs an invocation to the spirits for help and pity. They were conducted to the parade, where the French and the allied chiefs were already assembled, and Pemoussa thus addressed them: —

"My father, and all the nations here present, I come to ask for life. It is no longer ours, but yours. I bring you these seven women, who are my flesh, and whom I put at your feet, to be your slaves. But do not think that I am afraid to die; it is the life of our women and children that I ask of you." He then offered six wampum belts, in token that his followers owned themselves beaten, and begged for mercy. "Tell us, I pray you," — these were his last words, — "something that will lighten the hearts of my people when I go back to them."

Dubuisson left the answer to his allies. The appeal of the suppliant fell on hearts of stone. The whole concourse sat in fierce and sullen silence, and the envoys read their doom in the gloomy brows that surrounded them. Eight or ten of the allied savages presently came to Dubuisson, and one of them said in a low voice: "My father, we come to ask your leave to knock these four great chiefs in the head.

It is they who prevent our enemies from surrendering without conditions. When they are dead, the rest will be at our mercy."

Dubuisson told them that they must be drunk to propose such a thing. "Remember," he said, "that both you and I have given our word for their safety. If I consented to what you ask, your father at Montreal would never forgive me. Besides, you can see plainly that they and their people cannot escape you."

The would-be murderers consented to bide their time, and the wretched envoys went back with their tidings of despair.

"I confess," wrote Dubuisson to the governor, a few days later, "that I was touched with compassion; but as war and pity do not agree well together, and especially as I understood that they were hired by the English to destroy us, I abandoned them to their fate."

The firing began once more, and the allied hordes howled round the camp of their victims like troops of ravenous wolves. But a surprise awaited them. Indians rarely set guards at night, and they felt sure now of their prey. It was the nineteenth day of the siege.[1] The night closed dark and rainy, and when morning came, the enemy were gone. All among them that had strength to move had glided away through the gloom with the silence of shadows, passed the camps of their sleeping enemies, and

---

[1] According to the paper ascribed to Léry it was only the eighth.

reached a point of land projecting into the river opposite the end of Isle au Cochon, and a few miles above the French fort. Here, knowing that they would be pursued, they barricaded themselves with trunks and branches of trees. When the astonished allies discovered their escape, they hastily followed their trail, accompanied by some of the French, led by Vincennes. In their eagerness they ran upon the barricade before seeing it, and were met by a fire that killed and wounded twenty of them. There was no alternative but to forego their revenge and abandon the field, or begin another siege. Encouraged by Dubuisson, they built their wigwams on the new scene of operations; and, being supplied by the French with axes, mattocks, and two swivels, they made a wall of logs opposite the barricade, from which they galled the defenders with a close and deadly fire. The Mississagas and Ojibwas, who had lately arrived, fished and hunted for the allies, while the French furnished them with powder, ball, tobacco, Indian corn, and kettles. The enemy fought desperately for four days, and then, in utter exhaustion, surrendered at discretion.[1]

The women and children were divided among the victorious hordes, and adopted or enslaved. To the men no quarter was given. "Our Indians amused themselves," writes Dubuisson, "with shooting four

---

[1] The paper ascribed to Léry says that they surrendered on a promise from Vincennes that their lives should be spared, but that the promise availed nothing.

or five of them every day." Here, however, another surprise awaited the conquerors and abridged their recreation, for about a hundred of these intrepid warriors contrived to make their escape, and among them was the great war-chief Pemoussa.

The Outagamies were crippled, but not disabled, for but a part of the tribe was involved in this bloody affair. The rest were wrought to fury by the fate of their kinsmen, and for many years they remained thorns in the sides of the French.

There is a disposition to assume that events like that just recounted were a consequence of the contact of white men with red; but the primitive Indian was quite able to enact such tragedies without the help of Europeans. Before French or English influence had been felt in the interior of the continent, a great part of North America was the frequent witness of scenes still more lurid in coloring, and on a larger scale of horror. In the first half of the seventeenth century the whole country, from Lake Superior to the Tennessee, and from the Alleghanies to the Mississippi, was ravaged by wars of extermination, in which tribes, large and powerful by Indian standards, perished, dwindled into feeble remnants, or were absorbed by other tribes and vanished from sight. French pioneers were sometimes involved in the carnage, but neither they nor other Europeans were answerable for it.[1]

---

[1] *Dubuisson à Vaudreuil*, 15 *Juin*, 1712. This is Dubuisson's report to the governor, which soon after the event he sent to Montreal

by the hands of Vincennes. He says that the great fatigue through
which he has just passed prevents him from giving every detail,
and he refers Vaudreuil to the bearer for further information. The
report is, however, long and circumstantial.

*État de ce que M. Dubuisson a dépensé pour le service du Roy pour
s'attirer les Nations et les mettre dans ses intérêts afin de résister aux
Outagamis et aux Mascoutins qui étaient payés des Anglais pour détru-
ire le poste du Fort de Ponchartrain du Détroit*, 14 *Octobre*, 1712.
Dubuisson reckons his outlay at 2,901 livres.

These documents, with the narrative ascribed to the engineer
Léry, are the contemporary authorities on which the foregoing
account is based.

CHAPTER XIII.

1697–1750.

LOUISIANA.

The Mississippi to be occupied. — English Rivalry. — Iberville. — Bienville. — Huguenots. — Views of Louis XIV. — Wives for the Colony. — Slaves. — La Mothe-Cadillac. — Paternal Government. — Crozat's Monopoly. — Factions. — The Mississippi Company. — New Orleans. — The Bubble bursts. — Indian Wars. — The Colony firmly established. — The two Heads of New France.

At the beginning of the eighteenth century an event took place that was to have a great influence on the future of French America. This was the occupation by France of the mouth of the Mississippi, and the vindication of her claim to the vast and undefined regions which La Salle had called Louisiana. La Salle's schemes had come to nought, but they were revived, seven years after his death, by his lieutenant, the gallant and faithful Henri de Tonty, who urged the seizure of Louisiana for three reasons, — first, as a base of attack upon Mexico; secondly, as a dépôt for the furs and lead ore of the interior; and thirdly, as the only means of preventing the English from becoming masters of the West.[1]

[1] *Henri de Tonty à Cabart de Villermont,* 11 *Septembre,* 1694 (Margry, iv. 3).

Three years later, the Sieur de Rémonville, a friend of La Salle, proposed the formation of a company for the settlement of Louisiana, and called for immediate action as indispensable to anticipate the English.[1] The English were, in fact, on the point of taking possession of the mouth of the Mississippi, and were prevented only by the prompt intervention of the rival nation.

If they had succeeded, colonies would have grown up on the Gulf of Mexico after the type of those already planted along the Atlantic: voluntary immigrants would have brought to a new home their old inheritance of English freedom; would have ruled themselves by laws of their own making, through magistrates of their own choice; would have depended on their own efforts, and not on government help, in the invigorating consciousness that their destinies were in their own hands, and that they themselves, and not others, were to gather the fruits of their toils. Out of conditions like these would have sprung communities, not brilliant, but healthy, orderly, well rooted in the soil, and of hardy and vigorous growth.

But the principles of absolutism, and not those of a regulated liberty, were to rule in Louisiana. The new French colony was to be the child of the Crown. Cargoes of emigrants, willing or unwilling, were to be shipped by authority to the fever-stricken banks

---

[1] *Mémoire sur le Projet d'establir une nouvelle Colonie au Missis-sippi*, 1697 (Margry, iv. 21).

of the Mississippi, — cargoes made up in part of those whom fortune and their own defects had sunk to dependence; to whom labor was strange and odious, but who dreamed of gold mines and pearl fisheries, and wealth to be won in the New World and spent in the Old; who wore the shackles of a paternal despotism which they were told to regard as of divine institution; who were at the mercy of military rulers set over them by the King, and agreeing in nothing except in enforcing the mandates of arbitrary power and the withering maxim that the labor of the colonist was due, not to himself, but to his masters. It remains to trace briefly the results of such conditions.

The before-mentioned scheme of Rémonville for settling the Mississippi country had no result. In the next year the gallant Le Moyne d'Iberville — who has been called the Cid, or, more fitly, the Jean Bart, of Canada — offered to carry out the schemes of La Salle and plant a colony in Louisiana.[1] One thing had become clear, — France must act at once, or lose the Mississippi. Already there was a movement in London to seize upon it, under a grant to two noblemen. Iberville's offer was accepted; he was ordered to build a fort at the mouth of the great river, and leave a garrison to hold it.[2] He sailed with two frigates, the "Badine" and the "Marin,"

---

[1] *Iberville au Ministre,* 18 *Juin,* 1698 (Margry, iv. 51).

[2] *Mémoire pour servir d'Instruction au Sieur d'Iberville* (Margry, iv. 72).

and towards the end of January, 1699, reached
Pensacola. Here he found two Spanish ships, which
would not let him enter the harbor. Spain, no less
than England, was bent on making good her claim to
the Mississippi and the Gulf of Mexico, and the two
ships had come from Vera Cruz on this errand.
Three hundred men had been landed, and a stockade
fort was already built. Iberville left the Spaniards
undisturbed and unchallenged, and felt his way westward along the coasts of Alabama and Mississippi,
exploring and sounding as he went. At the beginning of March his boats were caught in a strong
muddy current of fresh water, and he saw that he
had reached the object of his search, the "fatal river"
of the unfortunate La Salle. He entered it, encamped,
on the night of the third, twelve leagues above its
mouth, climbed a solitary tree, and could see nothing
but broad flats of bushes and canebrakes.[1]

Still pushing upward against the current, he
reached in eleven days a village of the Bayagoula
Indians, where he found the chief attired in a blue
capote, which was probably put on in honor of the
white strangers, and which, as the wearer declared,
had been given him by Henri de Tonty, on his
descent of the Mississippi in search of La Salle, thirteen years before. Young Le Moyne de Bienville,
who accompanied his brother Iberville in a canoe,
brought him, some time after, a letter from Tonty
which the writer had left in the hands of another

---

[1] *Journal d'Iberville* (Margry, iv. 131).

chief, to be delivered to La Salle in case of his arrival, and which Bienville had bought for a hatchet. Iberville welcomed it as convincing proof that the river he had entered was in truth the Mississippi.[1] After pushing up the stream till the twenty-fourth, he returned to the ships by way of lakes Maurepas and Ponchartrain.

Iberville now repaired to the harbor of Biloxi, on the coast of the present State of Mississippi. Here he built a small stockade fort, where he left eighty men, under the Sieur de Sauvolle, to hold the country for Louis XIV.; and this done, he sailed for France. Thus the first foundations of Louisiana were laid in Mississippi.

Bienville, whom his brother had left at Biloxi as second in command, was sent by Sauvolle on an exploring expedition up the Mississippi with five men in two canoes. At the bend of the river now called English Turn, — *Tour à l'Anglais*, — below the site of New Orleans, he found an English corvette of ten guns, having, as passengers, a number of French Protestant families taken on board from the Carolinas, with the intention of settling on the Mississippi. The commander, Captain Louis Bank,

---

[1] This letter, which D'Iberville gives in his Journal, is dated "Du Village des Quinipissas, le 20 Avril, 1685." Iberville identifies the Quinipissas with the Bayagoulas. The date of the letter was evidently misread, as Tonty's journey was in 1686. See "La Salle and the Discovery of the Great West," ii. 199, *note*. Iberville's lieutenant, Sugères, commanding the "Marin," gives the date correctly. *Journal de la Frégate le Marin*, 1698, 1699 (Margry, iv.).

LE MOYNE DE BIENVILLE.

declared that his vessel was one of three sent from
London by a company formed jointly of Englishmen
and Huguenot refugees for the purpose of founding
a colony.[1]   Though not quite sure that they were
upon the Mississippi, they were on their way up the
stream to join a party of Englishmen said to be
among the Chickasaws, with whom they were trading
for Indian slaves.   Bienville assured Bank that he
was not upon the Mississippi, but on another river
belonging to King Louis, who had a strong fort there
and several settlements.   "The too-credulous Englishman," says a French writer, "believed these inventions and turned back."[2]   First, however, a
French engineer in the service of Bank contrived to
have an interview with Bienville, and gave him a
petition to the King of France, signed by four
hundred Huguenots who had taken refuge in the
Carolinas after the revocation of the Edict of Nantes.
The petitioners begged that they might have leave
to settle in Louisiana, with liberty of conscience,
under the French Crown.   In due time they got

---

[1] *Journal du Voyage du Chevalier d'Iberville sur le Vaisseau du
Roy la Renommée en* 1699 (Margry, iv. 395).

[2] Gayarré, *Histoire de la Louisiane* (1846), i. 69.   Bénard de la
Harpe, *Journal historique* (1831), 20.   Coxe says, in the preface to
his *Description of Carolana* (1722), that "the present proprietor of
Carolana, my honour'd Father, . . . was the author of this English voyage to the Mississippi, having in the year 1698 equipp'd and
fitted out Two Ships for Discovery by Sea, and also for building
a Fortification and settling a Colony by land; there being in both
vessels, besides Sailors and Common Men, above Thirty English
and French Volunteers."   Coxe adds that the expedition would have
succeeded if one of the commanders had not failed to do his duty.

their answer. The King replied, through the minister, Ponchartrain, that he had not expelled heretics from France in order that they should set up a republic in America.[1] Thus, by the bigotry that had been the bane of Canada and of France herself, Louis XIV. threw away the opportunity of establishing a firm and healthy colony at the mouth of the Mississippi.

So threatening was the danger that England would seize the country, that Iberville had scarcely landed in France when he was sent back with a reinforcement. The colonial views of the King may be gathered from his instructions to his officer. Iberville was told to seek out diligently the best places for establishing pearl-fisheries, though it was admitted that the pearls of Louisiana were uncommonly bad. He was also to catch bison calves, make a fenced park to hold them, and tame them for the sake of their wool, which was reputed to be of value for various fabrics. Above all, he was to look for mines, the finding of which the document declares to be "la grande affaire." [2]

On the eighth of January, Iberville reached Biloxi, and soon after went up the Mississippi to that remarkable tribe of sun-worshippers, the Natchez, whose villages were on and near the site of the city that now bears their name. Some thirty miles above he

---

[1] Gayarré, *Histoire de la Louisiane* (1846), i. 69.

[2] *Mémoire pour servir d'Instruction au Sieur d'Iberville* (Margry, iv 348).

found a kindred tribe, the Taensas, whose temple took fire during his visit, when, to his horror, he saw five living infants thrown into the flames by their mothers to appease the angry spirits.[1]

Retracing his course, he built a wooden redoubt near one of the mouths of the Mississippi to keep out the dreaded English.

In the next year he made a third voyage, and ordered the feeble establishment at Biloxi to be moved to the bay of Mobile. This drew a protest from the Spaniards, who rested their claims to the country on the famous bull of Pope Alexander VI. The question was referred to the two Crowns. Louis XIV., a stanch champion of the papacy when his duties as a Catholic did not clash with his interests as a king, refused submission to the bull, insisted that the Louisiana country was his, and declared that he would hold fast to it because he was bound, as a son of Holy Church, to convert the Indians and keep out the English heretics.[2] Spain was then at peace with France, and her new King, the Duc d'Anjou, grandson of Louis XIV., needed the support of his powerful kinsman; hence his remonstrance against French encroachment was of the mildest.[3]

---

[1] *Journal du Voyage du Chevalier d'Iberville sur le Vaisseau du Roy la Renommée*, 1699, 1700.

[2] *Mémoire de la Junte de Guerre des Indes. Le Ministre de la Marine au Duc d'Harcourt* (Margry, iv. 553, 568).

[3] Iberville wrote in 1701 a long memorial, in which he tried to convince the Spanish court that it was for the interest of Spain that the French should form a barrier between her colonies and those of

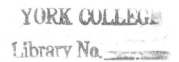
YORK COLLEGE
Library No.

Besides Biloxi and Mobile Bay, the French formed a third establishment at Dauphin Island. The Mississippi itself, which may be called the vital organ of the colony, was thus far neglected, being occupied by no settlement and guarded only by a redoubt near one of its mouths.

Of the emigrants sent out by the court to the new land of promise, the most valuable by far were a number of Canadians who had served under Iberville at Hudson Bay. The rest were largely of the sort who are described by that officer as "beggars sent out to enrich themselves," and who expected the government to feed them while they looked for pearls and gold mines. The paternal providence of Versailles, mindful of their needs, sent them, in 1704, a gift of twenty marriageable girls, described as "nurtured in virtue and piety, and accustomed to work." Twenty-three more came in the next year from the same benignant source, besides seventy-five soldiers, five priests, and two nuns. Food, however, was not sent in proportion to the consumers; and as no crops were raised in Louisiana, famine and pestilence followed, till the starving colonists were forced to live on shell-fish picked up along the shores.

Disorder and discord filled the land of promise. Nicolas de la Salle, the *commissaire ordonnateur*, an official answering to the Canadian intendant, wrote to the minister Ponchartrain that Iberville and his

England, which, he says, were about to seize the country as far as the Mississippi and beyond it.

brothers, Bienville and Chateauguay, were "thieves and knaves."[1] La Vente, curé of Mobile, joined in the cry against Bienville, and stirred soldiers and settlers to disaffection; but the bitterest accuser of that truly valuable officer was the worthy matron who held the unenviable post of directress of the "King's girls," — that is, the young women sent out as wives for the colonists. It seems that she had matrimonial views for herself as well as for her charge; and she wrote to Ponchartrain that Major Boisbriant, commander of the garrison, would certainly have married her if Bienville had not interfered and dissuaded him. "It is clear," she adds, "that M. de Bienville has not the qualities necessary for governing the colony."[2]

Bienville was now chief in authority. Charges of peculation and other offences poured in against him, and at last, though nothing was proved, one De Muys was sent to succeed him, with orders to send him home a prisoner if on examination the accusations should prove to be true. De Muys died on the voyage. D'Artaguette, the new intendant, proceeded to make the inquiry, but refused to tell Bienville the nature of the charges against him, saying that he had orders not to do so. Nevertheless, when he had finished his investigation he reported to the minister

---

[1] *Nicolas de la Salle au Ministre, 7 Septembre,* 1706.

[2] "Il est clair que M. de Bienville n'a pas les qualités nécessaires pour bien gouverner la colonie." Gayarré found this curious letter in the Archives de la Marine.

that the accused was innocent; on which Nicolas de la Salle, whom he had supplanted as intendant, wrote to Ponchartrain that D'Artaguette had deceived him, being no better than Bienville himself. La Salle further declared that Barrot, the surgeon of the colony, was an ignoramus, and that he made money by selling the medicines supplied by the King to cure his Louisianian subjects. Such were the trans-atlantic workings of the paternalism of Versailles.

Bienville, who had been permitted to resume his authority, paints the state of the colony to his masters, and tells them that the inhabitants are dying of hunger, — not all, however, for he mentions a few exceptional cases of prosperity. These were certain thrifty colonists from Rochelle, who, says Bienville, have grown rich by keeping dram-shops, and now want to go back to France; but he has set a watch over them, thinking it just that they should be forced to stay in the colony.[1] This was to add the bars of a prison to the other attractions of the new home.

As the colonists would not work, there was an attempt to make Indian slaves work for them; but as these continually ran off, Bienville proposed to open a barter with the French West Indies, giving three red slaves for two black ones, — an exchange which he thought would be mutually advantageous, since the Indians, being upon islands, could no longer escape. The court disapproved the plan, on the ground that the West Indians would give only their

[1] *Dépêche de Bienville*, 12 *Octobre*, 1708.

worst negroes in exchange, and that the only way to get good ones was to fetch them from Guinea.

Complaints against Bienville were renewed till the court sent out La Mothe-Cadillac to succeed him, with orders to examine the charges against his predecessor, whom it was his interest to condemn, in order to keep the governorship. In his new post, Cadillac displayed all his old faults; began by denouncing the country in unmeasured terms, and wrote in his usual sarcastic vein to the colonial minister: "I have seen the garden on Dauphin Island, which had been described to me as a terrestrial paradise. I saw there three seedling pear-trees, three seedling apple-trees, a little plum-tree about three feet high, with seven bad plums on it, a vine some thirty feet long, with nine bunches of grapes, some of them withered or rotten and some partly ripe, about forty plants of French melons, and a few pumpkins. This is M. d'Artaguette's terrestrial paradise, M. de Rémonville's Pomona, and M. de Mandeville's Fortunate Islands. Their stories are mere fables." Then he slanders the soil, which, he declares, will produce neither grain nor vegetables.

D'Artaguette, no longer fancying himself in Eden, draws a dismal picture of the state of the colony. There are, he writes, only ten or twelve families who cultivate the soil. The inhabitants, naturally lazy, are ruined by the extravagance of their wives. "It is necessary to send out girls and laboring-men. I am convinced that we shall easily discover mines when persons are sent us who understand that business." [1]

The colonists felt no confidence in the future of Louisiana. The King was its sole support, and if, as was likely enough, he should tire of it, their case would be deplorable. When Bienville ruled over them, they had used him as their scapegoat; but that which made the colony languish was not he, but the vicious system it was his business to enforce. The royal edicts and arbitrary commands that took the place of law proceeded from masters thousands of miles away, who knew nothing of the country, could not understand its needs, and scarcely tried to do so.

In 1711, though the mischievous phantom of gold and silver mines still haunted the colony, we find it reported that the people were beginning to work, and were planting tobacco. The King, however, was losing patience with a dependency that cost him endless expense and trouble, and brought little or nothing in return, — and this at a time when he had a costly and disastrous war on his hands, and was in no mood to bear supernumerary burdens. The plan of giving over a colony to a merchant, or a company of merchants, was not new. It had been tried in other French colonies with disastrous effect. Yet it was now tried again. Louisiana was farmed out for fifteen years to Antoine Crozat, a wealthy man of

---

[1] D'Artaguette in Gayarré, *Histoire de la Louisiane.* This valu able work consists of a series of documents, connected by a thread of narrative.

business.   The countries made over to him extended
from the British colonies on the east to New Mexico
on the west, and the Rio del Norte on the south,
including the entire region watered by the Mississippi,
the Missouri, the Ohio, and their tributaries, as far
north as the Illinois.   In comparison with this immense domain, which was all included under the
name of Louisiana, the present State so called is but
a small patch on the American map.

To Crozat was granted a monopoly of the trade,
wholesale and retail, domestic and foreign, of all
these countries, besides the product of all mines,
after deducting one-fourth reserved for the King.
He was empowered to send one vessel a year to
Guinea for a cargo of slaves.   The King was to pay
the governor and other Crown officers, and during
the first nine years the troops also; though after that
time Crozat was to maintain them till the end of his
term.

In consideration of these and other privileges, the
grantee was bound to send to Louisiana a specified
number of settlers every year.   His charter provided
that the royal edicts and the *Coutume de Paris* should
be the law of the colony, to be administered by a
council appointed by the King.

When Louisiana was thus handed over to a specu-
lator for a term of years, it needed no prophet to
foretell that he would get all he could out of it, and
put as little into it as possible.   When Crozat took
possession of the colony, the French court had been

thirteen years at work in building it up. The result of its labors was a total population, including troops, government officials, and clergy, of 380 souls, of whom 170 were in the King's pay. Only a few of the colonists were within the limits of the present Louisiana. The rest lived in or around the feeble stockade forts at Mobile, Biloxi, Ship Island, and Dauphin Island. This last station had been partially abandoned; but some of the colonists proposed to return to it, in order to live by fishing, and only waited, we are told, for help from the King. This incessant dependence on government relaxed the fibres of the colony and sapped its life-blood.

The King was now exchanged for Crozat and his grinding monopoly. The colonists had carried on a modest trade with the Spaniards at Pensacola in skins, fowls, Indian corn, and a few other articles, bringing back a little money in return. This, their only source of profit, was now cut off; they could sell nothing, even to one another. They were forbidden to hold meetings without permission; but some of them secretly drew up a petition to La Mothe-Cadillac, who was still the official chief of the colony, begging that the agents of Crozat should be restricted to wholesale dealings, and that the inhabitants might be allowed to trade at retail. Cadillac denounced the petition as seditious, threatened to hang the bearer of it, and deigned no other answer.

He resumed his sarcasms against the colony. "In my opinion this country is not worth a straw (*ne vaut*

pas un fétu).   The inhabitants are eager to be taken
out of it.   The soldiers are always grumbling, and
with reason."   As to the council, which was to be
the only court of justice, he says that no such thing
is possible, because there are no proper persons to
compose it; and though Duclos, the new intendant,
has proposed two candidates, the first of these, the
Sieur de Lafresnière, learned to sign his name only
four months ago, and the other, being chief surgeon
of the colony, is too busy to serve.[1]

Between Bienville, the late governor, and La
Mothe-Cadillac, who had supplanted him, there was
a standing quarrel; and the colony was split into
hostile factions, led by the two disputants.   The
minister at Versailles was beset by their mutual
accusations, and Bienville wrote that his refusal to
marry Cadillac's daughter was the cause of the
spite the governor bore him.[2]

The indefatigable curé De la Vente sent to Ponchartrain a memorial, in the preamble of which he
says that since Monsieur le Ministre wishes to be
informed exactly of the state of things in Louisiana,
he, La Vente, has the honor, with malice to nobody,
to make known the pure truth; after which he goes
on to say that the inhabitants "are nearly all drunk-
ards, gamblers, blasphemers, and enemies of every-

---

[1] *La Mothe-Cadillac au Ministre*, in Gayarré, i. 104, 105.

[2] " Que si M. de Lamothe-Cadillac lui portoit tant d'animosité,
c'étoit à cause du refus qu'il avoit fait d'épouser sa fille." — *Bienville in Gayarré*, i. 116.

thing good;" and he proceeds to illustrate the statement with many particulars.[1]

As the inhabitants were expected to work for Crozat, and not for themselves, it naturally followed that they would not work at all; and idleness produced the usual results.

The yearly shipment of girls continued; but there was difficulty in finding husbands for them. The reason was not far to seek. Duclos, the intendant, reports the arrival of an invoice of twelve of them, "so ugly that the inhabitants are in no hurry to take them."[2] The Canadians, who formed the most vigorous and valuable part of the population, much preferred Indian squaws. "It seems to me," pursues the intendant, "that in the choice of girls, good looks should be more considered than virtue." This latter requisite seems, at the time, to have found no more attention than the other, since the candidates for matrimony were drawn from the Parisian hospitals and houses of correction, from the former of which Crozat was authorized to take one hundred girls a year, "in order to increase the population." These hospitals were compulsory asylums for the poor and vagrant of both sexes, of whom the great Hôpital Général of Paris contained at one time more than six thousand.[3]

---

[1] *Mémoire du Curé de la Vente*, 1714.

[2] The earlier cargoes of girls seem to have been better chosen, and there was no difficulty in mating them. Serious disputes sometimes rose from the competition of rival suitors. — Dumont, *Mémoires historiques de la Louisiane*, chap. v.

[3] Prominent officials of the colony are said to have got wives

Crozat had built his chief hopes of profit on a trade, contraband or otherwise, with the Mexican ports; but the Spanish officials, faithful instruments of the exclusive policy of their government, would not permit it, and were so vigilant that he could not elude them. At the same time, to his vexation, he found that the King's officers in Louisiana, with more address or better luck, and in contempt of his monopoly, which it was their business to protect, carried on, for their own profit, a small smuggling trade with Vera Cruz. He complained that they were always thwarting his agents and conspiring against his interests. At last, finding no resource left but an unprofitable trade with the Indians, he gave up his charter, which had been a bane to the colony and a loss to himself. Louisiana returned to the Crown, and was soon passed over to the new Mississippi Company, called also the Western Company.[1]

That charlatan of genius, the Scotchman John Law, had undertaken, with the eager support of the Regent Duke of Orleans, to deliver France from financial ruin through a prodigious system of credit, of which Louisiana, with its imaginary gold mines, was made the basis. The government used every

---

from these sources. Nicolas de la Salle is reported to have had two in succession, both from the hospitals. Bénard de la Harpe, 107 (ed. 1831).

[1] *Lettres patentes en forme d'Édit portant établissement de la Compagnie d'Occident,* in Le Page du Pratz, *Histoire de la Louisiane,* i. 47.

means to keep up the stock of the Mississippi Company. It was ordered that the notes of the royal bank and all certificates of public debt should be accepted at par in payment for its shares. Powers and privileges were lavished on it. It was given the monopoly of the French slave-trade, the monopoly of tobacco, the profits of the royal mint, and the farming of the revenues of the kingdom. Ingots of gold, pretending to have come from the new Eldorado of Louisiana, were displayed in the shop-windows of Paris. The fever of speculation rose to madness, and the shares of the company were inflated to monstrous and insane proportions.

When Crozat resigned his charter, Louisiana, by the highest estimates, contained about seven hundred souls, including soldiers, but not blacks or Indians. Crozat's successors, however, say that the whole number of whites, men, women, and children, was not above four hundred.[1] When the Mississippi Company took the colony in charge, it was but a change of despots. Louisiana was a prison. But while no inhabitant could leave it without permission of the authorities, all Jews were expelled, and all Protestants excluded. The colonists could buy nothing except from the agents of the company, and sell nothing except to the same all-powerful masters, always at prices fixed by them. Foreign vessels were forbidden to enter any port of Louisiana, on pain of confiscation.

The coin in circulation was nearly all Spanish, and

[1] *Règlement de Régie,* 1721.

in less than two years the Company, by a series of
decrees, made changes of about eighty per cent in its
value.   Freedom of conscience, freedom of speech,
of trade, and of action, were alike denied.   Hence
voluntary immigration was not to be expected; "but,"
says the Duc de Saint-Simon, "the government
wished to establish effective settlements in these vast
countries, after the example of the English; and
therefore, in order to people them, vagabonds and
beggars, male and female, including many women of
the town, were seized for the purpose both in Paris
and throughout France."[1]   Saint-Simon approves
these proceedings in themselves, as tending at once
to purge France and people Louisiana, but thinks the
business was managed in a way to cause needless
exasperation among the lower classes.

In 1720 it was ordered by royal edict that no more
vagabonds or criminals should be sent to Louisiana.
The edict, it seems, touched only one sex, for in the
next year eighty girls were sent to the colony from
the Parisian House of Correction called the Sal-
pêtrière.   There had been a more or less constant
demand for wives, as appears by letters still preserved
in the archives of Paris, the following extract from
one of which is remarkable for the freedom with
which the writer, a M. de Chassin, takes it upon him
to address a minister of State in a court where
punctilio reigned supreme.   "You see, Monseigneur,
that nothing is wanting now to make a solid settle-

[1] Saint-Simon, *Mémoires* (ed. Chéruel), xvii. 461.

ment in Louisiana but a certain piece of furniture which one often repents having got, and with which I shall dispense, like the rest, till the Company sends us girls who have at least some show of virtue. If there happens to be any young woman of your acquaintance who wants to make the voyage for love of me, I should be much obliged to her, and would do my best to show her my gratitude." [1]

The Company, which was invested with sovereign powers, began its work by sending to Louisiana three companies of soldiers and sixty-nine colonists. Its wisest act was the removal of the governor, L'Épinay, who had supplanted La Mothe-Cadillac, and the reappointment of Bienville in his place. Bienville immediately sought out a spot for establishing a permanent station on the Mississippi. Fifty men were sent to clear the ground, and in spite of an inundation which overflowed it for a time, the feeble foundations of New Orleans were laid. Louisiana, hitherto diffused through various petty cantonments, far and near, had at last a capital, or the germ of one.

It was the sixth of September, 1717, when the charter of the Mississippi Company was entered in the registers of the Parliament of Paris; and from that time forward, before the offices of the Company in the Rue Quincampoix, crowds of crazed speculators jostled and fought from morning till night to get their names inscribed among the stockholders.

[1] *De Chassin au Ministre,* 1 *Juillet,* 1722, in Gayarré, i. 190.

Within five years after, the huge glittering bubble had burst. The shares, each one of which had seemed a fortune, found no more purchasers, and in its fall the Company dragged down with it its ally and chief creditor, the bank. All was dismay and despair, except in those who had sold out in time, and turned delusive paper into solid values. John Law, lately the idol and reputed savior of France, fled for his life, amid a howl of execration.

Yet the interests of the kingdom required that Louisiana should be sustained. The illusions that had given to the Mississippi Company a morbid and intoxicated vitality were gone, but the Company lingered on, and the government still lent it a helping hand. A French writer remarks that the few Frenchmen who were famishing on the shores of the Mississippi and the Gulf of Mexico had cost the King, since the colony began, more than 150,000 livres a year. The directors of the Company reported that they had shipped 7,020 persons to the colony, besides four hundred already there when they took possession, and that 5,420 still remained, the rest having died or escaped.[1] Besides this importation of whites, they had also brought six hundred slaves from Guinea. It is reckoned that the King, Crozat, and the Mississippi Company had spent among them

---

[1] A considerable number of the whites brought to Louisiana in the name of the Company had been sent at the charge of persons to whom it had granted lands in various parts of the colony. Among these was John Law himself, who had the grant of large tracts on the Arkansas.

about eight million livres on Louisiana, without any return.[1]

The bursting of the Mississippi bubble did not change the principles of administration in Louisiana. The settlers, always looking to France to supply their needs and protect them against their own improvidence, were in the habit of butchering for food the livestock sent them for propagation. The remedy came in the shape of a royal edict forbidding any colonist to kill, without permission of the authorities, any cow, sheep, or lamb belonging to himself, on pain of a fine of three hundred livres; or to kill any horse, cow, or bull belonging to another, on pain of death.

Authority and order were the watchwords, and disorder was the rule. The agents of power quarrelled among themselves, except when they leagued together to deceive their transatlantic masters and cover their own misdeeds. Each maligned the other, and it was scarcely possible for the King or the Company to learn the true state of affairs in their distant colony.

Accusations were renewed against Bienville, till in 1724 he was ordered to France to give account of his conduct, and the Sieur Perier was sent out to take his place. Perier had no easy task. The Natchez Indians, among whom the French had made a settlement and built a fort called Fort Rosalie, suddenly rose on their white neighbors and massacred nearly

[1] Bénard de la Harpe, 371 (ed. 1831).

all of them.[1] Then followed a long course of Indian
wars. The French believed that there was a general
conspiracy among the southern tribes for their destruction, — though this was evidently an exaggeration of
the danger, which, however, was serious. The
Chickasaws, a brave and warlike people, living
chiefly in what is now western Tennessee and
Kentucky, made common cause with the Natchez,
while the more numerous Choctaws, most of whose
villages were in the present State of Mississippi,
took part with the French. More than a thousand
soldiers had been sent to Louisiana; but Perier pronounced them "so bad that they seem to have been
made on purpose for the colony."[2] There were also
about eight hundred militia. Perier showed little
vigor, and had little success. His chief resource was
to set the tribes against one another. He reports
that his Indian allies had brought him a number of
Natchez prisoners, and that he had caused six of
them, four men and two women, to be burned alive,
and had sent the rest as slaves to St. Domingo. The
Chickasaws, aided by English traders from the
Carolinas, proved formidable adversaries, and when
attacked, ensconced themselves in stockade forts so
strong that, as the governor complains, there was no
dislodging the defenders without cannon and heavy
mortars.

---

[1] *Lettre du Père le Petit*, in *Lettres Édifiantes ;* Dumont, *Mémoires
historiques*, chap. xxvii.

[2] "Nos soldats, qui semblent être faits exprès pour la colonie,
tants ils sont mauvais." — *Dépêche de Perier*, 18 *Mars*, 1730.

In this state of things the directors of the Mississippi Company, whose affairs had gone from bad to worse, declared that they could no longer bear the burden of Louisiana, and begged the King to take it off their hands. The colony was therefore transferred from the mercantile despotism of the Company to the paternal despotism of the Crown, and it profited by the change. Commercial monopoly was abolished. Trade between France and Louisiana was not only permitted, but encouraged by bounties and exemption from duties; and instead of paying to the Company two hundred per cent of profit on indispensable supplies, the colonists now got them at a reasonable price.

Perier was removed, and again Bienville was made governor. Diron d'Artaguette, who came with him as intendant, reported that the colonists were flying the country to escape starvation, and Bienville adds that during the past year they had subsisted for three months on the seed of reeds and wild grasses.[1] The white population had rather diminished than increased during the last twelve years, while the blacks, who had lately conspired to massacre all the French along the Mississippi, had multiplied to two thousand.[2] A French writer says: "There must have been a worm gnawing the root of the tree that had been transplanted into so rich a soil, to make it wither instead

[1] *Mémoire de Bienville*, 1730.

[2] For a curious account of the discovery of this negro plot, see Le Page du Pratz, iii. 304.

of growing.   What it needed was the air of liberty."
But the air of liberty is malaria to those who have
not learned to breathe it.   The English colonists
throve in it because they and their forefathers had
been trained in a school of self-control and self-
dependence; and what would have been intoxication for others, was vital force to them.

Bienville found the colony again threatened with
a general rising, or, as he calls it, a revolt, of the
Indian tribes.   The Carolina traders, having no
advantage of water-ways, had journeyed by land with
pack-horses through a thousand miles of wilderness,
and with the aid of gifts had instigated the tribes
to attack the French.   The Chickasaws especially,
friends of the English and arch-enemies of Louisiana,
became so threatening that a crushing blow against
them was thought indispensable.   The forces of the
colony were mustered to attempt it; the enterprise
was mismanaged, and failed completely.[1]   Bienville
tried to explain the disaster, but his explanation
was ill received at court; he was severely rebuked,
reproved at the same time for permitting two families
to emigrate to St. Domingo, and sharply ordered to
suffer nobody to leave Louisiana without express
license from Versailles.   Deeply wounded, he offered
his resignation, and it was accepted.   Whatever his
failings, he had faithfully served the colony, and
gained from posterity the title of Father of Louisiana.

[1] *Dépêche de Bienville*, 6 *Mai*, 1740.   Compare Le Page du Pratz,
iii. chap. xxiv.

With the help of industrious nursing, — or, one might almost say, in spite of it, — Louisiana began at last to strike roots into the soil and show signs of growth, though feebly as compared with its sturdy rivals along the Atlantic seaboard, which had cost their King nothing, and had been treated, for the most part, with the coolest neglect. Cavelier de la Salle's dream of planting a firm settlement at the mouth of the Mississippi, and utilizing, by means of it, the resources of the vast interior, was, after half a century, in some measure realized. New France (using that name in its broadest geographical sense) had now two heads, — Canada and Louisiana; one looking upon the Gulf of St. Lawrence, and the other upon the Gulf of Mexico. Canada was not without jealousy of her younger and weaker sister, lest she might draw away, as she had begun to do at the first, some of the most active and adventurous elements of the Canadian population; lest she might prove a competitor in the fur-trade; and lest she should encroach on the Illinois and other western domains, which the elder and stronger sister claimed as her own. These fears were not unfounded; yet the vital interests of the two French colonies were the same, and each needed the help of the other in the prime and all-essential task of keeping the British colonies in check. The chiefs of Louisiana looked forward to a time when the great southern tribes, — Creeks, Cherokees, Choctaws, and even the dreaded Chickasaws, — won over by French missionaries to the

Church, and therefore to France, should be turned against the encroaching English to stop their westward progress and force them back to the borders of the Atlantic.   Meanwhile the chiefs of Canada were maturing the plan — pursued with varying assiduity, but always kept in view — of connecting the two vital extremities of New France by a chain of forts to control the passes of the West, keep communications open, and set English invasion at defiance.

CHAPTER XIV.

1700–1732.

THE OUTAGAMIE WAR.

The Western Posts. — Detroit. — The Illinois. — Perils of the West. — The Outagamies. — Their Turbulence. — English Instigation. — Louvigny's Expedition. — Defeat of Outagamies. — Hostilities renewed. — Lignery's Expedition. — Outagamies attacked by Villiers; by Hurons and Iroquois. — La Butte des Morts. — The Sacs and Foxes.

The rulers of Canada labored without ceasing in their perplexing task of engrossing the fur-trade of the West and controlling the western tribes to the exclusion of the English. Every day made it clearer that to these ends the western wilderness must be held by forts and trading-posts; and this policy of extension prevailed more and more, in spite of the league of merchants, who wished to draw the fur-trade to Montreal, — in spite of the Jesuits, who felt that their influence over the remoter tribes would be compromised by the presence among them of officers, soldiers, and traders; and in spite of the King himself, who feared that the diffusion of the colony would breed disorder and insubordination.

Detroit, the most important of the western posts, struggled through a critical infancy in the charge of its founder, La Mothe-Cadillac, till, by a choice not very judicious, he was made governor of Louisiana. During his rule the population had slowly increased to about two hundred souls; but after he left the place it diminished to a point that seemed to threaten the feeble post with extinction. About 1722 it revived again; *voyageurs* and discharged soldiers settled about the fort, and the parish register shows six or eight births in the course of the year.[1]

Meanwhile, on the banks of the Mississippi another settlement was growing up which did not owe its birth to official patronage, and yet was destined to become the most noteworthy offspring of Canada in the West. It was known to the French as "the Illinois," from the name of the group of tribes belonging to that region. La Salle had occupied the banks of the river Illinois in 1682; but the curious Indian colony which he gathered about his fort on the rock of St. Louis[2] dispersed after his death, till few or none were left except the Kaskaskias, a sub-tribe of the Illinois. These still lived in the meadow below Fort St. Louis, where the Jesuits Marquette, Allouez, Rale, Gravier, and Marest labored in turn for their conversion, till, in 1700, they or some of them followed Marest to the Mississippi and set up their wigwams where the town of Kaskaskia now stands, near the mouth of the little river which bears the same name. Charlevoix, who was here in 1721, calls this

---

[1] Rameau, *Notes historiques sur la Colonie Canadienne du Detroit.*
[2] See " La Salle and the Discovery of the Great West," ii. 59.

the oldest settlement of the Illinois,[1] — though there is some reason to believe that the village of Cahokia, established as a mission by the Jesuit Pinet, sixty miles or more above Kaskaskia, and nearly opposite the present city of St. Louis, is, by a few weeks, the elder of the two. The *voyageurs, coureurs de bois,* and other roving Canadians made these young settlements their resort, took to wife converted squaws,[2] and ended with making the Illinois their home. The missions turned to parishes, the missionaries to curés, and the wigwams to those compact little Canadian houses that cause one to marvel at the ingenuity which can store so multitudinous a progeny within such narrow limits.

White women from Canada or Louisiana began to find their way to these wilderness settlements, which with every generation grew more French and less Indian. The river Mississippi was at once their friend and their enemy. It carried their produce to New Orleans, but undermined their rich alluvial shores, cut away fields and meadows, and swept them in its turbid eddies thirteen hundred miles southward, as a contribution to the mud-banks of the delta.

When the Mississippi Company came into power, the Illinois, hitherto a dependency of Canada, was

---

[1] " Ce poste, le premier de tous par droit d'antiquité." — *Journal historique,* 403 (ed. 1744).

[2] The old parish registers of Kaskaskia are full of records of these mixed marriages. See Edward G. Mason, *Illinois in the Eighteenth Century.*

annexed to Louisiana.   Pierre Dugué de Boisbriant
was sent to take command of it, and under his direction a fort was built on the bank of the Mississippi
sixteen miles above Kaskaskia.   It was named Fort
Chartres, in honor of the Duc de Chartres, son of the
Regent, who had himself once borne the same title.
This work, built at first of wood and earth, was
afterwards rebuilt of stone, and became one of the
chief links in the chain of military communication
between Canada and Louisiana.

Here, with the commandant at its head, sat the
council of three which ruled over the little settlement.[1]   Here too was a garrison to enforce the
decrees of the council, keep order among the settlers,
and give them a protection which they greatly
needed, since they were within striking distance of
the formidable Chickasaws, the effects of whose
hostility appear year after year on the parish register
of deaths at Kaskaskia.   Worse things were in store;
for the gallant young Pierre d'Artaguette, who was
appointed to the command in 1734, and who marched
against the Chickasaws with a band of Frenchmen
and Indians, was defeated, captured, and burned
alive, astonishing his torturers by the fortitude with
which he met his fate.   The settlement had other
foes not less dangerous.   These were the Outagamies,

---

[1] The two other members were La Loire des Ursins, director of
the Mississippi Company, and Michel Chassin, its commissary, —
he who wrote the curious letter to Ponchartrain, asking for a wife,
quoted in the last chapter, pp. 317–318.

or Foxes, between whom and the tribes of the Illinois there was a deadly feud. We have seen how, in 1712, a band of Outagamies, with their allies, the Mascoutins, appeared at Detroit and excited an alarm, which, after a savage conflict, was ended with their ruin. In 1714 the Outagamies made a furious attack upon the Illinois, and killed or carried off seventy-seven of them.[1] A few years later they made another murderous onslaught in the same quarter. They were the scourge of the West, and no white man could travel between Canada and Louisiana except at the risk of his life.

In vain the French parleyed with them; threats and blandishments were useless alike. Their chiefs would promise, sometimes in good faith, to keep the peace and no more offend their father Onontio; but nearly all the tribes of the Lake country were their hereditary enemies, and some bloody revenge for ancient wrongs would excite their young warriors to a fury which the elders could not restrain. Thus, in 1722 the Saginaws, a fierce Algonquin band on the eastern borders of Michigan, killed twenty-three Outagamies; the tribesmen of the slain returned the blow, other tribes joined the fray, and the wilderness was again on fire.[2]

The Canadian authorities were sorely perplexed, for this fierce inter-tribal war threatened their whole system of western trade. Meanwhile the English

---

[1] *Vaudreuil au Ministre,* 16 *Septembre,* 1714.

[2] *Idem,* 2 *Octobre,* 1723.

and Dutch of New York were sending wampum belts to the Indians of the upper lakes, inviting them to bring their furs to Albany; and Ramesay, governor of Montreal, complains that they were all disposed to do so. "Twelve of the upper tribes," says Lord Cornbury, "have come down this year to trade at Albany;" but he adds that as the Indians have had no presents for above six years, he is afraid "we shall lose them before next summer."[1] The governor of Canada himself is said to have been in collusion with the English traders for his own profit.[2] The Jesuits denied the charge, and Father Marest wrote to the governor, after the disaster to Walker's fleet on its way to attack Quebec, "The protection you have given to the missions has drawn on you and the colony the miraculous protection of God."[3]

Whether his accusers did him wrong or not, Vaudreuil felt the necessity of keeping the peace among the western Indians and suppressing the Outagamie incendiaries. In fact, nothing would satisfy him but their destruction. "They are the common enemies of all the western tribes," he writes. "They have lately murdered three Frenchmen and five Hurons at Detroit. The Hurons ask for our help against them, and we must give it, or all the tribes will despise us."[4]

[1] *N. Y. Col. Docs.*, v. 65.
[2] *Mémoire présenté au Comte de Ponchartrain par M. d'Auteuil, procureur-général du Roy*, 1708.
[3] *Marest à Vaudreuil*, 21 *Janvier*, 1712.
[4] *Vaudreuil et Bégon au Ministre*, 15 *Novembre*, 1713.

He put his chief trust in Louvigny, formerly commandant at Michilimackinac. That officer proposed
to muster the friendly tribes and march on the
Outagamies just as their corn was ripening, fight
them if they stood their ground, or if not, destroy
their crops, burn their wigwams, and encamp on the
spot till winter; then send out parties to harass them
as they roamed the woods seeking a meagre subsist-
ence by hunting. In this way he hoped to cripple, if
not destroy them.[1]

The Outagamies lived at this time on the Fox
River of Green Bay, — a stream which owes its name
to them.[2] Their chief village seems to have been
between thirty and forty miles from the mouth of the
river, where it creeps through broad tracts of rushes,
willows, and wild rice. In spite of their losses at
Detroit in 1712, their strength was far from being
broken.

During two successive summers preparations were
made to attack them; but the march was delayed,
once by the tardiness of the Indian allies, and again
by the illness of Louvigny. At length, on the first
of May, 1716, he left Montreal with two hundred
and twenty-five Frenchmen, while two hundred more
waited to join him at Detroit and Michilimackinac,
where the Indian allies were also to meet him. To

---

[1] *Vaudreuil au Ministre,* 16 *Septembre,* 1714.

[2] " Les Renards [Outagamies] sont placez sur une rivière qui
tombe dans la Baye des Puants [Green Bay]." — *Registre du Conseil
de la Marine,* 28 *Mars,* 1716.

save expense in pay and outfit, the Canadians recruited for the war were allowed to take with them
goods for trading with the Indians. Hence great
disorder and insubordination, especially as more than
forty barrels of brandy were carried in the canoes, as
a part of these commercial ventures, in consequence
of which we hear that when French and Indians were
encamped together, "hell was thrown open." [1]

The Outagamies stood their ground. Louvigny
says, with probable exaggeration, that when he made
his attack their village held five hundred warriors,
and no less than three thousand women, — a disparity
of sexes no doubt due to the inveterate fighting
habits of the tribe. The wigwams were enclosed by a
strong fence, consisting of three rows of heavy oaken
palisades. This method of fortification was used
also by tribes farther southward. When Bienville
attacked the Chickasaws, he was foiled by the solid
wooden wall that resisted his cannon, being formed
of trunks of trees as large as a man's body, set
upright, close together, and made shot-proof by
smaller trunks, planted within so as to close the
interstices of the outer row. [2]

The fortified village of the Outagamies was of a
somewhat different construction. The defences consisted of three rows of palisades, those of the middle
row being probably planted upright, and the other

[1] "Où il y a des François et des sauvages, c'est un **enfer
ouvert**." — *Registre du Conseil de Marine,* 28 *Mars,* 1716.

[2] Le Page du Pratz.

two set aslant against them. Below, along the inside of the triple row, ran a sort of shallow trench or rifle-pit, where the defenders lay ensconced, firing through interstices left for the purpose between the palisades.[1]

Louvigny had brought with him two cannon and a mortar; but being light, they had little effect on the wooden wall, and as he was provided with mining tools, he resolved to attack the Outagamie stronghold by regular approaches, as if he were besieging a fortress of Vauban. Covered by the fire of three pieces of artillery and eight hundred French and Indian small-arms, he opened trenches during the night within seventy yards of the palisades, pushed a sap sixty feet nearer before morning, and on the third night burrowed to within about twenty-three yards of the wall. His plan was to undermine and blow up the palisades.

The Outagamies had made a furious resistance, in which their women took part with desperation; but dreading the threatened explosion, and unable to resist the underground approaches of their enemy, they asked for a parley, and owned themselves beaten. Louvigny demanded that they should make peace with all tribes friendly to the French, give up all

---

[1] *Louvigny au Ministre*, 14 *Octobre*, 1716. Louvigny's account of the Outagamie defences is short, and not very clear. La Mothe-Cadillac, describing similar works at Michilimackinac, says that the palisades of the innermost row alone were set close together, those of the two other rows being separated by spaces of six inches or more, through which the defenders fired from their loopholes. The plan seems borrowed from the Iroquois.

prisoners, and make war on distant tribes, such as the Pawnees, in order to take captives who should supply the place of those they had killed among the allies of the French; that they should pay, in furs, the costs of the war, and give six chiefs, or sons of chiefs, as hostages for the fulfilment of these conditions.[1]

On the twelfth of October Louvigny reached Quebec in triumph, bringing with him the six hostages.

The Outagamie question was settled for a time. The tribe remained quiet for some years, and in 1718 sent a deputation to Montreal and renewed their submission, which the governor accepted, though they had evaded the complete fulfilment of the conditions imposed on them. Yet peace was not secure for a moment. The Kickapoos and Mascoutins would not leave their neighbors, the Illinois, at rest; the Saginaws made raids on the Miamis; and a general war seemed imminent. "The difficulty is inconceivable of keeping these western tribes quiet," writes the governor, almost in despair.[2]

At length the crisis came. The Illinois captured the nephew of Oushala, the principal Outagamie war-chief, and burned him alive; on which the Outagamies attacked them, drove them for refuge to the top of the rock on which La Salle's fort of St. Louis had been built, and held them there at mercy. They would have starved to death, had not the victors,

---

[1] Dépêche de Vaudreuil, 14 Octobre, 1716.
[2] Vaudreuil au Conseil de Marine, 28 Octobre, 1719.

dreading the anger of the French, suffered them to escape.[1] For this they took to themselves great credit, not without reason, in view of the provocation. At Versailles, however, their attack on the Illinois seemed an unpardonable offence, and the next ship from France brought a letter from the colonial minister declaring that the Outagamies must be effectually put down, and that "his Majesty will reward the officer who will reduce, or rather destroy, them."[2]

The authorities of Canada were less truculent than their masters at the court, or were better able to count the costs of another war. Longueuil, the provisional governor, persisted in measures of peace, and the Sieur de Lignery called a council of the Outagamies and their neighbors, the Sacs and Winnebagoes, at Green Bay. He told them that the Great Onontio, the King, ordered them, at their peril, to make no more attacks on the Illinois; and they dutifully promised to obey, while their great chief, Oushala, begged that a French officer might be sent to his village to help him keep his young warriors from the war-path.[3] The pacific policy of Longueuil was not approved by Desliettes, then commanding in the Illinois country; and he proposed to settle accounts with the Outagamies by exterminating them.

---

[1] *Paroles des Renards* [Outagamies] *dans un Conseil tenu le 6 Septembre,* 1722.

[2] *Réponse du Ministre à la lettre du Marquis de Vaudreuil du 11 Octobre,* 1723.

[3] *Mémoire sur les Renards,* 27 *Avril,* 1727.

"This is very well," observes a writer of the time; "but to try to exterminate them and fail would be disastrous."[1]

The Marquis de Beauharnois, who came out as governor of Canada in 1726, was averse to violent measures, since if an attempt to exterminate the offending tribe should be made without success, the life of every Frenchman in the West would be in jeopardy.[2] Lignery thought that if the Outagamies broke the promises they had made him at Green Bay, the forces of Canada and Louisiana should unite to crush them. The missionary, Chardon, advised that they should be cut off from all supplies of arms, ammunition, and merchandise of any kind, and that all the well-disposed western tribes should then be set upon them, — which, he thought, would infallibly bring them to reason.[3]

The new governor, perplexed by the multitude of counsellors, presently received a missive from the King, directing him not to fight the Outagamies if he could help it, "since the consequences of failure would be frightful."[4] On the other hand, Beauharnois was told that the English had sent messages to the Lake tribes urging them to kill the French in their country, and that the Outagamies had promised to do

---

[1] *Mémoire concernant la Paix que M. de Lignery a faite avec les Chefs des Renards, Sakis* [Sacs], *et Puants* [Winnebagoes], 7 *Juin,* 1726.

[2] *Mémoire sur les Renards,* 27 *Avril,* 1727.

[3] *Ibid.*

[4] *Mémoire du Roy,* 29 *Avril,* 1727.

so. "This," writes the governor, "compels us to make war in earnest. It will cost sixty thousand livres." [1]

Dupuy, the intendant, had joined with Beauharnois in this letter to the minister; but being at the time in a hot quarrel with the governor, he soon after sent a communication of his own to Versailles, in which he declares that the war against the Outagamies was only a pretext of Beauharnois for spending the King's money, and enriching himself by buying up all the furs of the countries traversed by the army.[2]

Whatever the motives of the expedition, it left Montreal in June, under the Sieur de Lignery, followed the rugged old route of the Ottawa, and did not reach Michilimackinac till after midsummer. Thence, in a flotilla of birch canoes carrying about a thousand Indians and five hundred French, the party set out for the fort at the head of Green Bay.[3] Here they caught one Outagamie warrior and three Winnebagoes, whom the Indian allies tortured to death. Then they paddled their canoes up Fox River, reached a Winnebago village on the twenty-fourth of August, followed the channel of the stream, a ribbon of lazy water twisting in a vague, perplexing way through the broad marsh of wild rice and flags, till they saw the chief village of the Outagamies

[1] *Beauharnois et Dupuy au Ministre, 25 Octobre,* 1727.

[2] *Mémoire de Dupuy,* 1728.

[3] Desliettes came to meet them, by way of Chicago, with five hundred Illinois warriors and twenty Frenchmen. *La Perrière et La Fresnière à Beauharnois,* 10 *Septembre,* 1728.

on a tract of rising ground a little above the level of the bog.[1] It consisted of bark wigwams, without palisades or defences of any kind. Its only inmates were three squaws and one old man. These were all seized, and, to the horror of Père Crespel, the chaplain, were given to the Indian allies, who kept the women as slaves, and burned the old man at a slow fire.[2] Then, after burning the village and destroying the crop of maize, peas, beans, and squashes that surrounded it, the whole party returned to Michili-mackinac.[3]

The expedition was not a success. Lignery had hoped to surprise the enemy; but the alert and nimble savages had escaped him. Beauharnois makes the best of the miscarriage, and writes that "the army did good work;" but says a few weeks later that something must be done to cure the contempt which the western allies of the French have conceived for them "since the last affair."[4]

Two years after Lignery's expedition, there was another attempt to humble the Outagamies. Late in the autumn of 1730 young Coulon de Villiers, who twenty-four years later defeated Washington at Fort Necessity, appeared at Quebec with news that the Sieur de Villiers, his father, who commanded the

---

[1] *Guignas à Beauharnois, 29 Mai,* 1728.

[2] *Dépêche de Beauharnois,* 1 *Septembre,* 1728.

[3] The best account of this expedition is that of Père Emanuel Crespel. Lignery made a report which seems to be lost, as it does not appear in the Archives.

[4] *Beauharnois au Ministre,* 15 *Mai,* 1729; *Ibid.,* 21 *Juillet,* 1729.

post on the St. Joseph, had struck the Outagamies a deadly blow and killed two hundred of their warriors, besides six hundred of their women and children. The force under Villiers consisted of a body of Frenchmen gathered from various western posts, another body from the Illinois, led by the Sieurs de Saint-Ange, father and son, and twelve or thirteen hundred Indian allies from many friendly tribes.[1]

The accounts of this affair are obscure and not very trustworthy. It seems that the Outagamies began the fray by an attack on the Illinois at La Salle's old station of Le Rocher, on the river Illinois. On hearing of this, the French commanders mustered their Indian allies, hastened to the spot, and found the Outagamies intrenched in a grove which they had surrounded with a stockade. They defended themselves with their usual courage, but, being hard pressed by hunger and thirst, as well as by the greatly superior numbers of their assailants, they tried to escape during a dark night, as their tribesmen had done at Detroit in 1712. The French and

[1] *Beauharnois et Hocquart au Ministre,* 2 *Novembre,* 1730. An Indian tradition says that about this time there was a great battle between the Outagamies and the French, aided by their Indian allies, at the place called Little Butte des Morts, on the Fox River. According to the story, the Outagamies were nearly destroyed. Perhaps this is a perverted version of the Villiers affair. (See *Wisconsin Historical Collections,* viii. 207.) Beauharnois also reports, under date of 6 May, 1730, that a party of Outagamies, returning from a buffalo hunt, were surprised by two hundred Ottawas, Ojibwas, Menominies, and Winnebagoes, who killed eighty warriors and three hundred women and children.

their allies pursued, and there was a great slaughter, in which many warriors and many more women and children were the victims.[1]

The offending tribe must now, one would think, have ceased to be dangerous; but nothing less than its destruction would content the French officials. To this end, their best resource was in their Indian allies, among whom the Outagamies had no more deadly enemy than the Hurons of Detroit, who, far from relenting in view of their disasters, were more eager than ever to wreak their ire on their unfortunate foe. Accordingly, they sent messengers to the converted Iroquois at the Mission of Two Mountains, and invited them to join in making an end of the Outagamies. The invitation was accepted, and in the autumn of 1731 forty-seven warriors from the Two Mountains appeared at Detroit. The party was soon made up. It consisted of seventy-four Hurons, forty-six Iroquois, and four Ottawas. They took the trail to the mouth of the river St. Joseph, thence around the head of Lake Michigan to the Chicago portage, and thence westward to Rock River. Here were the villages of the Kickapoos and Mascoutins, who had been allies of the Outagamies, but having lately quarrelled with them, received the strangers as friends and gave them guides. The party now filed northward, by forests and prairies, towards the

---

[1] Some particulars of this affair are given by Ferland, *Cours d'Histoire du Canada*, ii. 437; but he does not give his authority I have found no report of it by those engaged.

Wisconsin, to the banks of which stream the Outagamies had lately removed their villages. The warriors
were all on snow-shoes, for the weather was cold and
the snow deep. Some of the elders, overcome by the
hardships of the way, called a council and proposed
to turn back; but the juniors were for pushing on at
all risks, and a young warrior declared that he would
rather die than go home without killing somebody.
The result was a division of the party; the elders
returned to Chicago, and the younger men, forty
Hurons and thirty Iroquois, kept on their way.

At last, as they neared the Wisconsin, they saw
on an open prairie three Outagamies, who ran for
their lives. The Hurons and Iroquois gave chase,
till from the ridge of a hill they discovered the principal Outagamie village, consisting, if we may believe
their own story, of forty-six wigwams, near the bank
of the river. The Outagamie warriors came out to
meet them, in number, as they pretended, much
greater than theirs; but the Huron and Iroquois
chiefs reminded their followers that they had to do
with dogs who did not believe in God, on which they
fired two volleys against the enemy, then dropped
their guns and charged with the knife in one hand
and the war-club in the other. According to their
own story, which shows every sign of mendacity,
they drove back the Outagamies into their village,
killed seventy warriors, and captured fourteen more,
without counting eighty women and children killed,
and a hundred and forty taken prisoners. In short,

they would have us believe that they destroyed the
whole village, except ten men, who escaped entirely
naked, and soon froze to death. They declared
further that they sent one of their prisoners to the
remaining Outagamie villages, ordering him to tell
the inhabitants that they had just devoured the better
part of the tribe, and meant to stay on the spot two
days; that the tribesmen of the slain were free to
attack them if they chose, but in that case, they
would split the heads of all the women and children
prisoners in their hands, make a breastwork of the
dead bodies, and then finish it by piling upon it
those of the assailants.[1]

Nothing is more misleading than Indian tradition,
which is of the least possible value as evidence. It
may be well, however, to mention another story,
often repeated, touching these dark days of the
Outagamies. It is to the effect that a French trader
named Marin, whom they had incensed by levying
blackmail from him, raised a party of Indians, with
whose aid he surprised and defeated the unhappy
tribe at the Little Butte des Morts, that they retired
to the Great Butte des Morts, higher up Fox River,
and that Marin here attacked them again, killing or
capturing the whole. Extravagant as the story
seems, it may have some foundation, though various
dates, from 1725 to 1746, are assigned to the alleged
exploit, and contemporary documents are silent con-

---

[1] *Relation de la Défaite des Renards par les Sauvages Hurons et
Iroquois, le 28 Février,* 1732. (Archives de la Marine.)

cerning it. It is certain that the Outagamies were not destroyed, as the tribe exists to this day.[1]

In 1736 it was reported that sixty or eighty Outagamie warriors were still alive.[2] Their women, who when hard pushed would fight like furies, were relatively numerous and tolerably prolific, and their villages were full of sturdy boys, likely to be dangerous in a few years. Feeling their losses and their weakness, the survivors of the tribe incorporated themselves with their kindred and neighbors, the Sacs, Sakis, or Saukies, the two forming henceforth one tribe, afterwards known to the Americans as the Sacs and Foxes. Early in the nineteenth century they were settled on both banks of the upper Mississippi. Brave and restless like their forefathers, they were a continual menace to the American frontiersmen, and in 1832 they rose in open war, under their famous chief, Blackhawk, displaying their hereditary prowess both on foot and on horseback, and more than once defeating superior numbers of American mounted militia. In the next year that excellent artist,

[1] The story is told in Snelling, *Tales of the Northwest* (1830), under the title of *La Butte des Morts,* and afterwards, with variations, by the aged Augustus Grignon, in his *Recollections,* printed in the *Collections of the Wisconsin Historical Society,* iii. ; also by Judge M. L. Martin and others. Grignon, like all the rest, was not born till after the time of the alleged event. The nearest approach to substantial evidence touching it is in a letter of Beauharnois, who writes in 1730 that the Sieur Dubuisson was to attack the Outagamies with fifty Frenchmen and five hundred and fifty Indians, and that Marin, commander at Green Bay, was to join him. *Beauharnois au Ministre,* 25 *Juin,* 1730.

[2] *Mémoire sur le Canada,* 1736.

SACS AND FOXES.

Charles Bodmer, painted a group of them from life,
— grim-visaged savages, armed with war-club, spear,
or rifle, and wrapped in red, green, or brown blankets,
their heads close shaven except the erect and bristling
scalp-lock, adorned with long eagle-plumes, while
both heads and faces are painted with fantastic
figures in blue, white, yellow, black, and vermilion.[1]

Three or four years after, a party of their chiefs
and warriors was conducted through the country by
order of the Washington government, in order to
impress them with the number and power of the
whites. At Boston they danced a war-dance on the
Common in full costume, to the delight of the boy
spectators, of whom I was one.

---

[1] Charles Bodmer was the artist who accompanied Prince Maximilian of Wied in his travels in the interior of North America.

The name Outagamie is Algonquin for a fox. Hence the French called the tribe Renards, and the Americans, Foxes. They called themselves Musquawkies, which is said to mean " red earth," and to be derived from the color of the soil near one of their villages.

CHAPTER XV.

1697–1741.

FRANCE IN THE FAR WEST.

FRENCH EXPLORERS. — LE SUEUR ON THE ST. PETER. — CANA-
DIANS ON THE MISSOURI. — JUCHEREAU DE SAINT-DENIS. —
BÉNARD DE LA HARPE ON RED RIVER. — ADVENTURES OF DU
TISNÉ. — BOURGMONT VISITS THE COMANCHES. — THE BROTHERS
MALLET IN COLORADO AND NEW MEXICO. — FABRY DE LA
BRUYÈRE.

THE occupation by France of the lower Mississippi
gave a strong impulse to the exploration of the West,
by supplying a base for discovery, stimulating enterprise by the longing to find gold mines, open trade
with New Mexico, and get a fast hold on the countries
beyond the Mississippi in anticipation of Spain; and
to these motives was soon added the hope of finding
an overland way to the Pacific. It was the Canadians, with their indomitable spirit of adventure,
who led the way in the path of discovery.

As a bold and hardy pioneer of the wilderness, the
Frenchman in America has rarely found his match.
His civic virtues withered under the despotism of
Versailles, and his mind and conscience were kept in
leading-strings by an absolute Church; but the forest
and the prairie offered him an unbridled liberty,
which, lawless as it was, gave scope to his energies,

till these savage wastes became the field of his most noteworthy achievements.

Canada was divided between two opposing influences. On the one side were the monarchy and the hierarchy, with their principles of order, subordination, and obedience; substantially at one in purpose, since both wished to keep the colony within manageable bounds, domesticate it, and tame it to soberness, regularity, and obedience. On the other side was the spirit of liberty, or license, which was in the very air of this wilderness continent, reinforced in the chiefs of the colony by a spirit of adventure inherited from the Middle Ages, and by a spirit of trade born of present opportunities; for every official in Canada hoped to make a profit, if not a fortune, out of beaver-skins. Kindred impulses, in ruder forms, possessed the humbler colonists, drove them into the forest, and made them hardy woodsmen and skilful bush-fighters, though turbulent and lawless members of civilized society.

Time, the decline of the fur-trade, and the influence of the Canadian Church gradually diminished this erratic spirit, and at the same time impaired the qualities that were associated with it. The Canadian became a more stable colonist and a steadier farmer; but for forest journeyings and forest warfare he was scarcely his former self. At the middle of the eighteenth century we find complaints that the race of *voyageurs* is growing scarce. The taming process was most apparent in the central and lower parts of the colony, such as the Côte de Beaupré and the opposite shore of the St. Lawrence, where the hands of the government and of the Church were strong; while at the head of the colony, — that is, about Montreal and its neighborhood, — which touched the primeval wilderness, an uncontrollable spirit of adventure still held its own. Here, at the beginning of the century, this spirit was as strong as it had ever been, and achieved a series of explorations and discoveries which revealed the plains of the Far West long before an Anglo-Saxon foot had pressed their soil.

The expedition of one Le Sueur to what is now the State of Minnesota may be taken as the starting-point of these enterprises. Le Sueur had visited the country of the Sioux as early as 1683. He returned thither in 1689 with the famous *voyageur* Nicolas Perrot.[1] Four years later, Count Frontenac sent him to the Sioux country again. The declared purpose of the mission was to keep those fierce tribes at peace with their neighbors; but the governor's enemies declared that a contraband trade in beaver was the true object, and that Frontenac's secretary was to have half the profits.[2] Le Sueur returned after two years, bringing to Montreal a Sioux chief and his squaw, — the first of the tribe ever seen there. He then went to France, and represented to the court that he had built a fort at Lake Pepin, on the

[1] *Journal historique de l'Établissement des Français à la Louisiane,* 43.
[2] *Champigny au Ministre,* 4 *Novembre,* 1693.

upper Mississippi; that he was the only white man
who knew the languages of that region; and that if
the French did not speedily seize upon it, the English, who were already trading upon the Ohio, would
be sure to do so.   Thereupon he asked for the command of the upper Mississippi, with all its tributary
waters, together with a monopoly of its fur-trade for
ten years, and permission to work its mines, promising that if his petition were granted, he would secure
the country to France without expense to the King.
The commission was given him.   He bought an outfit and sailed for Canada, but was captured by the
English on the way.   After the peace he returned to
France and begged for a renewal of his commission.
Leave was given him to work the copper and lead
mines, but not to trade in beaver-skins.   He now
formed a company to aid him in his enterprise, on
which a cry rose in Canada that under pretence of
working mines he meant to trade in beaver, — which
is very likely, since to bring lead and copper in bark
canoes to Montreal from the Mississippi and Lake
Superior would cost far more than the metal was
worth.   In consequence of this clamor his commission
was revoked.

Perhaps it was to compensate him for the outlays
into which he had been drawn that the colonial
minister presently authorized him to embark for
Louisiana and pursue his enterprise with that infant
colony, instead of Canada, as his base of operations.
Thither, therefore, he went; and in April, 1700, set

out for the Sioux country with twenty-five men, in a small vessel of the kind called a "felucca," still used in the Mediterranean. Among the party was an adventurous youth named Penecaut, a ship-carpenter by trade, who had come to Louisiana with Iberville two years before, and who has left us an account of his voyage with Le Sueur.[1]

The party slowly made their way, with sail and oar, against the muddy current of the Mississippi, till they reached the Arkansas, where they found an English trader from Carolina.   On the tenth of June, spent with rowing, and half starved, they stopped to rest at a point fifteen leagues above the mouth of the Ohio.   They had staved off famine with the buds and leaves of trees; but now, by good luck, one of them killed a bear, and, soon after, the Jesuit Limoges arrived from the neighboring mission of the Illinois, in a canoe well stored with provisions.   Thus refreshed, they passed the mouth of the Missouri on the thirteenth of July, and soon after were met by three Canadians, who brought them a letter from the Jesuit Marest, warning them that the river was infested by war-parties.   In fact, they presently saw seven canoes of Sioux warriors, bound against the Illinois; and not long after, five Canadians appeared, one of whom had been badly wounded in a recent encounter with a band of Outagamies, Sacs, and

---

[1] *Relation de Penecaut.* In my possession is a contemporary manuscript of this narrative, for which I am indebted to the kind-ness of General J. Meredith Reade.

Winnebagoes bound against the Sioux. To take one
another's scalps had been for ages the absorbing business and favorite recreation of all these Western
tribes. At or near the expansion of the Mississippi
called Lake Pepin, the voyagers found a fort called
Fort Perrot, after its builder;[1] and on an island near
the upper end of the lake, another similar structure,
built by Le Sueur himself on his last visit to the
place. These forts were mere stockades, occupied
from time to time by the roving fur-traders as their
occasions required.

Towards the end of September, Le Sueur and his
followers reached the mouth of the St. Peter, which
they ascended to Blue Earth River. Pushing a
league up this stream, they found a spot well suited
to their purpose, and here they built a fort, of which
there was great need, for they were soon after joined
by seven Canadian traders, plundered and stripped to
the skin by the neighboring Sioux. Le Sueur named
the new post Fort l'Huillier. It was a fence of
pickets, enclosing cabins for the men. The neighboring plains were black with buffalo, of which the
party killed four hundred, and cut them into quarters,

---

[1] Penecaut, *Journal. Procès-verbal de la Prise de Possession du
Pays des Nadouessioux, etc., par Nicolas Perrot*, 1689. Fort Perrot
seems to have been built in 1685, and to have stood near the outlet
of the lake, probably on the west side. Perrot afterwards built
another fort, called Fort St. Antoine, a little above, on the east
bank. The position of these forts has been the subject of much
discussion, and cannot be ascertained with precision. It appears
by the *Prise de Possession*, cited above, that there was also, in 1689,
a temporary French post near the mouth of the Wisconsin.

which they placed to freeze on scaffolds within the enclosure. Here they spent the winter, subsisting on the frozen meat, without bread, vegetables, or salt, and, according to Penecaut, thriving marvellously, though the surrounding wilderness was buried five feet deep in snow.

Band after band of Sioux appeared, with their wolfish dogs and their sturdy and all-enduring squaws burdened with the heavy hide coverings of their teepees, or buffalo-skin tents. They professed friendship and begged for arms. Those of one band had blackened their faces in mourning for a dead chief, and calling on Le Sueur to share their sorrow, they wept over him, and wiped their tears on his hair. Another party of warriors arrived with yet deeper cause of grief, being the remnant of a village half exterminated by their enemies. They, too, wept profusely over the French commander, and then sang a dismal song, with heads muffled in their buffalo-robes.[1] Le Sueur took the needful precautions against his dangerous visitors, but got from them a large supply of beaver-skins in exchange for his goods.

When spring opened, he set out in search of mines, and found, not far above the fort, those beds of blue and green earth to which the stream owes its name. Of this his men dug out a large quantity, and select-

---

[1] This weeping over strangers was a custom with the Sioux of that time mentioned by many early writers. La Mothe-Cadillac marvels that a people so brave and warlike should have such a fountain of tears always at command.

ing what seemed the best, stored it in their vessel as a precious commodity. With this and good store of beaver-skins, Le Sueur now began his return voyage for Louisiana, leaving a Canadian named D'Éraque and twelve men to keep the fort till he should come back to reclaim it, promising to send him a canoe-load of ammunition from the Illinois. But the canoe was wrecked, and D'Éraque, discouraged, abandoned Fort l'Huillier, and followed his commander down the Mississippi.[1]

Le Sueur, with no authority from government, had opened relations of trade with the wild Sioux of the Plains, whose westward range stretched to the Black Hills, and perhaps to the Rocky Mountains. He reached the settlements of Louisiana in safety, and sailed for France with four thousand pounds of his worthless blue earth.[2] Repairing at once to Versailles, he begged for help to continue his enterprise. His petition seems to have been granted. After long delay, he sailed again for Louisiana, fell ill on the voyage, and died soon after landing.[3]

Before 1700, the year when Le Sueur visited the St. Peter, little or nothing was known of the country west of the Mississippi, except from the report of

---

[1] In 1702 the geographer De l'Isle made a remarkable MS. map entitled *Carte de la Rivière du Mississippi, dressée sur les Mémoires de M. Le Sueur.*

[2] According to the geologist Featherstonhaugh, who examined the locality, this earth owes its color to a bluish-green silicate of iron.

[3] Besides the long and circumstantial *Relation de Penecaut*, an account of the earlier part of La Sueur's voyage up the Mississippi is contained in the *Mémoire du Chevalier de Beaurain*, which, with

Indians. The romances of La Hontan and Mathieu
Sâgean were justly set down as impostures by all but
the most credulous. In this same year we find Le
Moyne d'Iberville projecting journeys to the upper
Missouri, in hopes of finding a river flowing to the
Western Sea. In 1703, twenty Canadians tried to
find their way from the Illinois to New Mexico, in
hope of opening trade with the Spaniards and dis-
covering mines.[1] In 1704 we find it reported that
more than a hundred Canadians are scattered in
small parties along the Mississippi and the Missouri;[2]
and in 1705 one Laurain appeared at the Illinois,
declaring that he had been high up the Missouri and
had visited many tribes on its borders.[3] A few
months later, two Canadians told Bienville a similar
story. In 1708 Nicolas de la Salle proposed an
expedition of a hundred men to explore the same
mysterious river; and in 1717 one Hubert laid before
the Council of Marine a scheme for following the
Missouri to its source, since, he says, "not only may
we find the mines worked by the Spaniards, but also
discover the great river that is said to rise in the
mountains where the Missouri has its source, and is
believed to flow to the Western Sea." And he
advises that a hundred and fifty men be sent up the

other papers relating to this explorer, including portions of his
Journal, will be found in Margry, vi. See also *Journal historique
de l'Établissement des Français à la Louisiane*, 38–71.

[1] *Iberville à ——, 15 Février*, 1703 (Margry, vi. 180).
[2] *Bienville au Ministre, 6 Septembre*, 1704.
[3] Beaurain, *Journal historique*.

river in wooden canoes, since bark canoes would be dangerous, by reason of the multitude of snags.[1]

In 1714 Juchereau de Saint-Denis was sent by La Mothe-Cadillac to explore western Louisiana, and pushed up Red River to a point sixty-eight leagues, as he reckons, above Natchitoches. In the next year, journeying across country towards the Spanish settlements, with a view to trade, he was seized near the Rio Grande and carried to the city of Mexico. The Spaniards, jealous of French designs, now sent priests and soldiers to occupy several points in Texas. Juchereau, however, was well treated, and permitted to marry a Spanish girl with whom he had fallen in love on the way; but when, in the autumn of 1716, he ventured another journey to the Mexican borders, still hoping to be allowed to trade, he and his goods were seized by order of the Mexican viceroy, and, lest worse should befall him, he fled empty-handed, under cover of night.[2]

In March, 1719, Bénard de la Harpe left the feeble little French post at Natchitoches with six soldiers and a sergeant.[3] His errand was to explore the country, open trade if possible with the Spaniards, and establish another post high up Red River. He and his party soon came upon that vast entanglement

[1] Hubert, *Mémoire envoyé au Conseil de la Marine.*

[2] Penecaut, *Relation*, chaps. xvii., xviii. Le Page du Pratz, *Histoire de la Louisiane*, i. 13–22. Various documents in Margry, vi. 193–202.

[3] For an interesting contemporary map of the French establishment at Natchitoches, see Thomassy, *Géologie pratique de la Louisiane.*

of driftwood, or rather of uprooted forests, afterwards known as the Red River raft, which choked the stream and forced them to make their way through the inundated jungle that bordered it. As they pushed or dragged their canoes through the swamp, they saw with disgust and alarm a good number of snakes, coiled about twigs and boughs on the right and left, or sometimes over their heads. These were probably the deadly water-moccason, which in warm weather is accustomed to crawl out of its favorite element and bask itself in the sun, precisely as described by La Harpe. Their nerves were further discomposed by the splashing and plunging of alligators lately wakened from their wintry torpor. Still, they pushed painfully on, till they reached navigable water again, and at the end of the month were, as they thought, a hundred and eight leagues above Natchitoches. In four days more they reached the Nassonites.

These savages belonged to a group of stationary tribes, only one of which, the Caddoes, survives to our day as a separate community. Their enemies, the Chickasaws, Osages, Arkansas, and even the distant Illinois, waged such deadly war against them that, according to La Harpe, the unfortunate Nassonites were in the way of extinction, their numbers having fallen, within ten years, from twenty-five hundred souls to four hundred.[1]

La Harpe stopped among them to refresh his men,

[1] Bénard de la Harpe, in Margry, vi. 264.

and build a house of cypress-wood as a beginning of the post he was ordered to establish; then, having heard that a war with Spain had ruined his hopes of trade with New Mexico, he resolved to pursue his explorations.

With him went ten men, white, red, and black, with twenty-two horses bought from the Indians, for his journeyings were henceforth to be by land. The party moved in a northerly and westerly course, by hills, forests, and prairies, passed two branches of the Wichita, and on the third of September came to a river which La Harpe calls the southwest branch of the Arkansas, but which, if his observation of latitude is correct, must have been the main stream, not far from the site of Fort Mann. Here he was met by seven Indian chiefs, mounted on excellent horses saddled and bridled after the Spanish manner. They led him to where, along the plateau of the low, treeless hills that bordered the valley, he saw a string of Indian villages, extending for a league and belonging to nine several bands, the names of which can no longer be recognized, and most of which are no doubt extinct. He says that they numbered in all six thousand souls; and their dwellings were high, dome-shaped structures, built of clay mixed with reeds and straw, resting, doubtless, on a frame of bent poles.[1]

[1] Beaurain says that each of these bands spoke a language of its own. They had horses in abundance, descended from Spanish stock. Among them appear to have been the Ouacos, or Huecos, and the Wichitas, — two tribes better known as the Pawnee Picts. See Marcy, *Exploration of Red River.*

With them were also some of the roving Indians of the plains, with their conical teepees of dressed buffalo-skin.

The arrival of the strangers was a great and amazing event for these savages, few of whom had ever seen a white man. On the day after their arrival the whole multitude gathered to receive them and offer them the calumet, with a profusion of songs and speeches. Then warrior after warrior recounted his exploits and boasted of the scalps he had taken. From eight in the morning till two hours after midnight the din of drums, songs, harangues, and dances continued without relenting, with a prospect of twelve hours more; and La Harpe, in desperation, withdrew to rest himself on a buffalo-robe, begging another Frenchman to take his place. His hosts left him in peace for a while; then the chiefs came to find him, painted his face blue, as a tribute of respect, put a cap of eagle-feathers on his head, and laid numerous gifts at his feet. When at last the ceremony ended, some of the performers were so hoarse from incessant singing that they could hardly speak.[1]

La Harpe was told by his hosts that the Spanish settlements could be reached by ascending their river; but to do this was at present impossible. He began his backward journey, fell desperately ill of a fever, and nearly died before reaching Natchitoches.

[1] Compare the account of La Harpe with that of the Chevalier de Beaurain; both are in Margry, vi. There is an abstract in *Journal historique.*

Having recovered, he made an attempt, two years later, to explore the Arkansas in canoes, from its mouth, but accomplished little besides killing a good number of buffalo, bears, deer, and wild turkeys. He was confirmed, however, in the belief that the Comanches and the Spaniards of New Mexico might be reached by this route.

In the year of La Harpe's first exploration, one Du Tisné went up the Missouri to a point six leagues above Grand River, where stood the village of the Missouris. He wished to go farther, but they would not let him. He then returned to the Illinois, whence he set out on horseback with a few followers across what is now the State of Missouri, till he reached the village of the Osages, which stood on a hill high up the river Osage. At first he was well received; but when they found him disposed to push on to a town of their enemies, the Pawnees, forty leagues distant, they angrily refused to let him go. His firmness and hardihood prevailed, and at last they gave him leave. A ride of a few days over rich prairies brought him to the Pawnees, who, coming as he did from the hated Osages, took him for an enemy and threatened to kill him. Twice they raised the tomahawk over his head; but when the intrepid traveller dared them to strike, they began to treat him as a friend. When, however, he told them that he meant to go fifteen days' journey farther, to the Padoucas, or Comanches, their deadly enemies, they fiercely forbade him; and after planting a French flag in their village, he returned as he had come, guiding his way by compass, and reaching the Illinois in November, after extreme hardships.[1]

Early in 1721 two hundred mounted Spaniards, followed by a large body of Comanche warriors, came from New Mexico to attack the French at the Illinois, but were met and routed on the Missouri by tribes of that region.[2] In the next year, Bienville was told that they meant to return, punish those who had defeated them, and establish a post on the river Kansas; whereupon he ordered Boisbriant, commandant at the Illinois, to anticipate them by sending troops to build a French fort at or near the same place. But the West India Company had already sent one Bourgmont on a similar errand, the object being to trade with the Spaniards in time of peace, and stop their incursions in time of war.[3] It was hoped also that, in the interest of trade, peace might be made between the Comanches and the tribes of the Missouri.[4]

Bourgmont was a man of some education, and well acquainted with these tribes, among whom he had

[1] *Relation de Bénard de la Harpe. Autre Relation du même. Du Tisné à Bienville.* Margry, vi. 309, 310, 313.

[2] *Bienville au Conseil de Régence,* 20 *Juillet,* 1721.

[3] *Instructions au Sieur de Bourgmont,* 17 *Janvier,* 1722. Margry, vi. 389.

[4] The French had at this time gained a knowledge of the tribes of the Missouri as far up as the Arickaras, who were not, it seems, many days' journey below the Yellowstone, and who told them of "prodigiously high mountains," — evidently the Rocky Mountains. *Mémoire de la Renaudière,* 1723.

traded for years. In pursuance of his orders he built
a fort, which he named Fort Orléans, and which
stood on the Missouri not far above the . mouth
of Grand River. Having thus accomplished one
part of his mission, he addressed himself to the
other, and prepared to march for the Comanche
villages.

Leaving a sufficient garrison at the fort, he sent
his ensign, Saint-Ange, with a party of soldiers and
Canadians, in wooden canoes, to the villages of the
Kansas higher up the stream, and on the third of
July set out by land to join him, with a hundred and
nine Missouri Indians and sixty-eight Osages in his
train. A ride of five days brought him again to
the banks of the Missouri, opposite a Kansas town.
Saint-Ange had not yet arrived, the angry and turbid
current, joined to fevers among his men, having
retarded his progress. Meanwhile Bourgmont drew
from the Kansas a promise that their warriors should
go with him to the Comanches. Saint-Ange at last
appeared, and at daybreak of the twenty-fourth the
tents were struck and the pack-horses loaded. At
six o'clock the party drew up in battle array on a hill
above the Indian town, and then, with drum beating
and flag flying, began their march. "A fine prairie
country," writes Bourgmont, "with hills and dales
and clumps of trees to right and left." Sometimes
the landscape quivered under the sultry sun, and
sometimes thunder bellowed over their heads, and
rain fell in floods on the steaming plains.

Renaudière, engineer of the party, one day stood by the side of the path and watched the whole procession as it passed him. The white men were about twenty in all. He counted about three hundred Indian warriors, with as many squaws, some five hundred children, and a prodigious number of dogs, the largest and strongest of which dragged heavy loads. The squaws also served as beasts of burden; and, says the journal, "they will carry as much as a dog will drag." Horses were less abundant among these tribes than they afterwards became, so that their work fell largely upon the women.

On the sixth day the party was within three leagues of the river Kansas, at a considerable distance above its mouth. Bourgmont had suffered from dysentery on the march, and an access of the malady made it impossible for him to go farther. It is easy to conceive the regret with which he saw himself compelled to return to Fort Orléans. The party retraced their steps, carrying their helpless commander on a litter.

First, however, he sent one Gaillard on a perilous errand. Taking with him two Comanche slaves bought for the purpose from the Kansas, Gaillard was ordered to go to the Comanche villages with the message that Bourgmont had been on his way to make them a friendly visit, and, though stopped by illness, hoped soon to try again, with better success.

Early in September, Bourgmont, who had arrived

safely at Fort Orléans, received news that the mission
of Gaillard had completely succeeded; on which,
though not wholly recovered from his illness, he set
out again on his errand of peace, accompanied by his
young son, besides Renaudière, a surgeon, and nine
soldiers. On reaching the great village of the Kansas
he found there five Comanche chiefs and warriors,
whom Gaillard had induced to come thither with
him. Seven chiefs of the Otoes presently appeared,
in accordance with an invitation of Bourgmont; then
six chiefs of the Iowas and the head chief of the
Missouris. With these and the Kansas chiefs a
solemn council was held around a fire before Bourgmont's tent; speeches were made, the pipe of peace
was smoked, and presents were distributed.

On the eighth of October the march began, the
five Comanches and the chiefs of several other
tribes, including the Omahas, joining the cavalcade.
Gaillard and another Frenchman named Quesnel were
sent in advance to announce their approach to the
Comanches, while Bourgmont and his followers moved
up the north side of the river Kansas till the eleventh,
when they forded it at a point twenty leagues from
its mouth, and took a westward and southwestward
course, sometimes threading the grassy valleys of
little streams, sometimes crossing the dry upland
prairie, covered with the short, tufted dull-green
herbage since known as "buffalo grass." Wild
turkeys clamored along every watercourse; deer
were seen on all sides, buffalo were without number,

sometimes in grazing droves, and sometimes dotting the endless plain as far as the eye could reach. Ruffian wolves, white and gray, eyed the travellers askance, keeping a safe distance by day, and howling about the camp all night. Of the antelope and the elk the journal makes no mention. Bourgmont chased a buffalo on horseback and shot him with a pistol, — which is probably the first recorded example of that way of hunting.

The stretches of high, rolling, treeless prairie grew more vast as the travellers advanced. On the seventeenth, they found an abandoned Comanche camp. On the next day as they stopped to dine, and had just unsaddled their horses, they saw a distant smoke towards the west, on which they set the dry grass on fire as an answering signal. Half an hour later a body of wild horsemen came towards them at full speed, and among them were their two couriers, Gaillard and Quesnel, waving a French flag. The strangers were eighty Comanche warriors, with the grand chief of the tribe at their head. They dashed up to Bourgmont's bivouac and leaped from their horses, when a general shaking of hands ensued, after which white men and red seated themselves on the ground and smoked the pipe of peace. Then all rode together to the Comanche camp, three leagues distant.[1]

[1] This meeting took place a little north of the Arkansas, apparently where that river makes a northward bend, near the twenty-second degree of west longitude. The Comanche villages were several days' journey to the southwest. This tribe is always

Bourgmont pitched his tents at a pistol-shot from the Comanche lodges, whence a crowd of warriors presently came to visit him. They spread buffalo-robes on the ground, placed upon them the French commander, his officers, and his young son; then lifted each, with its honored load, and carried them all, with yells of joy and gratulation, to the lodge of the Great Chief, where there was a feast of ceremony lasting till nightfall.

On the next day Bourgmont displayed to his hosts the marvellous store of gifts he had brought for them, — guns, swords, hatchets, kettles, gunpowder, bullets, red cloth, blue cloth, hand-mirrors, knives, shirts, awls, scissors, needles, hawks' bells, vermilion, beads, and other enviable commodities, of the like of which they had never dreamed. Two hundred savages gathered before the French tents, where Bourgmont, with the gifts spread on the ground before him, stood with a French flag in his hand, surrounded by his officers and the Indian chiefs of his party, and harangued the admiring auditors.

He told them that he had come to bring them a message from the King, his master, who was the Great Chief of all the nations of the earth, and whose will it was that the Comanches should live in peace with his other children, — the Missouris, Osages, Kansas, Otoes, Omahas, and Pawnees, — with whom

mentioned in the early French narratives as the Padoucas, — a name by which the Comanches are occasionally known to this day. See Whipple and Turner, *Reports upon Indian Tribes*, in *Explorations and Surveys for the Pacific Railroad* (Senate Doc., 1853, 1854).

they had long been at war; that the chiefs of these tribes were now present, ready to renounce their old enmities; that the Comanches should henceforth regard them as friends, share with them the blessing of alliance and trade with the French, and give to these last free passage through their country to trade with the Spaniards of New Mexico. Bourgmont then gave the French flag to the Great Chief, to be kept forever as a pledge of that day's compact. The chief took the flag, and promised in behalf of his people to keep peace inviolate with the Indian children of the King. Then, with unspeakable delight, he and his tribesmen took and divided the gifts.

The next two days were spent in feasts and rejoicings. "Is it true that you are men?" asked the Great Chief. "I have heard wonders of the French, but I never could have believed what I see this day." Then, taking up a handful of earth, "The Spaniards are like this; but you are like the sun." And he offered Bourgmont, in case of need, the aid of his two thousand Comanche warriors. The pleasing manners of his visitors, and their unparalleled generosity, had completely won his heart.

As the object of the expedition was accomplished, or seemed to be so, the party set out on their return. A ride of ten days brought them again to the Missouri; they descended in canoes to Fort Orléans, and sang Te Deum in honor of the peace.[1]

---

[1] *Relation du Voyage du Sieur de Bourgmont, Juin-Novembre,* 1724, in Margry. vi. 398. Le Page du Pratz, iii. 141.

No farther discovery in this direction was made for the next fifteen years. Though the French had explored the Missouri as far as the site of Fort Clark and the Mandan villages, they were possessed by the idea — due, perhaps, to Indian reports concerning the great tributary river, the Yellowstone — that in its upper course the main stream bent so far southward as to form a waterway to New Mexico, with which it was the constant desire of the authorities of Louisiana to open trade. A way thither was at last made known by two brothers named Mallet, who with six companions went up the Platte to its South Fork, which they called River of the Padoucas, — a name given it on some maps down to the middle of this century. They followed the South Fork for some distance, and then, turning southward and southwestward, crossed the plains of Colorado. Here the dried dung of the buffalo was their only fuel; and it has continued to feed the camp-fire of the traveller in this treeless region within the memory of many now living. They crossed the upper Arkansas, and apparently the Cimarron, passed Taos, and on the twenty-second of July reached Santa Fé, where they spent the winter. On the first of May, 1740, they began their return journey, three of them crossing the plains to the Pawnee villages, and the rest descending the Arkansas to the Mississippi.[1]

[1] *Journal du Voyage des Frères Mallet, présenté à MM. de Bienville et Salmon.* This narrative is meagre and confused, but serves to establish the main points. *Copie du Certificat donné à Santa Fé aux*

The bold exploit of the brothers Mallet attracted great attention at New Orleans, and Bienville resolved to renew it, find if possible a nearer and better way to Santa Fé, determine the nature and extent of these mysterious western regions, and satisfy a lingering doubt whether they were not contiguous to China and Tartary.[1] A naval officer, Fabry de la Bruyère, was sent on this errand, with the brothers Mallet and a few soldiers and Canadians. He ascended the Canadian Fork of the Arkansas, named by him the St. André, became entangled in the shallows and quicksands of that difficult river, fell into disputes with his men, and, after protracted efforts, returned unsuccessful.[2]

While French enterprise was unveiling the remote Southwest, two indomitable Canadians were pushing still more noteworthy explorations into more northern regions of the continent.

sept [huit] *Français par le Général Hurtado,* 24 *Juillet,* 1739. *Père Rébald au Père de Beaubois, sans date. Bienville et Salmon au Ministre,* 30 *Avril,* 1741, in Margry, vi. 455–468.

[1] *Instructions données par Jean-Baptiste de Bienville à Fabry de la Bruyère,* 1 *Juin,* 1741. Bienville was behind his time in geographical knowledge. As early as 1724 Bénard de la Harpe knew that in ascending the Missouri or the Arkansas one was moving towards the "Western Sea," — that is, the Pacific, — and might, perhaps, find some river flowing into it. See *Routes qu'on peut tenir pour se rendre à la Mer de l'Ouest,* in *Journal historique,* 387.

[2] *Extrait des Lettres du Sieur Fabry.*

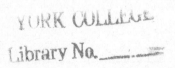
YORK COLLEGE
Library No.